ALL THE
COMMISSIONER'S
MEN

CHRIS BIRT

STENTORIAN
PUBLISHING LTD

A succinct commentary on the Thomas case, published in The Nation on 4 December 1980.

STENTORIAN
PUBLISHING LTD

Stentorian Publishing Ltd, 4 Starlight Arcade,
Taupo 3351, New Zealand

First published by Stentorian Publishing Ltd, 2012

Designed by Mark David
Typeset by The Art Group
Printed in Hong Kong by Regal Printing Ltd

National Library of New Zealand Cataloguing-in-Publication Data

* Birt, Chris.
* All The Commissioner's Men / Chris Birt.
* ISBN 978-0-473-20915-5
* 1. Crewe, Jeanette Lenore. 2. Crewe, David Harvey. 3. Murder victims—
New Zealand. 5. Murder—Investigation—New Zealand—Franklin District.
6. Police misconduct—New Zealand—Franklin District. I. Title.
364.1523099331—dc 23

www.crewemurders.com

Email for orders or inquiries
info@crewemurders.com

DEDICATION

To the late Inspector Jack Collins
and the men and women of the New Zealand
Police – past and future – who honour their
oath of office and set aside the temptation to put
their ego, arrogance, self-gratification or career
advancement above the rule of law and the
expectations of the community they are
sworn to serve.

ACKNOWLEDGEMENTS

To Adelina, who graciously accepted, as a literary widow, the countless lonely hours that flow from an undertaking of such magnitude and intricacy, who returned me to something akin to life at the end of the gruelling days that were followed by even more exhausting nights, and who displayed the patience of Job. I will remember always your determination that the good fight had to be fought in its entirety, not in abridged form, when others sought to blunt the impact of what I was striving to put before the public, based on my fervent belief that only through truth will justice flow. Less courageous women may have wilted in the face of such challenges and it is a testament to your faith in your man, and the rightness of the cause, that you never did. For that, I owe a great debt, and my eternal gratitude.

To my old travelling companion Nick, who regardless of the passage of time, has continued to insist that justice must be done for those persons and those families who were robbed of that by a system he loved and cherished, often more than life itself. That his faith in that system was so severely diminished as a consequence of the corrupted ambitions of a handful of practitioners of the law in the 1970s is itself a travesty.

To Pat, who had indeterminable faith in my abilities and who quickly grasped the intimate knowledge I had been able to acquire, not only of the tragic events which emerged at Pukekawa in the latter half of 1970, but of the actions of those sent to investigate them on behalf of the people of New Zealand. Through your deeds and your actions, and those of your kin over decades, you ensured that he whom you knew to be innocent was able to leave behind a decade of imprisonment as a free man and with an unencumbered character and name, which is all he had ever wished for. Your courage in standing beside your niece in her darkest of hours, and in the years until she was called to a more deserving place, warrants far greater recognition than you have ever been afforded. My earnest hope is that your contribution to justice in this country will one day be truly recognised and that you, too, will see justice done to all those who have been denied it thus far.

To Gerald and Peter, two warriors of the law who refused to be cowered by the powerful machine that is the State and whom, over many years, have continued to campaign for those infinitely less able to defend themselves. Our association may have been of relatively recent origin, but the willingness with which you imparted your great knowledge of these events, and your wise counsel, will always be valued.

To Kathryn and Mark, who worked tirelessly as this project drew closer to its conclusion and who provided the expertise required to ensure that it became a work of which I could be proud. Your encouragement at a time when hope was waning will be long cherished by me and by those who shared the absolute need to get this book into the public domain.

To Stephanie, Graeme and Linda of the Ministry of Justice, and to Vernon and his reference team at Archives New Zealand. My heartfelt appreciation for the professional manner in which you all responded to demands for official information from so many decades ago, the assistance you provided and the manner in which you went beyond the call of duty in a bid to satisfy what must have seemed at times to be an insatiable appetite for knowledge and for documents, many of them now long confined to your agency's respective archival systems. Your williness to assist rather than hinder is a fine tribute to openness and transparency and is one which other agencies of the State could well learn from.

To my legal team, and particularly Michael. My gratitude is with you, not only for the way in which you went about checking the text contained within the pages of this revealing book, but the interest you showed in this as a work worthy of publication. Your support in seeing that the events of the 1970s have finally been disclosed and the time you put into not only researching the relevant law, but in assimilating it into your legal opinion on the contents of *All The Commissioner's Men* is both deeply appreciated and highly valued.

And lastly to Desmond and those who are closest to him. It is difficult to capture in words the contribution you have made to the development and creation of this published work, and even more importantly, to the cause of justice in the country we call home. Just as your father steered a unwaivering path in his fight to clear such an honourable name, so have you taken up this most commendable of causes. Not once have you demonstrated even the slightest deviation from your belief that at some time the truth would emerge, and with it would come the judgment of those who brought such pain and suffering to your family. Without your patience in allowing me unfettered retention of the many transcripts and historic files that rightly ought to have been with you, *All The Commissioner's Men* could not have been researched and written. Much of the significant, and revealing, content of this book emanated from those files, which must now be preserved in perpetuity as a testament to just how far evil men will go to further their ends. Finally, without the support you have provided in recent months, this is a book that may never have seen the light of day, despite its merits. For that I owe immense gratitude, as should all those who populate this once great, but now all too often troubled land of our's.

Photographs used in this book were kindly supplied by the New Zealand Herald (Auckland) and the DominionPost (Wellington). The author and publisher wish to acknowledge the assistance and co-operation provided by the photographic staff of New Zealand's leading daily newspapers in searching their archives and providing the copyright waiver required to permit reproduction of these images. Individually and collectively, these historic images form an important part of the record of crimes committed 42 years ago and the events that followed.

Photographs supplied by Archives New Zealand - Department of Internal Affairs Te Tari Taiwhenua
Aerial of Crewe farm [Archives reference: COM 40/12]; Kitchen in Crewe house [Archives reference: COM 40/11]
Rochelle Crewe's cot [Archives reference: COM 40/11]; Junk from Thomas farm tip [Archives reference: COM 40/12]
Aerial of Thomas farm [Archives reference: COM 40/11]; Rusty old wheel rim [Archives reference: COM 40/12]
Composite trailer frame [Archives reference: COM 40/12]

'The greatest threat to the reputation of the police service
is criminals in uniform'

- Independent Police Complaints Commission chairman Nick Hardwick,
following the jailing of London Metropolitan Police Commander Ali Dizaei
for four years for trying to frame an innocent man and committing perjury
in a bid to cover his abuse of office.

The Right Honourable John Key
Prime Minister
Parliament Buildings
Wellington New Zealand

28th October 2010

Dear Prime Minister

I have noted through Internet coverage of the Crewe murder case that Rochelle Crewe is seeking an independent inquiry into the killing of her parents at Pukekawa in June 1970 and that this should be conducted by an overseas judge.

As the person who was falsely accused, at two Supreme Court trials, of being the woman who fed Rochelle and having had to live with the subsequent stigma of that for 40 years since, I support this call for an independent inquiry in the strongest possible terms.

Like Rochelle, I want to see the murders solved, if it is at all possible. I am aware also of the view that if the New Zealand public is ever to regain its confidence in its police force, the corruption and fabrication surrounding the investigation of these murders also needs to be fully exposed.

It is my view, and that of my family, relations and many friends in New Zealand, that not only was the failure to prosecute former Detective Inspector Bruce Hutton a grave mistake after the 1980 Royal Commission brought down its most damning findings, but that a number of others involved have not been exposed for their perjury and malpractice during that investigation.

It was unfortunate that the terms of reference for the Thomas Royal Commission specifically prohibited a full and exhaustive inquiry into many matters. In that respect the tribunal was unable to expose the full extent of what went on during the Crewe investigation and the subsequent prosecution of my former husband Arthur Allan Thomas and persecution and defamation of myself.

I am prepared to co-operate fully with any independent inquiry into this matter. Like Arthur, I was an innocent party in these crimes but we both became victims, as indeed Jeanette and Harvey Crewe and their surviving daughter Rochelle were innocent victims. The hurt and humiliation inflicted on me cannot be erased, but the great wrong done to me can be righted and I am seeking from you a mechanism to now do so.

Yours faithfully

Vivien Harrison

Vivien Harrison
Kingsthorpe, Queensland 4000, Australia.

THE CREWE MURDER INQUIRY AND THE THOMAS AFFAIR
Key characters in a real-life tragedy

A

Graham Abbott, Detective: exhibits officer Crewe inquiry
Robert Adams-Smith, QC: special investigator for Rob Muldoon
Percy Allen: Minister of Police (National)
George Austing, Assistant Commissioner: Officer in charge of
Auckland Police district

David Baragwanath

B

Wally Baker, Detective Inspector: Crewe inquiry overview
David Baragwanath: junior counsel at Thomas trials
George Barton: counsel for Royal Commission at High Court
Ted Bennett: former Chennells Estate manager
Peter Brant: former Army arms instructor
Jack Brewster: owner of .22 rifle
Howard Broad: Commissioner of Police
Keith Brown: Tuakau stock agent
Ken Burnside: Assistant Commissioner of Police, then Commissioner
Paddy Byrne, Detective Chief Superintendent

Frank Cairns

C

Frank Cairns (Dr): forensic pathologist
Maurice Casey: Appeal Court judge
Ronald Caughey (Dr): medical practitioner
Mike Charles, Detective Sergeant: Crewe inquiry squad
Howard Chennells: brother of Maisey Demler
Newman Chennells: father of Maisey Demler
Ron Chitty: nearest neighbour to Crewes
Jack Collins, Detective Sergeant: 2nd in charge Oliver Walker inquiry
Bill Cook, Detective Chief Inspector
Ian Cook: manager ICI (Imperial Chemical Industries)
Robin Cooke: Supreme Court judge
Heather Cowley: step-daughter of Charles Shirtcliffe
Harvey Crewe: murder victim June 1970
Jeanette Crewe: murder victim June 1970
Marie Crewe: mother of Harvey Crewe
Rochelle Crewe: sole survivor of June 1970 murders
Michael Crew: counsel assisting Royal Commission

Mike Charles

Len Demler

D

Paul Davison: counsel for Crown Prosecutor David Morris
Ronald Davison: President Court of Appeal
Mervyn Dedman, Detective: fingerprint specialist Crewe inquiry
Len Demler: father of Jeanette Crewe
Maisey (May) Demler: mother of Jeanette Crewe

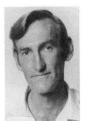

Alexander Fletcher

Norma Demler: second wife of Len Demler
Ian Devereux: defence scientist 2nd Thomas trial
Craig Duncan, Detective: Crewe inquiry squad

E

Thomas Eichelbaum: Counsel for Royal Commission at 1982 appeal
William Eggleton: Pukekohe jeweller
Len Elliott: vintage car enthusiast
Robert Elliott (Dr): medical practitioner
Ross Eyre: youngest son of Ruth Eyre
Ruth Eyre: mother of Eyre boys

F

Peter Gordon

Mike Fibbes, area controller police western district
John Fisher: owner of rolled gold watch
Rob Fisher: counsel for Police at Royal Commission
Martyn Finlay: Minister of Justice (Labour)
Robert Fleming: son of Pukekawa farmer Ross Fleming
Alexander Fletcher: engineer and farm worker
Ray Fox: Pukekawa farmer
Thomas Fox (Dr): first medical practitioner to view Rochelle

G

Pat Gaines, Inspector: Officer in charge of land and river search
Bernie Galvin: head of Prime Minister's Department
Peter Garratt: Pukekawa farmer
Kevin Gee, Detective: Crewe inquiry scene squad
Doug Gifford: assistant to Jim Sprott 2nd Thomas trial
Peter Gordon: Cabinet Minister (National) and Thomas Royal Commissioner
Nicholas Gresson: Crewe investigator, son of Justice Terence Gresson

H

John Hughes

Jack Handcock: relief manager Crewe farm
Vivien Harrison (Thomas): wife of Arthur Thomas
Ben Hawker: manager Chennells Estate 1951-1961
John Henry: counsel for police at Royal Commission
Trevor Henry: judge at 1st Thomas trial
Graeme Hewson: former employer and friend of Harvey Crewe
Les Higgins, Detective: Crewe inquiry scene squad
Michael Holland: Supreme Court judge
Keith Holyoake: Governor General who signed Thomas pardon
Michael Houghton: Anglican Minister at Howick
John Hughes, Detective Sergeant: Officer in charge of suspects Crewe inquiry
Bruce Hutton, Detective Inspector: Officer in charge of Crewe inquiry

Trevor Henry

J

Len Johnston

Brian Jackson: vintage car enthusiast
Brian James, Detective Inspector: southern division Otahuhu
Murray Jeffries, Detective Sergeant: Officer in charge of scene Crewe inquiry
Allen Johnston: former Anglican Archbishop and Royal Commissioner
Len Johnston, Detective: Officer in charge of axle inquiry Crewe inquiry

K

Stan Keith, Detective: clerk of Crewe inquiry
Anthony Keesing: Counsel for Attorney General 1982 appeal
David Keruse: vintage car enthusiast
Howard Keyte: counsel assisting Royal Commission
Maud Knox: close friend of Marie Crewe
Wyndham Knox: close friend of Marie Crewe

L

Stan Keith

David Lange: Prime Minister (Labour)
George Leighton: Foreman of CG Roeszler and Sons, engraver Melbourne
Rod Locker: scientist Meat Industry Research Institute
Samuel Ludbrook (Dr): medical practitioner

M

Ross Meurant

Duncan MacIntyre: deputy Prime Minister (National)
Steve Mackay: farm labourer on Demler farm
Ella McGuire: Mayoress of Tuakau
Donald McLean: Stipendary Magistrate at depositions
Dale McConachie: farmer at Glen Murray
Queenie McConachie: farmer at Glen Murray
George McGregor: retired Supreme Court judge
Jim McLay: Minister of Justice (National)
Ian MacArthur: Supreme Court judge
Duncan McMullin: Court of Appeal judge
Barney Metcalfe, Detective: Crewe inquiry squad
Ross Meurant, Detective on trial: Crewe inquiry scene squad
Ian Miller: Supreme Court registrar
Nick Milsum, Detective Sergeant: Crewe inquiry squad
Lester Moller: Supreme Court judge
Bob Moodie: national secretary of Police Association
David Morris: Crown Prosecutor
Rob Muldoon: Prime Minister (National)

N

David Morris

Paul Neazor: Solicitor General
Donald Nelson: scientist Department of Scientific and Industrial Research
Alfred North: President of Court of Appeal

Donald Nelson

O
Greg O'Connor: president of the Police Association
Pat O'Donovan, Detective Senior Sergeant: Crewe inquiry overview
Noel Ottaway: foreman and workmate of Rasmussen

P
Bruce Parkes, Detective: Crewe inquiry squad
Dave Payne: 2nd chairman Thomas Retrial Committee
John Payne, Detective: Crewe inquiry squad
Lester Payne, Detective: Crewe inquiry squad
Clifford Perry: judge at 2nd Thomas trial
Julie Priest: poultry farmer Pukekawa
Owen Priest: poultry farmer Pukekawa

Clifford Perry

R
Rod Rasmussen: engineer at Meremere
Ivor Richardson: Court of Appeal judge
Clifford Richmond: Court of Appeal judge
John Roberts, Detective: Crewe inquiry squad
Bob Rock: foreman 2nd Thomas trial jury
Bruce Roddick: Pukekawa farm labourer
Mal Ross, Detective Superintendent: regional co-ordinator Auckland CIB
Gerald Ryan: junior counsel for 2nd Thomas trial
Kevin Ryan, QC: counsel for 2nd Thomas trial and at Royal Commission

Bruce Roddick

S
David Schnauer: counsel for DSIR and Justice Department
Les Schultz, Detective Senior Sergeant: 2nd in charge Crewe inquiry
Phil Seaman, Detective Sergeant: Crewe inquiry squad
Rory Shanahan: scientist Department of Scientific and Industrial Research
Angus [Gus] Sharpe: Commissioner of Police
Charles Shirtcliffe: original builder of 1956 road trailer
Lin Sinton, Detective Sergeant: Crewe inquiry squad
Richard Smellie: counsel for DSIR and Justice Department
Edward Somers, QC: Supreme Court and Court of Appeal judge
Graham Speight: Supreme Court judge
Paul Spence, Constable: police diver
Jim Sprott: scientist and defence forensics advisor
John Staveley: head of forensic blood unit
Barry Stevens, Constable: police photographer
Buster Stuckey: brother-in-law of Arthur Thomas

Jim Sprott

T
Robert Taylor: New South Wales Supreme Court judge and
Royal Commission chairman
Paul Temm, QC: senior counsel at 1st Thomas trial
Allan G Thomas: father of Arthur Thomas

Allan G Thomas

Arthur Thomas: innocent man wrongly convicted of double murders
Des Thomas: brother of Arthur Thomas
Lloyd Thomas: brother of Arthur Thomas
Richard Thomas: brother of Arthur Thomas
Thomas Thorp: Supreme Court judge
David Tompkins QC: counsel for Hutton and Johnston 1982 appeal
Harry Todd: Government Analyst and DSIR scientist
Jim Tootill, Detective Sergeant: Crewe inquiry squad
Beverly Turner: sister of Harvey Crewe
Don Turner: brother in law of Harvey Crewe

V

Jim Toothill

Doug Vesey: uncle of Vivien Harrison (Thomas)
Pat Vesey: uncle of Vivien Harrison (Thomas) and first chairman
Thomas Retrial Committee

W

John Wallace QC: counsel Crown Prosecutor David Morris
Bob Walton: Assistant Commissioner of Police then Commissioner
Brian Webb: junior counsel 1st Thomas trial
Gordon Whyte: 2nd owner of 1956 road trailer
Richard Wild: Chief Justice
Brian Wilkinson, Detective Chief Superintendent: regional co-ordinator
Auckland CIB
Peter Williams, QC: counsel for Thomas at second referral to Court of
Appeal and Royal Commission
Barbara Willis: carer of Rochelle Crewe after murders
Gerald Wyllie, Constable: Tuakau policeman, first officer to scene

Bob Walton

Y

David Yallop: British author and crime writer

Foreword

This is not a book I ever intended writing. Indeed the reverse is true. During most of the decade since the publication *The Final Chapter*, my previous book on Pukekawa's infamous Crewe murders, I have resisted the notion that another effort of this nature was necessary, or even desirable. That book was intended to be the ultimate whodunnit of the murders of Jeanette and Harvey Crewe in June 1970. It was a work which focused entirely on bringing to public attention the extent and the detail of the 'evidence' the New Zealand Police assembled against Len Demler, Jeanette's father.

I know now that the homicide inquiry squad led by Detective Inspector Bruce Hutton, as he was at that time, actually gathered much more evidence on Demler than the Police ever revealed – infinitely more. As events have unfolded, it has become obvious that if one does not know that information exists, then clearly one is unable to ask for it. That is a tactic the police have used to great effect – not only to obstruct my efforts in the decades I have spent trying to get to the truth of the Crewe murders, but one which was used with such devastating effect to thwart the defence teams at two Supreme Court trials, in 1971 and 1973, and to obstruct the officers of the Royal Commission of Inquiry established in 1980 to probe these very matters.

The release of *The Final Chapter* a decade ago, should, as I have stated, have been the end of my dalliance with this piece of recent New Zealand history, in all its grisly and disturbing detail.

This long-running, mystifying saga first engulfed me on 5 November 1976. What began as a very ordinary day in reality signalled the start of an extraordinary journey – one, I suspect, that has yet to reach its ultimate conclusion. Its very foundation was a commotion in the newsroom of the Mount Maunganui office of the *Bay of Plenty Times* where I was, at that moment, the senior reporter. This involved a discussion between a younger colleague and a tall, balding man of athletic physique who was more than making his presence felt. He was Nicholas Gresson, the son of a former Judge of the Supreme Court, the late Terence. His impassioned plea was centred on the need of the news media to give more coverage to the terrible injustice that had befallen one Arthur Allan Thomas, who had found himself imprisoned for two particularly shocking murders committed in the Pukekawa district, south of Auckland, six years earlier.

I assigned myself to the story of Gresson's one-man campaign to expose the injustice that had been perpetrated on Thomas and then went on to other things, as is the life of a daily newspaper journalist. But clearly Gresson believed he had sniffed out a potential investigator and within a few days he was back, insisting that I join him on a trip to Pukekawa – to 'murder country' as he called it. The die, as they say, was cast. Unwittingly I became one of the legions of those who, in that tumultuous era, were seeking the truth about the killing of the Crewes and with it, justice for Thomas.

In the year that followed, the trips north to Pukekawa became more frequent and more intense as Gresson and I probed the circumstances of these murders. Memories were fresh then and much of the information offered by good, solid, dependable country folk has proved invaluable in the decades that have followed. The personal knowledge these residents of the Pukekawa district had of aspects of these crimes – and life in that locality generally – was, more often than not, never conveyed to the police, either because of their suspicion of the 'suits from the city' or because of the manner in which either they, or members of their family, were treated by detectives who did not understand the nature and character of rural dwellers.

The information provided by many of those long-time residents in the years that followed the Crewe murders remains, an indelible record of a tragic series of events in a tragic time for Pukekawa, and indeed, for New Zealand as a whole.

In more recent years, the Crewe murders have come to public attention once more, although to be fair, they are an issue that has never died, unlike the victims struck down so cruelly that cold windy night in June 1970. The catalyst for this renewed debate has, in no small part, been attributable to the comprehensive feature articles I wrote for *North & South* magazine in July 2010 and June 2011. The first focused on the anguish felt by Vivien Harrison, the wife of Arthur Thomas at the time of his arrest and incarceration. After more than 40 years, Vivien told of her hope and desire for an apology from the Crown for the wrongful description given to her as 'the woman who'd fed the baby'. It was a forlorn hope – nine months later, she died of cancer in Australia.

The second article related to the identity and actions of a woman whom, many believed, actually cared for and fed the Crewe's infant daughter for five days following the murders. It told of the knowledge the police had about the 'Phantom Woman of Pukekawa' from the very first days of this double homicide inquiry and how the country's top police officer, the Commissioner, prevented an investigation of her in the months immediately preceding the hearings of the Thomas Royal Commission.

Much of the information presented in *North & South* was sourced from a growing collection of documents extracted from the New Zealand Police slowly, and I might add painfully, via the mechanism of the Official Information Act. These documents – coupled with the information provided by Pukekawa residents during the mid 1970s – have caused an intensification of my disquiet over what actually took place within a criminal investigation unlike any seen in New Zealand, previously or since. As the police have continued – more than a little begrudgingly – to release documents from the Crewe homicide file, my focus has switched from the whodunit aspect of these unprovoked killings to the serious malpractice within the investigation that ensued. A new tragedy followed, perpetrated not by killers, but by those whom – as the Thomas Royal Commission observed a decade later – failed miserably in their duty to uphold the law.

It has always been assumed – quite wrongly in fact – that two police officers, acting in isolation from the rest of their squad, committed an act which sent a bewildered, trusting and most definitely innocent man to prison for almost 10 years. It has also been considered – from a public perspective anyway – that the single act that achieved this was the placement ('planting') of a cartridge case from this innocent man's rifle in the victims' garden. These acts were not, however, perpetrated by two detectives alone and nor was the planting of that cartridge case from the Thomas rifle in the Crewe garden the only unlawful act by members of the New Zealand Police in the course of that investigation and subsequent prosecution.

In this book, the methods by which members of the New Zealand Police set about constructing an entire case against a man whom some among them had determined was guilty of the vicious killing of two young people in their own home is placed under the microscope. So, too, is the part played by each of those involved in a case which remains a defining moment in our nation's legal history. Some of these actions, by those whom it must always be remembered were duty-bound to uphold the law, have been canvassed before – in the courts that tried and retried Thomas and especially at the Royal Commission established to investigate the circumstances of his arrest and convictions. But what will be demonstrated is that the juries, the judges and indeed the Royal Commissioners involved were never permitted to hear of, or view, many of the documents that tell the real story of his persecution and wrongful prosecution.

Until now, only those in the inner circle of the Crewe investigation squad have known of the actions they took in the name of the law, but which, in reality, were in direct contravention of it. What has become absolutely clear, however, is that those entrusted with delivering justice to Thomas throughout the 1970s were denied the opportunity to do so because the police suppressed, or failed to disclose, significant evidence that would have proved his innocence. The extent of that suppression, like so much of the tainted evidence collected during the Crewe homicide investigation, makes for disturbing reading.

The mystery of who killed Jeanette and Harvey Crewe, in the early evening of that cold, wet and miserable Wednesday in June 1970 endures. These were not random acts, but as Crown Prosecutor David Morris was aptly to observe, the simple, unprovoked, premeditated, cold-blooded killing of a trusting young couple. These acts, and the subsequent caring for the Crewe's 18-month old daughter for the five days before their disappearance was reported to police, remain New Zealand's ultimate cold case.

History records that a man went to prison – protesting his innocence as loudly and as often as he was able. That it took almost a decade before he was granted a pardon and released speaks volumes, not only about the way that some police officers went about their business, but about the inadequacies and failures of a system which many believed was designed to deliver justice to the people of New Zealand.

Following the pardon issued to Thomas, a Royal Commission found that two police officers – inquiry squad boss Bruce Hutton and one of his loyal followers, Detective Len Johnston – fabricated evidence by planting a cartridge case from his rifle in the Crewe garden in order to secure a conviction. What was not so readily known, or understood, by many was that subsequently Hutton, along with Johnston's family and two police organisations, sought to have the Royal Commission's findings ruled invalid. The Court of Appeal turfed out that action – as rightly it should have. In truth and in law, the formal findings of the Thomas Royal Commission remain intact. The Thomas case remains an indelible blot on the history of the New Zealand Police, no member of which was ever prosecuted for their unlawful acts.

That Royal Commission, given appropriate powers and the resources to do the job with which it had been entrusted, believed it had been able to determine the truth of what occurred within the Crewe homicide inquiry. However the limitations placed upon it's 1980 inquisition – by way of its carefully crafted and restrictive terms of reference and through a concerted and deliberate campaign by the police to deny it access to the most revealing documents of all – ensured that it was never quite able to put before the public the full extent of the malpractice that had occurred, nor to identify all of those responsible for what is undoubtedly the greatest travesty of justice this country has ever seen. This book seeks to remedy the inadequacies of that inquisition, while also balancing the books on behalf of those whose names and reputations were blackened simply because they had the courage to step up and tell the truth.

Chris Birt
06 April 2012

One

It was the last day of December 1969. Tasmanian school teacher Jennifer Mary Beard was seen in the company of a middle-aged man in a greeny-blue Vauxhall near Fox Glacier on the South Island's West Coast. Nine days later, her fiancée Reg Williams reported her missing after she failed to make their planned rendezvous at Milford Sound.

During the intervening period, on Saturday 3 January, an eight-year-old girl from an Oamaru family, having asked for a comfort stop, had seen a partially-clad woman lying under the Haast River bridge, some 100 kilometres south of the glacier. On returning to the family car, she told her parents, but they did not go to investigate and drove off. Thirteen days later, after a report from another family about the assistance given to a driver in a greeny-blue Vauxhall near that bridge, a detective went to the area and found the young Australian's body. It was badly decomposed after abandonment in the humid, midsummer conditions of South Westland and being awash in the river's rise and fall.

Four months after Jennifer Beard's murder, a 35-year-old mother of three, Betty McKay, disappeared near the Eastern Bay of Plenty settlement of Awakaponga. Two days beforehand, she had packed her possessions in a bag and had moved into her brother's home at nearby Thornton. The last confirmed sighting of Mrs McKay was at 12.30 am on Sunday 12 April when a male acquaintance dropped her off near the Thornton bridge. From there she had only about a kilometre and a half to walk to her brother's farm, but she did not make it and she was never seen again.

Rotorua teenager Olive Walker was a shy girl who, on Friday 15 May 1970, left her home to walk the 1.6 kilometres to her sister's house where she was to babysit her nieces and nephews. Piercing screams were heard a short time later, in nearby Malfroy Road, where her sister lived. Later that night, her body was found in a rest area 8 kilometres from the city on State Highway 5, the road to Taupo. She had been subjected to a frenzied attack with a blunt object, struck down so heavily that her skull was broken in seven places.

At 2.20pm on Monday, 22 June 1970, Tuakau police constable Gerald

Wyllie received a phone call from one Owen Priest, a poultry farmer of Pukekawa, a small rural settlement to the south of Auckland. On the basis of what Wyllie was told, he went first to Priest's house on State Highway 22, and then a kilometre or so further on, to the residence of Jeanette and Harvey Crewe, a young farming couple who had been living at Pukekawa for four years, since their marriage in 1966.

Wyllie arrived there at 2.55pm and within an hour local farmers had begun pouring onto the Crewe property, alerted to a mystery by phone calls which had spread around the district like a wildfire. Two police teams, involving both uniformed and Criminal Investigation Branch officers arrived, the first at 4pm and the second, having travelled from Auckland Central, at 5.10pm.

Hence, in the space of less than six months, New Zealand entered a new, unheard-of era. Five people were dead, police resources were stretched to the limit, and while there may have been suspects from the outset in each of these cases, no-one was 'in the can' so to speak. What was unusual was that so many people had been murdered in such a short period of time in a country with a population the size of a very small North American or European city – a far cry from the 70 or so murders experienced in New Zealand each year now.

Of the five murders – the killing of the Crewes are two events, not one – the latter two were the only ones to be 'resolved'. But in the eyes of the public, in law, and in the books of the New Zealand Police, all five murders remain officially unsolved to this day. Little is heard of the premature deaths of Jennifer Beard, Betty McKay and Olive Walker these days, although notable anniversaries do tend to refocus media attention on such cold cases. Occasionally too, police open the books again in a bid to jog the memories of those who may have always had crucial information to provide, or those whose consciences may have finally got the better of them. Mistakenly, some people ask for the Crewe case to be reopened, but the police themselves confirm – and have done so a number of times over recent years – it has never actually been closed. Nowhere in the Western world are cold case files closed unless the crimes are solved.

From the outset, the police investigators who swung into action at Pukekawa at 2.55pm on Monday, 22 June 1970, considered this to be a most baffling and unusual crime. The scene was one of a lounge covered in substantial bloodstains and a long eerie drag mark; a kitchen where watered-down blood was to be seen on kitchen cupboards; and an infant in her cot, where she had lain for five days, having obviously been changed and fed by an unknown person or persons. Bar a bent knitting needle and two slippers at opposite ends of the room, there was no sign of a struggle, and there were no bodies. Jeanette and Harvey Crewe had simply disappeared without trace.

A potted history of the murders of the husband and wife, and the investigation that followed is reproduced below, directly from the Royal Commission's report presented to Parliament a decade after the events. That report does not provide the detail of the hundreds of individuals – uniformed and plain clothed police, civilians, military and scientific personnel – who spent four months in the bone-chilling cold of that mid-winter period, nor the millions of dollars expended during that investigation, conducted alongside the dirty, flood-ravaged waters of the Waikato River.

The Royal Commission's report does however provide an excellent summary of events in the last six months of 1970 and covers the important aspects of the investigation that followed the murders, including the recovery of the Crewes' bodies – Jeanette's on 16 August and that of her husband exactly one month later. The Royal Commission's summary also outlines the main features of the police investigation into the murder of the Crewes and provides particulars of the judicial hearings and other legal steps taken to extricate Arthur Allan Thomas from the 'justice' system once he had been unjustly arrested, charged and convicted on two counts of the most serious crimes anyone can face in New Zealand.

Background

Jeanette Lenore Crewe was born in 1940, the elder daughter of Mr and Mrs L W [Len] and [Maisey] Demler. She grew up on their farm at Pukekawa and attended the local primary school, but completed her secondary education in Auckland. She trained as a teacher and taught in a number of places around the North Island after her training was completed. In 1961-1962 she travelled overseas and returned to New Zealand to teach in Maramarua and then in Wanganui.

In 1942 her younger sister, Heather Demler, was born. In 1950, upon the accidental death of an uncle, Jeanette and Heather Demler inherited his farm in equal shares. This farm had been known as the Chennells Estate. [Maisey Demler was a Chennells before her marriage in 1936 and she was raised on her family property next to that acquired by her new husband, Len Demler] and it was to be run by a series of managers until the sisters reached the age of 25.

David Harvey Crewe, usually known as Harvey, had a similar background to Jeanette Demler, in that he was born and raised in a farming district, in the lower North Island, but attended school in Wellington. Upon leaving school he was employed on various farms in the Woodville and Wanganui districts, and also spent 2 years as a shepherd in the Kumeroa area, employed by his friend from teenage years, Graeme Hewson.

It was while Jeanette Demler was living and teaching in Wanganui that she met Harvey Crewe. In June 1966 they married. At this time, Harvey Crewe bought Heather Demler's share of the [former] Chennells Estate. Thus when they moved on the farm it was as joint owners.

The property itself is located on [State] Highway 22, the house being some 60 yards [55 or so metres] off that road. The Crewes set to with vigour, determined to increase the efficiency and profitability of their farm. Perhaps this may account for the fact that Mr and Mrs Crewe appear to have made few friends in the ensuing 4 years. It seems that they retained a circle of friends who lived away from the area. Nevertheless this hardworking and competent couple appeared contented and happy. On 1 December 1968 their daughter Rochelle was born.

In February 1970 Jeanette Crewe's mother died. Lenard Demler continued to live by himself at his farm which adjoined the Crewe farm on Highway 22. Following his wife's death, Mr Demler became a regular visitor to the Crewe household for meals.

Arthur Allan Thomas was born in 1938, one of a family of nine children. He had four brothers and four sisters. He was raised on his parents' 272 acre [110 hectare] farm at Mercer Ferry Road, some 9 miles [14 kilometres] away from the Crewe farm. He attended the local primary school and left at the age of 14, having reached Standard 6.

On leaving school he began work on his father's dairy farm. Later he worked on an uncle's farm, then moved to the Roose Shipping Company as a labourer. He also spent some time in Maramarua as a forestry worker. Later he was an employee of Barr Brothers, an aerial topdressing firm.

In November 1964 Thomas married Vivien Carter who had recently arrived from England and was staying with her uncle in Wellsford. Following his marriage he worked on a number of farms until in June 1966 he entered into a 5-year lease with his father to take over the running of the family farm at Pukekawa. With his wife he farmed the property efficiently. Evidence suggests that they mixed well into the community as one would expect local persons to do, and to all appearances their marriage was a stable and happy one.

Police investigation

Detective Inspector [Bruce] Hutton, who became officer in charge of the case, had arrived at the house by 4pm on 22 June 1970, with a party of detectives. [Hutton's actual time of arrival was 5.10pm]. On that day, and in the following 7 weeks, he organised an investigation that was intense, thorough, and painstaking. It was however without result in two vital respects; neither body had been found, although it seemed likely from analysis of the many bloodstains, and from the small amount of brain tissue found on the arm of a chair, that both Mr and Mrs Crewe were dead. It had not been possible to obtain anything amounting to sufficient evidence against Demler, Mrs Crewe's father, who was initially Mr Hutton's main suspect.

The situation changed on 16 August 1970, when Mrs Crewe's body was found in the Waikato River. Fifteen fragments of the bullet from her head were recovered. These included one large fragment on the base of which the number eight had been embossed. The fragments were immediately sent to Dr D F [Donald] Nelson of the Department of Industrial and Scientific Research for comparison with bullets fired from rifles collected from relatives and associates of Mr and Mrs Crewe, and from residents within 5 miles [eight kilometres] of their farm, and from other persons who had in any way become involved with the inquiry. An intense search for a .22 cartridge case was also carried out in the house and the enclosure, both of which had been carefully searched in June.

Because police inquiries had revealed some association between Jeanette Crewe and Arthur Thomas in earlier years, Mr Thomas' .22 rifle was collected by the police on 17 August 1970. No .22 rifle was collected from Mr Demler because he was not registered as the owner of one, nor, despite a thorough investigation, could the police establish that he had had access to a .22 rifle at the time Mr and Mrs Crewe disappeared.

Dr Nelson told Mr Hutton on 19 August of his preliminary conclusion that neither Mr Thomas' rifle, nor one owned by the Eyre family, could be excluded as having fired the fatal bullet. The fragments of the bullet from the head of Harvey Crewe, also containing the remnants of a number 8 on the base, but more badly damaged and therefore of less assistance in identifying the rifle from which they were fired, were also taken by Dr Nelson following the discovery of Mr Crewe's body on 16

September 1970.

It was not however until later, between 13 and 16 October, that Dr Nelson confirmed his preliminary view that of the 64 rifles examined, only the Eyre rifle and the Thomas rifle could not be excluded as having fired the fatal bullets. It is clear to us that in this conversation he made Mr Hutton aware of a distinctive scoring mark in one of the 6 grooves in bullets test-fired from the Thomas rifle, and that such a mark had not been found on either of the fatal bullets. Therefore a positive identification of the fatal bullets as having come from the [Thomas] rifle could not be made. Dr Nelson's notes make it clear, and he and Mr Hutton should have realised, that it could not be stated affirmatively that the fatal bullets had come from Mr Thomas' rifle.

With Mr Crewe's body was recovered a car axle, which had obviously been tied to the body with wire as a weight, and was soon identified as coming from a 1928/29 Nash motor car series 420. By 13 October it had been established that, up until about August 1965, this had been in use on a trailer owned by Mr A A [Arthur] Thomas' father, Mr A G [Allan] Thomas. [The history of the car axle is disputed and there is now clear evidence that the original axle and running gear from the Thomas trailer never went back to their Pukekawa farm].

At about this time, two police officers, Detective Inspector [Wally] Baker [from Wellington] and Detective Sergeant [Pat] O'Donovan [from Christchurch], were sent to Auckland to conduct an overview of the Crewe homicide file. It is evident that they regarded the concentration on Mr Demler as the prime suspect by Mr Hutton's team as misguided, and that they encouraged the investigating team to search for other avenues of inquiry. During 2 weeks from 13 October 1970, the police investigating team did just this. While they had been unable during the previous 4 months to uncover a single item of hard evidence against their initial suspect, Mr Demler, they succeeded during this period in building up what amounted to virtually the whole case against Mr A A [Arthur] Thomas.

On 13 October, Detective [Len] Johnston picked up from Mr Thomas' farm a box of .22 ammunition, uncounted, which was to become exhibit 318. He also appears to have visited a tip on the [Thomas] farm that day, searching for parts connected with the axle. That evening the police conducted a reconstruction of the way in which Mr Crewe may have been shot, which involved the murderer shooting from outside the house, through the louvre windows with one foot on a brick parapet beside the steps leading to the back door, and the other foot on the windowsill.

On 14 October, other members of the Thomas family were interviewed concerning the axle [at Matakana, North Auckland]. On 15 October Mr Johnston was again on Mr Thomas' [Pukekawa] farm, this time looking for trailer parts and obtaining a statement which Mr Thomas had written out in his own hand. He returned on 20 October with Detective [Bruce] Parkes and located, after a cursory search of one of the three tips on the farm, two stub axles on which broken welds matched welding at either end of the axle itself. Wire samples, to be analysed and compared with wire taken from the two bodies, were also taken by Mr Johnston on 13 and 20 October. On that latter date [20 October] Mr Thomas' rifle was again uplifted [for the second time] by the police.

There is evidence from Mr and Mrs [Owen and Julie] Priest which establishes that two shots were fired by Mr Hutton and one other police officer, probably Mr Johnston, at the Crewe house at some time between 30 September 1970 and 27 October 1970. Extensive inquiries into the financial affairs of Mr Thomas were carried out by the police on 23 and 24 October. Finally, on 27 October 1970, Detective Sergeant [Mike] Charles and Detective Parkes were sent to the Crewe farm to search an area of garden beside the fence outside the back door of the house. It was thought that, if the murder of Mr Crewe had been carried out in the manner of the reconstruction of 13 October, a shellcase may have been ejected from the rifle into that garden. On any view of the matter, the garden had already been searched on two occasions, but [on 27 October] the two detectives located in the course of their sieve search a shellcase, later to become exhibit 350, within 2 hours of beginning the search. Mr A A Thomas was arrested and charged with the murders of Jeanette and Harvey Crewe on 11 November 1970.

Judicial and Other Proceedings on Both Counts of Murder

Mr Thomas first appeared in Court on 11 November 1970. He was remanded in custody until 25 November 1970 and then again to 14 December 1970 for the taking of depositions. The Lower Court hearing lasted until 22 December 1970, on which he was committed to the Supreme Court for trial on both charges.

The first trial took place between 15 February and 2 March 1971. The jury found him guilty of both charges. His appeal to the Court of

Appeal was dismissed by that Court on 18 June 1971.

In late 1971 Mr Thomas, his father Mr A G [Allan] Thomas and Mr P G F [Pat] Vesey submitted a petition to the Governor-General, pursuant to section 406 of the Crimes Act 1961, seeking a new trial. The material contained in that petition was considered by Sir George McGregor, a retired Judge of the Supreme Court. His report of 2 February 1972 gave as his view that no further reference to the Court should be granted; there had been, in his opinion, no miscarriage of justice. That recommendation notwithstanding, following a further petition of 2 June 1972, the matter was again put before the Court of Appeal on what has become known as the First Referral. Evidence and submissions were heard on four days between 5 February and 16 February 1973. On 26 February 1973 the Court of Appeal ordered a second trial.

That second trial [a retrial] began on 26 March 1973. It lasted until 16 April 1973, on which date Mr Thomas was convicted of both murders and again sentenced to life imprisonment. An appeal against this second conviction was dismissed by the Court of Appeal on 11 July 1973.

Mr Thomas' case had always attracted widespread publicity and public concern. A leading forensic scientist, Dr T J [Jim] Sprott, had given evidence on behalf of Mr Thomas at the second trial. After the trial he began, in the company of P J [Pat] Booth, to pursue an inquiry into a question raised late in the second trial, namely whether the cartridge case, exhibit 350, found by Detective Sergeant Charles could have any connection with the bullets found in the heads of Mr and Mrs Crewe.

Their efforts led to a further petition to the Governor-General, and the case was referred to the Court of Appeal for the second time. [The Second Referral]. The hearing took place between 9 December 1974 and 8 January 1975. On 29 January 1975 the five Judges of the Court of Appeal [a full Bench] gave a unanimous judgment that Thomas had not excluded a reasonable possibility that exhibit 350 contained a pattern 8 bullet.

The only other proceeding of a judicial nature in Mr Thomas' case was an attempt to appeal the judgment of the Court of Appeal at the Second Referral to the Privy Council. In 'Reasons for Judgment' dated 4 July 1978, the Privy Council advised that [it] had no jurisdiction to entertain such an appeal. [While the Royal Commission referred to this as a judgment, it was legally defined as an opinion of the Court of Appeal, provided to the Governor-General, and thus could not subsequently be ruled on by the Privy Council]. There was no slackening of effort on the part of those concerned with Mr Thomas' case however. Dr Sprott and Mr Booth particularly, continued their investigations into the cartridge case question following the judgment of the Court of Appeal on the Second Referral. Mr Booth published a book *Trial by Ambush* and Dr Sprott and Mr Booth jointly were responsible for the publication of the *ABC of Injustice*.

In 1978, British author, Mr D A [David] Yallop took an interest in the case. He spent a considerable time researching and writing his book *Beyond Reasonable Doubt?* This book stated his belief in Mr Thomas' innocence and his opinion that his conviction amounted to a serious miscarriage of justice. The nature and seriousness of the allegations made were such that the Prime Minister [Rob Muldoon] appointed Mr R A [Robert] Adams-Smith QC to report to him. Mr Adams-Smith gave two reports to the Prime Minister, dated 16 January 1979 and about December 1979. It was a consequence of the second that Mr Thomas received a free pardon pursuant to section 407 of the Crimes Act 1961. Shortly afterward, this [Royal] Commission [of Inquiry] was set up to investigate the circumstances of his conviction.

Two

The pardoning of Arthur Thomas on 17 December 1979 – he was released that same day from Hautu prison farm near Turangi – ended a fight between 'the people' and 'the Crown' which had spanned almost a decade, had seen his case examined in seven judicial hearings and had cost the New Zealand taxpayer many millions of dollars. The end result though was, in essence, a defeat for those who had concocted evidence, suppressed crucial information, bent the truth and obstructed justice in so many ways between 11 November 1970, when Thomas was arrested, and 17 December 1979, when he once again became a free man.

Over the subsequent three decades or so, there has been on-going debate about what the effect of a pardon actually means. To dispel the belief – as put over the years by any number of retired police officers – that Thomas' pardon was a technicality which had been 'engineered' by the Prime Minister of the day, Rob Muldoon, it is important to quote the letter of the law. Section 407 of the Crimes Act 1961 declares:

Whereas any person convicted of any offence is granted a free pardon by Her Majesty, or by the Governor-General in the exercise of any powers vested in him on that behalf, that person shall be deemed not to have committed that offence; provided that the granting of a free pardon shall not affect anything lawfully done or the consequences of anything unlawfully done before it is granted.

A subsequent ruling by the High Court, in response to action by police involved with the Crewe inquiry and the two police service associations – they sought to have the hearings of the Royal Commission terminated – is relevant to the pardon granted to Thomas. In a 60-page judgment, delivered on 29 August 1980, the Court determined:

In terms of the pardon Thomas is considered to have been wrongly convicted, and he cannot be charged again with the murder of either Harvey or Jeanette Crewe. He is, by reason of the pardon, deemed to have been wrongly convicted. The language of section 407 does not indicate any intention to create such radical departure from normal effect of a prerogative pardon as would be involved in reading into the language an intention to create a statutory fiction, the obliteration by force of law of the acts of the person pardoned. It is more sensibly read to be as, first a reaffirmation of the basic effect of the prerogative [pardon], and secondly, an attempt to minimise the residual legal disabilities or attainders.

In words that permit no confusion, Arthur Thomas is deemed not to have shot dead Jeanette and Harvey Crewe, at Pukekawa, on 17 June 1970.

Having seen Thomas released from prison, Justice Minister Jim McLay then set about having terms of reference drawn up for a Royal Commission of Inquiry. Those terms of reference were, themselves, a cause of great consternation from the pro-Thomas brigade, which by then had thousands of supporters scattered from one end of New Zealand to the other. While the general thrust of the impending inquiry was welcomed and the prospect of seeing the police involved with the Crewe inquiry put under a blowtorch for the first time celebrated, the Thomas Retrial Committee, in particular, wanted the conduct of the two Supreme Court trials and the actions of the two Crown Prosecutors examined by way of another distinctly separate term of reference. But that did not happen and to this day members of the Thomas family see it as the one regrettable deficiency in what was a Government-ordered and initiated independent inquiry into what had not only put an innocent man behind bars – with a double murder conviction to dwell on – but what had kept him there.

The terms of reference under which the Thomas Royal Commission was required to operate were as follows:

1. Whether the investigation into the deaths of David Harvey Crewe and Jeanette Lenore Crewe was carried out in a proper manner, and, in particular:-
a) Whether there was any impropriety on any person's part in the course of the investigation or subsequently, either in respect of the cartridge case (exhibit 350) or in respect of any other matter?
b) Whether any matters that should have been investigated were not investigated?
c) Whether proper steps were taken, after the arrest of Arthur Allan

Thomas, to investigate any matter or information, if any, which suggested he was not responsible for those deaths?

2. Whether the arrest and prosecution of Arthur Allan Thomas was justified?

3. Whether the prosecution failed at any stage to perform any duty it owed to the defence in respect of:-

a) The evidentiary material which might have assisted the defence?

b) Any other matter?

4. Whether in respect to the jury list for either trial:-

a) The Crown or the police or the defence obtained preference in respect of the time at which the list was supplied?

b) Any persons named on the list were approached by representatives of the Crown or the police or the defence before the jury was selected?

c) Anything was done other than in accordance with normal practice or was improper or was calculated to prejudice the fairness of the subsequent trial?

5. Whether, after each trial:-

a) The Crown or the police made an adequate investigation into new matters, if any, which may have related to the deaths of David Harvey Crewe and Jeanette Lenore Crewe or to the trial and which were placed before the Crown or the police by any person or persons?

b) Any relevant facts became known to the Crown or the police which were not known to them at the time of the trial?

6. What sum, if any, should be paid by way of compensation to Arthur Allan Thomas following upon the grant of a free pardon?

7. Such other matters as are directly relevant to the matters mentioned in paragraphs 1 to 6 of these presents:

But nothing in paragraphs 1 to 7 of these presents shall empower [the Royal Commission] to inquire into or report upon the actual conduct of the trials, whether by the Courts or on the part of the Crown or defence.

It was also tasked with determining what sum, if any, should be paid, by way of compensation to Thomas upon the grant of a free pardon, and to look at what other such matters were directly relevant to the five terms of reference it was to inquire into.

The proceedings of the Thomas Royal Commission took place over the course of most of 1980, and its final report is today freely available on the Internet. Many matters covered by that inquisitorial body will be referred to in this book, as they relate to individuals who were required to provide evidence, under oath, and to the evidence they gave in that forum. In doing so, it will be illustrated that even though an independent panel – each member of which had quite distinctly different skills and expertise – sought to get to the truth of the conviction of Arthur Thomas, even its best endeavours were thwarted, to one degree or another, by a collective of like-minded souls who shared a determination not to reveal all, nor to give effect to the oath they swore before entering the witness box – to speak 'the truth, the whole truth and nothing but the truth'.

Three

Hundreds of men, and a handful of women, were involved in the search for Jeanette and Harvey Crewe, and the investigation that followed their murders. They consisted of uniform police and CIB officers, farmers, navy divers and helicopter crews, scientists and medical officers and others. Each, in their own way, was a contributor to one of the biggest and most costly criminal inquiries ever mounted in New Zealand.

While most were volunteers – predominantly farmers – and military personnel engaged in combing the hills and valleys, the tomos and waterways, as the search for the missing couple ground relentlessly from one day to the next through late June and all of July, the inquiry into these baffling murders rested with a squad of detectives, which at its peak numbered around twenty. By early August – in the absence of bodies or any real hard evidence about the offender – this squad was reduced to a handful, as few as four at that time.

The officer who headed the Crewe inquiry specifically was Bruce Hutton, who had been a detective inspector for a little over two years when he was dispatched to the Crewe farm at Pukekawa in mid June 1970. Commanding the Auckland Police was Assistant Commissioner George Austing. As officer in charge of the region he had the duty of signing off the arrest of Arthur Thomas four months and 24 days after the Crewes were murdered. The CIB team in his region came under the stewardship of Detective Superintendent Mal Ross, to whom Hutton reported at a local level. Second in charge of the inquiry team was Detective Senior Sergeant Les Schultz – who by 13 October was off the case, having been rushed to Auckland hospital by ambulance from his home with a severe stomach ailment.

The document referred to as a wiring diagram – the organisational chart of the Crewe inquiry – records the identities of those most heavily involved in that investigation, although most had but a brief connection with it. This document shows that under Schultz's command was the inquiry clerk Stan Keith, couriers, typists and a reception and supply officer. Off to one side were the police photographers, scientists from the Department of Scientific and Industrial Research, pathologist Dr Frank Cairns, Lands and Survey staff, blood specialist Dr John Staveley and radio operators.

Detective Graham (Bud) Abbott was officer in charge of exhibits. The field search team was under the control of Inspector Pat Gaines, with uniformed officers, army and air force personnel, police and navy divers, locals and other members of the public, boat owners, dog handlers and officials from councils and Government departments to organise and manage.

The nerve centre of this particular investigation however was the line of the organisational chart that involved the real expertise, such as it was at that time – officer in charge of suspects Detective Sergeant John Hughes; officer in charge of inquiries Detective Sergeant Mike Charles: officer in charge of relatives Detective Sergeant Phil Seaman and officer in charge of the scene Detective Sergeant Murray Jeffries – the latter with Detective Constable Les Higgins, Detective Bruce Parkes, Detective Kevin Gee and detective-on-trial, Constable Ross Meurant.

This collection was finished off by the 'grunts' who went from one end of the Pukekawa district to the other in the area canvass, under the control of Detective Sergeant Jim Tootill. Working for him were Detective Barney Metcalfe, Detective John Roberts and the two Paynes, John and Lester, also detectives. A number of other CIB personnel were involved in this inquiry on an as-required basis – their job to get in, get their specific task done and then to go onto other inquiries. Detective Sergeant Lin Sinton, Detective Craig Duncan and Detective Sergeant Nick Milsum were also involved at one time or another.

On 18 September 1970, two days after Harvey Crewe's body – and an old car axle found on the riverbed below – were pulled out of the Waikato River, one Detective Lenrick [Len] Johnston joined the Crewe homicide inquiry squad, by then heavily depleted. His arrival was to have a profound effect on the direction of the inquiry itself, and ultimately on the fate of Arthur Thomas and all those around him.

The investigation of the Crewe murders kicked off on 22 June 1970, late in the afternoon. It carried on during the remainder of June, July and August, with Len Demler remaining the prime suspect until early October. This is now confirmed, despite Hutton's much later insistence that he had decided in mid August – upon the recovery of Jeanette Crewe's body from the Waikato River – to take Demler off the suspect list at that point. Documents now show that Demler was still the main suspect as late as 2 October. On that day a ground-breaking conference was held for the purposes of examining the evidence which had been assembled against Demler during three and a half months of one of the most extensive and determined homicide investigations ever mounted in this country.

Only remotely associated with Jeanette Crewe, by way of attendance at the same primary school and some romantic aspirations as a teenager, Arthur Thomas had in fact been excluded as a suspect in mid-August. His rifle, among many others, had been seized immediately after the recovery of Jeanette Crewe's body, but it was returned on 8 September, with the message that it was not in any way connected with the murders. But from early October, Thomas was brought into the fold, although as Hutton later disclosed, Demler was still number one on the suspect list at that time.

The sequence of events after 2 October 1970 will be referred to later in the analysis of what part each of the main players in the investigation took in building a formidable case against Thomas in a matter of weeks. For present purposes, the veritable goldmine of 'evidence' in the five weeks under consideration - in reality only a little over three weeks as there was a hiatus in the field work in the 12 days immediately preceding the arrest of Thomas - the main thrust was on an overview of the inquiry, carried out by two out-of-town detectives.

Detective Inspector Wally Baker, a big man with an even bigger reputation, and Detective Sergeant Pat O'Donovan, were directed to go north to provide an independent overview of the Crewe homicide inquiry – where it had gone, or more correctly had not gone – and where it was headed. On arrival in Auckland, the two detectives took control of what was supposed to be the full documentary file on the homicide and spent the next two and a half weeks pouring over it. They also took the time to evaluate Hutton's prime suspect, Demler, as the documentary record now reveals. Baker's assessment of the man who had, for almost four months, been harassed and harangued, maligned and mercilously interrogated, often for hours at a time – and about whom rumours had been spread by those seeking to ring a confession from him – is an illuminating document.

In later years, some of those with a vital interest in the Crewe case have expressed the view that the Baker-O'Donovan overview, ordered as it was by police headquarters, was a clear signal of increasing agitation and exasperation from then Assistant Commissioner Bob Walton that the Crewe murders remained unsolved after months of investigation. It was Walton who, as head of the CIB nationally, would bear the brunt of any failure to perform within the ranks of those attached to the 'plain clothes' unit within the New Zealand Police.

The Baker-O'Donovan overview concluded with the 19 October conference [see appendices] at which they put forward their views. The other six participants – Hutton, Schultz, Tootill, Johnston, Parkes and Keith – were the remnants of what had been a Crewe inquiry squad. The formal record of this last gathering with the overview detectives states:

- Conference considered that apart from Thomas and Demler, from the enquiries there does not appear to be any other person remotely concerned.
- Conference concluded that every effort must be made immediately to either confirm Thomas as a suspect or exclude him entirely from the enquiry.

The next day, their task completed, Baker returned to Wellington, while O'Donovan flew onward, further south to Christchurch. As they were packing their possessions that day, Detective Bruce Parkes and Detective Len Johnston arrived at the Thomas farm with instructions to uplift his rifle, for the second time. Seven days later, a cartridge case proved to have been fired in that rifle was found, by Detective Sergeant Mike Charles, in the garden at the murder scene. The missing link between Thomas and the deaths of Jeanette and Harvey Crewe was now firmly up Hutton's sleeve.

Four

On 21 May 1980, the Thomas Royal Commission formally opened its proceedings, an event long anticipated by the supporters of the man whose convictions and imprisonment were to be examined, in minute detail, but with trepidation and a sense of foreboding by the individuals who actions were to be put under a spotlight of the most intense kind, and by the State's law enforcement agency itself.

Publicly, the New Zealand Police claimed to welcome the inquisition that had emerged from a decade of controversy, acrimony and open hostility between the free-Thomas campaigners and the group of former and serving officers whose blue line was becoming thinner by the day. By then Bob Walton had his hand firmly on the police tiller nationally as Commissioner and after learning that a Royal Commission of Inquiry was to be convened, he declared:

> The police welcome the public inquiry as it gives us the opportunity to answer allegations. The police will co-operate to the full. Any issues that do arise will be fully investigated by the police.

But behind the scenes rearguard actions were mounted, with the fighting spirit so savagely demonstrated in Thomas' second Supreme Court trial and in the seven years that followed that historic retrial being renewed with equal intensity.

Within four weeks of Thomas being granted his pardon, police were at one of the prisons in which he had previously been incarcerated, questioning an inmate – a former prison 'friend'. It was the first of a string of disclosures aimed at diminishing the effect of the pardon which appeared over coming years.

On 9 June 1980 the Royal Commission began its hearings and from the outset, the just-retired New South Wales chief judge Robert Lindsay Taylor – he proved to be the best choice imaginable as the 'chairman of the board' on that inquiry - made it abundantly clear that he would not tolerate any attempt by the police to turn those proceedings into a third trial of Thomas:

Arthur Allan Thomas has been granted a free pardon in respect of his convictions for the murders of Jeanette and Harvey Crewe. He is deemed never to have committed the offence. You will readily perceive that no question of the guilt or innocence of this man can ever arise again. There will be no third trial.

This is a message that the New Zealand Police and its legal representatives should have heard loud and clear but that they did not. Examination of the evidence produced at those proceedings clearly demonstrates that not only did the police largely *not* accept the effect of the pardon, but that some of its members – past and present – continued with a covert campaign to 'dig the dirt' on Thomas.

The Royal Commission did have an early victory, convincing the Government to amend the law to give it full powers to summon witnesses, administer oaths and hear witnesses. This required an amendment to the Commissions of Inquiry Act 1908, and its validity was backed fully by the Parliamentary Opposition. Several new offences were also created. These included willfully interfering with or obstructing the Commission and contempt of the Commission. That the request for this law change came just four days after the Royal Commission began its formal hearings is a sign that the three-man panel entrusted with getting to the bottom of the prosecution and double conviction of Thomas believed that they were facing mistrust, anger and resentment along with a healthy dose of obstruction from the police witnesses already appearing before them.

Within days, the Royal Commission chairman found himself telling inquiry head Bruce Hutton:

If you want me to accept you as a witness of truth, you will not be evasive, otherwise I will be loath to accept you.

The next day Judge Taylor was on the offensive again, telling Detective Sergeant Murray Jeffries, the officer in charge of the scene search at the Crewe property a decade before:

I had expected the officers engaged on the Crewe murder inquiry to be reliable men, but ever since the police evidence started there has been a constant thrust to create the opposite impression.

The scene was now set for a battle of monumental proportions. The same day Taylor delivered his stern rebuke to Jeffries, the two counsel for the police, John Henry and Rob Fisher staged a dramatic walk-out following what the newspapers termed 'a heated exchange'. It was to be another week before they were seen by the Royal Commission again. To their embarrassment they then had to once again go through the formality of seeking leave to appear before the Commission.

Before recommencing hearings, Taylor addressed what he described as an impression that the hearing being conducted was some sort of third trial [of Thomas] and that he was being unduly critical of one side:

> It is not a trial and I am not sitting as a Judge, nor am I discharging judicial functions. I am sitting as a Royal Commissioner and the role of this Commission is inquisitorial. Its function is to ascertain the truth. To do that the members are entitled to cross-examine witnesses and are bound, in my view, to question evidence if it appears to them to be questionable. I make no apologies for the fact that, in cross-examination, I have at times been abrupt and derisive when I thought evidence I had heard was worthy of it. I believe that to properly discharge the task I have undertaken I have to do my best to find out the truth.

He also went on to observe that the Commission's rulings and observations on evidence appeared to have two major consequences – that it would not receive evidence that tended to establish that Thomas' rifle, or Thomas himself, was responsible for the killing of the Crewes and further, that the Commission would consider the issues on the basis that Thomas did not in fact commit the crimes.

However, July that year began as June had finished, with the Royal Commission's chairman and counsel for the police again engaged in terse exchanges. From the transcript dated 3 July 1980:

> *Fisher:* The Commission's refusal [to allow him to table a submission] is denying counsel the opportunity to publicly record the difficulties we are having in presenting the police case.
> *Taylor:* You are not facing difficulties. We have allowed police witnesses to go to their legal advisors, to prepare their own briefs with their help and to have pointed out to them where difficulties were likely to be. And to be fair to them we have allowed them to go into the

witness box and read their statements. This is entirely unprecedented in my experience but it is being allowed because the events being considered by this Commission occurred 10 years previously. The only thing we didn't do, and this is what you wanted to do, was to let you and Mr Henry order your case and select the issues you choose. That would be inviting the whole of the public to say 'here we go again, another Thomas case run by the police'. The result would have reflected on the credibility of this Commission. Your objection, really, is that I have cross-examined policemen hard.

Fisher denied this, saying that his submission outlined 40 major denials of right to a hearing.

Taylor: If you don't have the courage to stand up when you should have – you never rose to say anything – then there is no injustice. You should make a protest at the time.

Taylor's fellow Commissioners, eager to show that this was not a case of a hard-nosed Australian Judge versus the New Zealand Police, then entered the fray. Peter Gordon told Fisher the views of the chairman were shared by both himself and the other panel member, the Most Reverend Allen Johnston.

Five days after that exchange – one of many in what was, in effect, a series of skirmishes that began when the Royal Commission's hearings commenced in June and ended when they concluded in September – Taylor and his panel brought down a ruling that was to eliminate for all time any connection the Thomas rifle had with the murders of Jeanette and Harvey Crewe. On 8 July 1980, the Commissioners halted the proceedings after hearing the evidence of Detective Les Higgins and immediately prior to beginning that of Detective Ross Meurant. That formal finding [Appendix 1] declares, in summary, that the cartridge case found in the Crewe garden – proven to have come from the Thomas Browning rifle – was never connected with the bullets that killed the Crewes.

July 1980 came to an end with the Royal Commissioners ruling again that the hearings they were conducting would not be a third trial of Thomas and that the evidence put to both his Supreme Court trials would not be called, unless it was relevant to the terms of reference. If it was, witnesses would be called for examination and cross-examination.

A new dimension was added by Thomas himself in the last days of that month, with a formal complaint following his discovery that police were at prisons questioning inmates as to whether he had, at any time during his incarceration, 'confessed' to murdering the Crewes. Judge Taylor and his colleagues were outraged and Police Commissioner Bob Walton bore the brunt:

Taylor: Are you aware that police officers have been going around making inquiries to try to get evidence of Thomas' guilt?

Walton: I believe they are checking on issues raised. I think the police have a duty to record such matters in case questions are raised, although they can do nothing about them.

Taylor: The man is innocent. What business is it of your's or your police force to go around checking? You know that Mr Thomas has made complaints that the police have been to jails where he was imprisoned. They have been going to inmates asking them questions directed to showing that he made confessions. Did you authorise that?

Walton: I did not.

Taylor: Would you not accept that this man, in law and by Act of Parliament, has been declared innocent. Isn't he entitled to be treated as such and not be hounded by police officers going around questioning people to see if he could be discredited?

Taylor then asked Walton if he had read a complaint from Thomas that police had interviewed a man serving a life sentence with a view to getting evidence that Thomas had made admissions:

Taylor: Isn't it indecent to hound a man who has spent 10 years in jail after being wrongly convicted. He was wrongly convicted and you know that.

Walton: I will tell the police they must not pursue or harass Mr Thomas.

The following day, Taylor found it necessary to address that issue again, opening the proceedings with a declaration that he had never instructed the New Zealand Police to stop investigating the Crewe murders. The former archbishop, Allen Johnston, joined the throng, telling the once-again packed hearings room that documents in the possession of members of the panel showed without doubt that police officers had indeed been making further inquiries about Thomas since he was granted his pardon. The Royal Commission was not, however, seeking to assume any power to direct the police in their duties. Royal Commissioner Peter Gordon also viewed the police intrusion into matters relating to Thomas as disturbing:

> We had considered, before Mr Walton was cross-examined, that since Mr Thomas could never again be tried, such actions [by the police] are not only unwarranted, but morally wrong.

That very same day the police went to the High Court with an application for an injunction seeking an immediate halt to the Royal Commission's hearings. This was filed under the Judicature Amendment Act on behalf of Hutton, Jeffries, the New Zealand Police Association and the Police Officers Guild and but after a late-afternoon hearing, Justice Speight refused to accede to what would have amounted to a stay on the Royal Commission's proceedings.

The inquiry went on, but not before a further challenge was mounted as the former and current police officers concerned, and their two service organisations, sought once more to halt the Royal Commission's work on the basis of alleged bias, predetermination and unfair conduct. It was a bold claim, as the Royal Commission's counsel, Dr George Barton, described it, as its intent was to 'bring the work of the [Royal] Commission to a complete and total stop'. One of the key planks of that action was also to seek a ruling that would permit the police to continue making inquiries into the Crewe murders, whether or not those inquiries tended to implicate Thomas.

That hearing of the High Court – before Justices Moller, Holland and Thorp – lasted 10 days and delivered a judgment that the Royal Commission could continue to do the job with which it had been mandated by Parliament, the highest Court in the land.

The judges did, however, come out in favour of the plaintiffs in one respect, ruling that the Commission's chairman had wrongly interpreted the effect and meaning of the pardon granted to Thomas. The error was that Taylor had declared the pardon to mean that Thomas was innocent, whereas the correct interpretation is that he was, and still is, deemed not to have committed the crimes with which he had been charged. This may be a subtle difference, but the law is the law and the status of

Arthur Thomas is as it was before he was convicted.

The High Court's determination that there had been no pre-determination or bias was an important ruling, given subsequent allegations by those named by the Royal Commission as fabricators of evidence.

One interesting observation on the High Court's decision over the interpretation issue came from Thomas' counsel Kevin Ryan. Asked whether the High Court's judgment was a vindication of the action taken by Hutton, Jeffries and the two police organisations, the Auckland criminal lawyer quipped wryly: 'The British claimed that Dunkirk was a victory.'

While the High Court judgment may be seen as something of a rebuke for the Royal Commission, it also provided an opportunity for Taylor and the two lay members of his panel to seek a change in the terms of reference, on the basis that they now required amendment. That matter went to the Cabinet for consideration, but the request was turned down, privately satisfying the Royal Commissioners as the denial meant they were able to proceed with the terms they already had, without further inference from a court or the Government itself.

The finale to the 1980 Royal Commission of Inquiry came during September, but with retired police brought in to pack the public gallery in support of 'their men' – today this is a tactic referred to as a rent-a-crowd moment – the fireworks continued:

Taylor: Answer the questions instead of embarking on long irrelevant explanations.

Hutton: If you intend to stop me answering the questions, I can't help this Commission.

Taylor: Mind your manners.

Hutton: Perhaps you could do the same Sir. Don't bully me. I will not be bullied. There is no doubt about it. Stop it. You have asked me the question seven times now. Any New Zealand Judge would stop you.

The crowd went wild, the Thomas supporters finally hearing the type of exchange they had been awaiting a decade to hear and the contingent of both retired and serving police officers baying in the Hutton corner: 'You tell him'.

On 24 September 1980, the Thomas Royal Commission ended

its hearings, having heard final submissions from all the counsel representing the parties granted leave to be represented – Howard Keyte and Michael Crew for the Commission itself; Peter Williams and Kevin Ryan for Thomas; John Henry and Rob Fisher for the New Zealand Police; Richard Smellie and David Schnauer for the DSIR and Justice Department; and John Wallace QC and Paul Davison for David Morris, the Crown Prosecutor.

Very little of the detail of those submissions made it into the public arena, with most of the content being provided by way of written statements from the counsel who had endured 64 days of hearings, but extracts are interspersed in the chapters of this book, where I considered them to be relevant or desirable.

The Thomas Royal Commission was, and remains, the biggest inquisition into the actions of members of the New Zealand Police ever conducted. The formal findings of Robert Taylor, Peter Gordon and Allen Johnston were uncompromising in their condemnation and those who formulated them were just as unrelenting in their delivery. The Commissioners decreed:

> This Commission is privileged to have been given the task of righting wrongs done to Thomas, by exposing the injustice done to him by manufactured evidence. We cannot erase the wrong verdicts or allow the dismissed appeals.
>
> ▢▢▢▢
>
> This Commission was not in an adversary position. We have searched for the truth, probed, inquired and interrogated where we thought necessary; made our displeasure known at prevarication and reluctance to speak the truth. We have not been content with so much of the truth as some saw fit to put it before us.
>
> ▢▢▢▢
>
> Money cannot put right the wrongs done to Mr Thomas or remove the stain he will carry for the rest of his life. The high-handed and oppressive actions of those responsible for his convictions cannot be obliterated. Nevertheless all these elements are to be reflected in our assessment, as are also his suffering, loss of enjoyment and amenities of life, and his pecuniary loss.

The Royal Commission recommended an overall compensation payment, on an ex gratia basis, of $1.087 million, which included $38,287 for members of the Thomas family. Upon the receipt of that report, Parliament unanimously received its formal findings and adopted the recommendations in relation to compensation, no doubt thankful that one long, grueling and destructive chapter in its history had come to an end, with an outcome deemed by most of its Members at least to have been just and worthy.

Five

The Thomas Royal Commission delivered such damning findings that the front pages of national newspapers and news bulletins of television and radio were filled to overflowing for days after 28 November 1980.

The reaction from police was swift, vitriolic and concerted, with caution being thrown to the wind as the headquarters-based hierarchy and its allies in the service associations, and even among the ranks of serving senior officers, sought to blunt the attack, not only on two of its former members, but on its own reputation. The police may have taken a more cautious approach had the extent to which they had beavered away in the background to further discredit Thomas been known to the public. This was not known, however, because these particular proceedings were conducted behind the Royal Commission's closed doors and are only now being brought to public attention, 32 years after the event.

The police tactics involved the use of jailhouse snitches, whom, according to contemporary accounts, are usually persons serving a long sentence and whom see there is benefit to be gained by turning State's evidence. In the dying days of the Thomas Royal Commission, two such persons emerged, brought forward at the insistence of the police. They did so, it must be noted, *after* Thomas had been pardoned.

The first two witnesses were serving inmates prepared to swear on oath that Thomas had 'confessed' to them that he had killed the Crewes. A third witness was a local driver who had provided a statement at the time of the murders, only to come back a decade later with much more defamatory and highly-damaging allegations against Thomas. The Commissioners initially resisted hearing evidence from these witnesses, considering their allegations to be both scurrilous and a waste of time. But following the High Court ruling of early September, a more cautionary approach had been adopted and, under protest, the testimony was heard.

By any objective evaluation, this was yet another cynical and calculated attempt by the police to further erode the credibility of a man who had not only been granted a free pardon, but was well on his way to receiving a lump-sum compensation payout, expected to run into seven figures. That was not a point missed by Thomas' counsel, Peter Williams QC, who told the Royal Commission:

> If this type of police harassment continues, we will be duty-bound to up the ante in terms of the compensation being sought.

In its formal report to Parliament, the Royal Commission canvassed this issue, reporting:

> Police made available the briefs of evidence of these witnesses, who had *not* previously given evidence [at the trials]. In both cases, their evidence was designed to associate Thomas with the murders. It was put forward as establishing that, if it was accepted that he had committed the murders, it was surely likely that he had dropped exhibit 350 in the [Crewe] garden. No doubt because of what emerged as to the dubious nature of the evidence, and of those persons giving it, the police were reluctant to put forward these people as witnesses they were asking to be called. They preferred to suggest that, having seen that the briefs disclosed relevant evidence, we should no doubt wish to hear it. That suggestion we regard as merely playing with words. There is no doubt but that these witnesses were put forward to us by the police.

The first witness had recently been released from what the Commission chairman referred to as a 'lunatic asylum'. This witness had been in that secure establishment from 1969 to 1974, but was later sent to prison. The basis of his 'evidence' was that Thomas had 'confessed' to the murders while in prison, had drawn maps and sketched outlines of his own house and the Crewe house. A psychiatrist who heard his evidence to the Royal Commission said this witness represented 'a classical case of grandiose paranoid schizophrenia', an assessment that was then confirmed by another medical professional.

What followed then may now seem bizarre, but this is as it is recorded:

> In the light of the doctor's evidence, we directed counsel assisting us not to lead any further evidence from the witness. We indicated to counsel for the police that, in our view, the evidence clearly

established the man's unreliability, that he was mentally ill, and to continue his examination was inhumane. We invited counsel [for the police] to seek instructions that he not ask the witness any questions and we adjourned for that purpose. Counsel for the police informed us that he was unable to obtain those instructions and he continued his examination.

The second witness, brought in to collaborate the testimony of the mentally ill inmate, had also spent many years in prison and had a long string of criminal convictions for offences including fraud. He opted not to give evidence, even though he had been delivered by the police to the witness box for precisely that purpose. His reason for refusing was that there may be reprisals from other prisoners and that these could take the form of physical violence. The transcript makes it patently obvious that he believed that if word got out he was testifying against Thomas – whom most inmates had come to regard as being innocent – he could have been attacked himself. Nevertheless the Royal Commissioners accepted, and properly considered, the briefs of evidence put before them in relation to his information. They did however record:

This second inmate was prepared some years ago to break the law for the purposes of personal gain. He is, as a consequence, serving an exceptionally long sentence. His prison file reveals him as shrewd, cunning, devious and manipulative, and a man who would go to considerable lengths to shorten his sentence. In addition, evidence we have received established that he has been a police informer on other matters. This second inmate would have had every reason to lie in support of the first. He must have hoped, realistically or not, that the police would use their influence to shorten his sentence or improve conditions for him. The only possible disadvantage which his story could bring him would be a prosecution for perjury. It may be that he refused to give evidence before us because he feared such a prosecution.

The Royal Commission recorded its view that the 'prison confessions' by Thomas never took place:

The evidence of the two prisoners was a tissue of lies and it causes us grave concern that police officers were so obviously ready to place credence on such unreliable, self-interested, and in the case of the first inmate, deluded evidence. It was but another instance of the police being unwilling to accept the pardon.

...ught forward in closed session was a local ...uth Auckland area. His name was withheld ...nily at that time but it is known to many now. ...dated 24 June 1970, two days after the Crewes ...he came forward to with a new statement 10 ...homas had been pardoned and released from

...new] evidence was that at 7am on the morning ...driving past the Crewe farm. In a lay-by just ...saw Thomas' car and trailer and on the trailer ...ese claims had been omitted from in his earlier ...mission later recorded:

...ce that was produced to us revealed that the man could not have been in the vicinity of the Crewe farm until 9am on 18 June 1970 and there is evidence that convinces us that Thomas could not have been there at that time. Furthermore, his evidence revealed envy of Thomas for the attention which his case had received from the news media and for the compensation which public opinion suggests he will receive from the Government following our report. All of these factors, taken with the demeanor of the man as he gave evidence, lead us unhesitatingly to reject his evidence as a total fabrication.

The police of course knew that the Royal Commission was not only reluctant to hear the two inmates and the driver who came out of the closet 10 years after the murders with a version of events so radically divergent from what he had reported in June 1970, but that it intended to dismiss what had been presented to it. In that context, what followed requires answers. On 28 September 1980, after the Royal Commission had finished its hearings but before it had presented its formal report to Parliament, the *Sunday News* carried a major article, with banner headlines – spread over two pages and accompanied by a photograph – which 'disclosed' that Thomas' car had been seen near the Crewes with 'two bundles on his trailer' the morning after the crimes had been committed.

Examination of that article is warranted.

The opening paragraph of that article, written by Michael Smith, points a clue as to the origin of what was, formally, suppressed evidence:

> Secret evidence allegedly heard behind closed doors at the Thomas Commission inquiry has been leaked to *Sunday News*. The man at the centre of this evidence is living in fear of his life. He has refused to be interviewed, but he did confirm that he had appeared before the Royal Commission.

Sunday News had agreed to refer to him only as Mr X to protect his identity, but it then went on to provide the actual detail of what he had told the Royal Commission.

The real issue that emerges is who provided the *Sunday News* with either his statement or the transcripts of a closed session of the Royal Commission, or both? It was certainly not the lawyers representing Thomas, the counsel acting for the Royal Commission, nor the three Commissioners themselves. The other parties with access to this information – it would be a travesty to call it evidence – were, through a process of elimination, few in number.

The Royal Commissioners had their attention drawn to this 'exclusive' as they were pondering the many months of evidence put before them and while preparing their final report. To a man they were unimpressed at this new attempt to discredit Thomas:

> The evidence of the last witness to whom we have referred was the subject of a front page article in a newspaper called *Sunday News* on 28 September 1980, after our public hearings had concluded. That action was quite improper. The publication of the material, which is shown by the cross-examination recorded in the transcript to be wholly unreliable, seems to us to have been an act of calculated and callous cynicism on the part of the newspaper.

The Royal Commission might have equally felt justified in leveling the accusation of being an act of calculated and callous cynicism against the party which actually leaked the information to the *Sunday News*. The question may also be fairly asked why the truck driver, along with the less ill of the two jailhouse snitches, were themselves not charged with perjury and put before a court?

Fresh from what may been seen as a voyage in a leaky boat, the police elite, by way of their industry association, then began attacking the Thomas Royal Commission through the media. On 12 November 1980 the chairman of the Police Officers' Guild, Detective Chief Inspector Bruce Scott, declared that he and his colleagues had no faith in the findings – its formal report had not even been hand-delivered to the hallowed halls of Parliament at that time:

> There is no doubt in our mind that grave allegations may be made against the police. The evidence giving support to any such findings may well be impossible to justify in the cold, hard light of day.

The guild, which represented serving officers from the rank of inspector to commissioner, viewed the conduct of the Royal Commission and the way it had brought its hearings to an 'abrupt end' as cause for deep concern. Grave disquiet was being felt, not only at the manner in which the Royal Commission had been functioning, but also at the apparent preconceived views it appeared to have, Scott insisted.

These observations – made by one of New Zealand's highest-ranking police officers – are interesting given that the High Court had previously ruled that the allegations of bias and predetermination by the three Royal Commissioners had no foundation.

The comments from that group of New Zealand's top police drew a gentle rebuke from the Government official who had overseen the creation of the Royal Commission, Justice Minister Jim McLay. He stressed that everyone should wait to see what was in the report before commenting. The Thomas Retrial Committee's chairman, Dave Payne, was not so diplomatic in his approach:

> The unprecedented comment from the Police Officers Guild in advance of the release of the Royal Commission's findings should be a matter of grave public concern. Police officers take an oath of allegiance to the Crown. The Royal Commission was appointed to represent the Queen and for the police to say they have no faith in the findings is almost treasonable.

Allan Thomas, the head of a long-suffering clan, added:
The police are blatantly trying to denigrate the Royal Commission of

Inquiry and play down the importance of its findings. This is as fine a group of men as you could possibly get together for such a task.

On the eve of the Royal Commission's report being presented, the Police Association went to Prime Minister Rob Muldoon in a last-ditched effort to get its publication delayed on the grounds that action through the Court of Appeal was being considered. Muldoon listened 'sympathetically' to the case put by representatives of those who were about to become condemned men, then instructed that the report be released, cunningly ruling that it should be tabled in the Parliament, thereby giving it the protection of full unfettered privilege. The event that Thomas, his supporters, and many thousands of people around New Zealand had waited a decade for took place on 28 November 1980.

Thomas, like every other member of his family – and those connected with them by tentacles that spread in so many different directions – still believed that justice would not only be seen to be done, but would actually be done. The day before the Royal Commission's findings hit the headlines he declared:

It is bringing to justice those who deserve it and will look into the system to prevent it happening again.

History however proved that the trust in the system which got Thomas two life sentences – not once but twice – remained misplaced. The New Zealand Police merely came together as one, as they had done from the time the first officer rode into town to collect his warrant of appointment from Governor George Grey, ruler of the new British colony, in October 1846.

Six

On the afternoon of the Baker-O'Donovan overview conference, 19 October 1970, the Crewe inquiry squad had precious little of substance on which to build a case against Arthur Thomas, by then firmly in the sights of Hutton and 'close' members of his squad.

What they had is detailed in the notes of the conference of that day, but police national headquarters has vehemently resisted any attempt to gain access to the full record of that gathering. What is available is an edited segment of that crucial gathering which relate to Demler. The Thomas 'evidence' has been deleted on the grounds of 'protecting a natural person'. This is inexplicable, given that the actions and activities of the man in question have been thoroughly scrutinised in the public domain for more than 40 years. A picture can however be built of the 'probable cause' aspect from the evidence produced at Thomas' two trials, the testimony given at the Royal Commission and the multitude of public statements recorded by the media since 1970. On that basis, it has to be said that the reason for suspecting Thomas at that very moment was particularly thin on the ground.

Thomas' alleged motive was in the mix – a teenage infatuation with a local girl that, a decade later, prompted him to 'execute her and her husband'. The Royal Commission concluded that was not motive at all, but the Crown used it to justify its willful prosecution of Thomas.

The other 'evidence' emanated from several pieces of timber found on the Thomas farm which *could* have matched that from an old trailer which *could* once have carried an old car axle which *could* have been tied to the body of Harvey Crewe. The Royal Commission concluded this 36 and a half pound [16.5 kilogram] piece of steel never had any connection with Thomas personally so was irrelevant.

The matter of 'probable cause' interested the Royal Commission. Its chairman, Robert Taylor, interrogated Hutton at length on this matter and in doing so obtained an admission about the extent of the evidence that had exclusively led the Crewe team down the Thomas path from 19 October 1970:

Taylor: Doesn't that mean that at that time you were considering the question of whether or not he should be dismissed as a suspect on 19 October?

Hutton: Not dismissed, because we had found some timber from that [trailer].

This statement, made by Hutton on oath, is at variance with the facts. The timber to which he was referring was not found on the Thomas farm tip until 21 October and was subsequently used to 'create' a skeleton trailer, the photographs of which were presented to the trial juries as depicting something that did not actually exist.

The Royal Commission chairman was not finished:

Taylor: I am not asking what you found, I am asking what that means. 'Conference concluded that every effort must be made immediately either to confirm Thomas as a suspect or exclude him altogether'. You had to get further evidence from him than what you had on 19 October, or he was not even a suspect. That is right isn't it?

Hutton: Not exactly a suspect.

Taylor: That is your words.

Hutton: There was a suggestion of a suspect. The next day there was a search warrant and the tip was searched.

Taylor: That means that if you didn't get more evidence Thomas was out, doesn't it?

Hutton: No it does not.

Taylor: Confirm him as a suspect?

Hutton: Find other evidence as to how this trailer came to be on his farm.

Taylor: Find other evidence to implicate him further in the crime, or he was no longer a suspect. That was the frame of mind on 19 October?

Hutton: Don't define my frame of mind please.

Taylor: Detective Inspector Hutton, the senior officer there?

Hutton: Yes.

Taylor: Who said at the conclusion of the conference 'every effort must be made'. Who said that?

Hutton: I don't remember. If it is down there that I said it, [then] I said it.

Taylor: If it is down there, you as the person in charge of the conference, the senior officer there, held that opinion?

Hutton: I held that opinion and as I have told you, either confirm or exclude him.

Taylor: As a suspect?

Hutton: For the inquiries, certainly.

With only the motive that was no motive and some pieces of timber which were irrelevant in its armory, the Hutton-led squad went about the business of solving the Crewe murders like a pack of terriers in hot pursuit of a rat. Within seven days a veritable goldmine of 'evidence' was on hand – on October 20, stub axles from the Thomas farm dump that fitted with the axle and the Thomas .22 rifle, along with galvanised wire that 'matched' that wrapped around the body of Harvey Crewe; on 21 October rusty and damaged old wheels and a towbar deemed to have come from the Thomas trailer which had 'indisputably' once hosted the axle that had been found with Crewe's body; and on the 27 October, in the garden of the Crewe house, a .22 cartridge that was subsequently proved to have come from the Thomas rifle.

At the Otahuhu CIB office, the relief was palpable. One miraculous discovery after the next, which together with a motive of the most powerful kind, would prove more than adequate to not only arrest Thomas, but to subsequently secure two murder convictions against him in two separate Supreme Court trials. But ultimately none of this counted for anything. Ten years after Hutton had formally charged Thomas with murdering Jeanette and Harvey Crewe, a Royal Commission of Inquiry brought down its own findings against Hutton and Johnston, the latter by then two years dead.

By 1980, Bob Walton, former head of the CIB, was Commissioner of Police. Walton had received an advance copy of the Royal Commission's formal report, as would have been expected, and he and his executive team braced themselves for the onslaught they knew would follow.

On the day the Royal Commission report was tabled, Walton sprang to the defence of his two former officers, declaring that no evidence could be found that would support a criminal charge against Hutton or Johnston, or indeed any other police officer.

Where is the evidence to support the conclusion that the two persons named, members of the police at the time of the investigation, actually planted a .22 cartridge case, later exhibit 350, in the Crewe garden? It cannot be denied that the circumstances could give rise to a suspicion of planting, but in the absence of evidence against the persons named, such an accusation is repugnant. The [Royal] Commission reported that it was most unfortunate that Detective Johnston was dead and not able to give evidence as he may have been able to give satisfactory explanations, but then it proceeded to condemn him and Mr Hutton without any trial.

Walton then rounded on other aspects of the Royal Commission's findings, including that which determined that there had been a double switching of another cartridge exhibit, labeled exhibit 343:

> Such conduct would amount to a criminal offence but again there is no evidence to support a charge.

Walton's statements drew this resolute response from Royal Commissioner Peter Gordon:

> The Commission felt no reluctance in stating outright that policemen had planted the shellcase which became the cornerstone of the Crown evidence against Mr Thomas. My fellow Commissioners and I are unanimous in believing policemen put the shellcase in the murdered couple's garden.

Unappeased, other members of the New Zealand Police, past and present, joined the chorus. Former commander of Auckland Police Gideon Tait publicly announced that he intended resigning from the National Party as a result of the Royal Commission's findings – retaliation presumably for the Muldoon Government's decision to appoint this inquisitorial body and then to support its findings upon release. A former detective inspector described the Commission's damning of the two police officers as 'itself nothing short of criminal' while former colleagues of Johnston organised a petition in his defence.

As the controversy swirled and reactions of supporters of the Royal Commission on one side and opponents on the other intensified, Police Commissioner Walton announced that 'in order to ensure impartiality' he was referring the matter to the Solicitor-General, Paul Neazor, to conduct an independent evaluation of whether there were grounds to prosecute Hutton. Having previously declared, categorically, that the 'evidence' heard by the Royal Commission would not stand up in a Court of law, this must be viewed as a disingenuous response at best.

The Thomas Retrial Committee, from the outset, had no faith that Neazor's investigation would deliver the justice its members and supporters had long sought, and nor did it. Delivered on 21 December 1981, that report formed the same view as that held by the Commissioner of Police, namely that there was insufficient evidence to put Hutton on trial. This, despite a very clear determination by the Solicitor-General that cartridges from the Thomas farm and his rifle *could* have been available to Hutton and Johnston in the relevant period between the second seizure of that firearm on 20 October 1970 and the finding of the cartridge case in the Crewe's garden seven days later. On this point alone, should the matter not have been put before a court of law for adjudication?

The December 1981 Neazor report, running to 17 pages, was prepared with the assistance of two police officers, one of them being Stan Keith, the original clerk of the Crewe inquiry who went on to maintain the homicide file throughout the 1970s and into the 1980s, when the Royal Commission held its hearings. This was a role he retained right through until 2010. Given that he was one of the officers whose actions the Solicitor-General looked at during that evaluation of the evidence which had emerged against Hutton and Johnston, any involvement by Keith in Neazor's own separate inquiry would, on the face of it, appear to have been injudicious.

Even while Neazor was dwelling on the issue before him, declarations by the police hierarchy continued, with Police Association secretary Bob Moodie reporting that meetings were being held with Hutton and Johnston's family to look at avenues available to those 'who have been so savagely and wrongly condemned by the Thomas Commission of Inquiry'.

A significant omission on Moodie's part, of course, was recognition that a pardon is entrenched in the British justice system and that commissions of inquiry are specifically legislated for in cases where the Government determines that there needs to be an external examination of a matter which is of grave public concern, as the Thomas case was.

The extent of resentment from within police circles against the Royal Commission and its findings can be seen in a decision, taken on 23 January 1981, following meetings in all 18 of the police union's divisions across the country. As a result, every constable and non-commissioned officer was levied $10 a week for two months to provide a $50,000 'fighting fund' aimed at overturning the Royal Commission's findings. It was subsequently reported that all but one district supported the proposed legal challenge, with a two-thirds majority agreeing to the levy.

In March 1982, just a matter of months after presentation of the Neazor report to the Government, a new challenge to the Royal Commission's finding was launched, this time in the Court of Appeal. These proceedings were also initiated by Hutton and the family of Johnston, with the backing of the two police service associations which had previously counted these officers in their membership. It may well have been better for 'the force' to have let sleeping dogs lie.

The Royal Commission engaged Thomas Eichelbaum – later that year to become a Judge of the Supreme Court, then New Zealand's 11th Chief Justice and a Sir – to conduct its defence. At that time Eichelbaum was president of the New Zealand Law Society, and a Queen's Counsel, and in taking the attack to those representing the forces of law and order in New Zealand, he prized open a door which, prior to that court action beginning, had only been slightly ajar in the Royal Commission's formal report.

Whereas the focus of the Royal Commission's report had been on the 'planting' of evidence by way of a cartridge case from the Thomas rifle, Eichelbaum put before the Court of Appeal a schedule of 43 improprieties by the police which had been uncovered during that 1980 inquisition. Moreover he stressed that his list was, indeed, not exhaustive, there being another 20 examples which 'could easily' be added to that schedule.

Eichelbaum gave the following explanation of the term 'impropriety', which he submitted was a broad one:

> It encompasses acts that amount to a substantial departure from the right conduct; conduct that is not desirable in the circumstances; which is discreditable or dishonourable; or which amounts to a serious or substantial breach of recognised standards of rectitude; something that is seriously reprehensible on the part of the person occupying the particular position.

He went on to submit that it was inconceivable that the intention had been that the Royal Commission was empowered to find impropriety on the part of a group or class of persons but without the power to name the individual or individuals concerned:

> Although, in theory, this involved a substantial number of persons, that is the police force as a whole, it is obvious that, on investigation, any impropriety in regard to any specific matter – such as the fabrication of an exhibit – could only involve those involved in the investigation of the deaths. It is not credible that the intention was that the whole of the group should be left under suspicion if the [Royal] Commission was in a position to nominate the person or persons involved.

Before this Court of Appeal hearing, proceedings had been lodged in the High Court. The respondents at this third judicial review were the three Royal Commissioners – Robert Taylor, Peter Gordon and Allen Johnston – the Attorney General and the New Zealand Police. The magnitude of the action can be demonstrated by the fact that the Full Bench of the Court of Appeal was involved – Chief Justice Sir Ronald Davison as president, with Justices Cooke, Richardson, Somers and Casey. The case essentially resolved around the allegation that the High Court had been wrong in finding that the Royal Commission was not biased and had not prejudged the issues and that its findings should be set aside.

The appellants claimed that the respondents were disqualified by bias, that they had prejudged the issue of the impropriety of the police with the result that they did not have a fair opportunity to present their case and that the first respondents [the Commissioners] were not able to interpret the evidence fairly. They requested the Court of Appeal, upon accepting those propositions, to rule that the Commission's findings relating to the planting of the shell case by Hutton and Johnston be ruled unauthorised and invalid, and be set aside as a consequence. The appellants went on to allege that the Royal Commission's terms of reference did not allow it to find that the named persons [Hutton and Johnston] had committed crimes. The Court of Appeal was further told that the Royal Commission's findings had resulted in Hutton and Johnston being exposed to extensive adverse publicity and that the dead detective's widow was likely to be seriously affected by being caused serious personal distress and embarrassment.

Several extracts from that hearing of almost two weeks are worthy of record. One was the evidence from the Royal Commission's counsel, Howard Keyte, in relation to whether he should have put to Hutton the allegation that he [Hutton] had been involved with planting the cartridge case:

> I did not intend at the start of my examination to put this to Mr Hutton, but I received such unsatisfactory answers during the course of my examination that the matter jelled in my mind and I thought it proper to put it to him.

Another concerned the role and rights of Royal Commissions and arose from an assertion from David Tompkins QC, for the appellants, that it was the unalienable right of any person not to be found guilty of criminal conduct except by the due process of law – namely a trial. This argument was countered by Anthony Keesing, on behalf of the Attorney General and the New Zealand Police, who noted the Government's right to appoint commissioners to inquire into any matter on which it needed help must be preserved:

> It should be for the Government to decide what weight to give to the report of the Commissioners, to assess any shortcomings in it and to act upon it to the extent it wishes, if at all.

On the last day of July 1982, the full Bench of the Court of Appeal formally rejected the bid for absolution on behalf of the two former police officers. Rather than overturning the Royal Commission's findings on Hutton and Johnston's involvement in the fabrication of evidence – via the planting of exhibit 350 in the Crewe garden to ensure Thomas was convicted – the Court of Appeal did the opposite, determining that the Royal Commission did indeed have the jurisdiction to make such findings. The highest Court in the land at that time, outside Parliament itself, adjudged that the Thomas Royal Commission had not acted in breach of its obligations of natural justice regarding allegations against Hutton and Johnston and that two paragraphs in the Royal Commission's report were, in substance, a finding that the persons named had committed the crime of fabricating evidence.

The biggest battle ever conducted on behalf of members of the New Zealand Police had been fought and lost and the findings of the Thomas Royal Commission remain inviolate to this day.

Seven

The issue of the planting of exhibit 350 – a .22 cartridge proved to have come from the Browning rifle of Arthur Allan Thomas – has been debated and argued about from almost from the day it was found in such suspicious circumstances on 27 October 1970.

According to records, exhibit 350 was a long rifle .22 brass cartridge, one of about 40,000 of the 400,000 produced by ICI Australia each day and then shipped to New Zealand. The formal finding of the Thomas Royal Commission was that this cartridge case had been planted in order to secure the conviction of an innocent man. The perpetrators of this act were identified as being the Crewe inquiry boss Detective Inspector Bruce Thomas Newton Hutton and the late Detective Lenrick Johnston, who had died in 1978.

In the end the categorisation of cartridge cases destroyed the police case against Thomas. The undisputed reality is that this .22 long rifle cartridge had never been put together with a number 8 bullet, the type which killed Jeanette and Harvey Crewe. It took almost a decade to get that acceptance, but on 8 July 1980 this long-elusive belief was established as fact as the Royal Commission demolished one of the key planks of the Crown case. While the cartridge case was not the only strategic piece of evidence used to secure the conviction of Thomas, it was the one the police felt they could rely on to sway the juries in the desired direction.

Not only is there evidence to demonstrate that such a criminal act took place but that some members of the Crewe inquiry squad celebrated that event, that this nation's leaders had subsequent knowledge that exhibit 350 had indeed been 'planted' and that the Royal Commission knew that this act of perversion of the course of justice had taken place before it opened its formal proceedings on 21 May 1980.

In a 1982 hearing of the Court of Appeal, Hutton and his co-plaintiffs alleged, through their counsel, that the Royal Commission was not entitled to name them and that it had demonstrated bias in its dealing with him and the deceased Johnston, who was obviously not able to defend himself and his actions in that forum. They asserted that this bias demonstrated itself in a number of ways, from the vigor in which Judge

Taylor had interrogated police witnesses to an alleged preconception that criminal acts had been perpetrated by those inquiring into the deaths of the murders. What the Bench of the Court of Appeal at that time could not have known however is that the Royal Commission had gone into its inquiry armed with a crucial piece of evidence, in the form of an alleged 'confession' – more aptly perhaps, an admission – from the late Len Johnston as to his part in the planting of exhibit 350.

The account of what took place, as relayed to me many years later, goes like this. Johnston was ill for some six months before he died at his home on 11 June 1978. His funeral was held at the All Saints Anglican Church in Howick, presided over by the Reverend Michael Houghton. Knowing he was dying, Johnston had confided to the clergyman about his involvement in the cartridge case aspect of the Crewe investigation, particularly focusing on his part in securing the conviction of Arthur Thomas. Either at Johnston's insistence or as a sequel to his 'admission' Houghton provided that information to then Prime Minister Robert Muldoon upon the former detective's passing.

Coincidentally or not, within four months of the detective's passing, Muldoon took the step of appointing Robert Adams-Smith QC to the role of independent Crewe inquisitor, offering him the powers of a commission of inquiry if need be. This proved to be unnecessary, but it can be fairly said that the investigations by that Queen's Counsel led directly to the pardon of Thomas a year later.

Confirmation, or denial, of the Johnston 'admission' by the Reverend Houghton – and whether or not he imparted that information to the Prime Minister of the day – is no longer possible. I did locate the man of the cloth – he had left his Howick parishioners and had moved to a South Auckland retirement village – but a request for an interview regarding the Johnston 'admission', was delayed as he became gravely ill. His wife noted at that time that the Anglican Minister 'was not able to assist me at that time'. He died in July 2010, in his 81st year, with his funeral being conducted in the same church where Johnston's family and friends, among them many police colleagues, had 32 years earlier farewelled their own loved one.

Those closely associated with the late Prime Minister are scarce on the ground and from those who remain no confirmation that Muldoon knew of the Johnston matter has been forthcoming. But Gerald Ryan, the older twin brother, but junior to Kevin, is able to provide validity to this claim. The sole remaining member of that renowned legal team reveals that his brother heard about Johnston's admission and he understands talked with the Reverend Houghton about it:

> It was either the Minister or someone close to him, but I'm 99 per cent sure Kevin talked with the Reverend Houghton himself. Quite a few people in legal and political circles in Auckland knew about it at that time, but I don't think it was common knowledge.

The senior Thomases and those who represented the family as legal practitioners over more than a decade firmly believe that Johnston did make this admission. This may explain what was viewed as an oddity in relation to the appointment of one member of the three-man panel which made up the Thomas Royal Commission. Apart from being beyond reproach – in terms of honour, commitment and impartiality – the reason for the appointment of the Most Reverend Allen Johnston to sit alongside Judge Taylor as a Royal Commissioner has never been explained, although many have wondered about it over the decades. Unlike the third panel member, former National Government Transport Minister Peter Gordon, who was a close Muldoon ally, the immediate past head of the Anglican Church in New Zealand seemed like the odd man out. The Anglican connection – on the one hand a long-serving parish Minister and on the other his equally-long serving Archbishop – may not be coincidental.

The planting of exhibit 350 – the .22 cartridge from the Thomas rifle – in the Crewe garden took on a new dimension in 2001 following the publication of my book *The Final Chapter* a decade ago. Initially this development came through a letter from a bar worker who had served what appears to have been a small, but often boisterous, collection of detectives from within the ranks of the Crewe homicide inquiry team.

This hotel worker was at that time engaged in duties at the Bader Drive Hotel in Mangere and while questions may be asked as to why this information only surfaced 30 years after the event, there is an explanation. It was fear – firstly of the potential loss of a job which at that time was badly needed due to family circumstances, and secondly of the machine that is the New Zealand Police in general and of individuals within the Crewe homicide squad in particular – that kept this witness silent for three decades. These were different times, an era when the man in the street did not question the police, and certainly did not challenge members of that force, or their actions, to the degree people do today.

Secret Witness A's information, contained in a formally sworn statutory declaration, attests to the use of the Bader Drive Hotel by some members, but certainly not by all, of the Crewe homicide squad. That these premises were so used has been confirmed by two members of that team, although in the formal response to an Official Information Act request on that matter – provided by police headquarters – there was something of an attempt to play down the true extent of those visits. The verification of use of this hotel, at that time, came from Stan Keith, the former clerk of the Crewe inquiry, after consultation with Hutton.

Secret Witness A tells of the nightly gatherings in a house bar that was closed to the public and in which the bar staff were sworn to secrecy. In such a secure environment, the Crewe inquiry detectives who participated in the wind-down sessions after hard, long, cold winter days in the fields of Pukekawa were able to let their hair down. One in particular took up this opportunity with gusto, bringing his wife, usually on Friday nights and at weekends, but unashamedly having a woman who was not his wife in for drinks on other evenings.

Secret Witness A's sworn declaration states:

Throughout my time working in the house bar, I heard bits of the conversations of the police who were drinking there. As the nights wore on and the drinks flowed, the voices got louder and the discussions became less restricted. I remember hearing that evidence had been planted against Arthur Allan Thomas and that this had been easy as the policemen who were drinking at my bar considered him to be a 'half-wit', to use their words. I was very disturbed by these revelations but the police officers who were there at that time thought it was a great joke – hilarious. I remember the conversations about the planting of the evidence against Thomas very clearly. It began with someone saying that they would now be able to put Thomas away. Someone else mentioned that no-one would know that the evidence had been planted. The group there at the time all laughed about it.

Secret Witness A's statutory declaration puts Bruce Hutton at the scene on the evening the planting of evidence was discussed, and that informant has sworn on oath a declaration attesting that to be the truth. It is also this witness' testimony that as soon as Thomas was arrested, a few weeks later, the Bader Drive Hotel's house bar was abandoned as the favoured drinking hole of members of the Crewe inquiry team and the facility was re-opened to the public.

A copy of this declaration was provided to then Assistant Commissioner Peter Marshall in August 2006, as part of a comprehensive file relating to the identity of the so-called 'mystery' woman who had fed Rochelle Crewe. That specific information regarding the bragging in the bar about the planting of exhibit 350 has not been acted on, insofar as Secret Witness A having never been interviewed or even contacted by police to this day, six years after the delivery of that file.

In an interview with former Police Commissioner Walton at his Wellington home in May 2006 – the last interview he ever gave before he died – The Master, as some of his loyal disciples saw fit to call him, quite innocently referred to police officers, in effect, giving themselves away in relation to the planting of evidence by way of loose talk and laughing about their actions.

Walton revealed that in early 1972, as a result of televised allegations that the Thomas cartridge case had been planted in the Crewe garden, then Police Minister Percy Allen became agitated. Not liking what he had seen on television the evening before, Allen hauled Police Commissioner Angus Sharp into his office and 'read the riot act'. As head of the national CIB, Walton was told by his boss to get to Auckland to determine the truth, or otherwise, of the allegations being made. That inquiry included signs that higher ranks look for that are relevant to the matter of police admitting fabrication of evidence. Walton told me:

> Now you don't understand the police, but if it [exhibit 350] had been planted, someone would have been laughing and poking the borax and that is what you rely on, to get a breakthrough and learn if it had been planted or not. Usually someone is bragging about it or throwing off about it and I could not find any of that when I went to Auckland.

The inquiry Walton refers to was conducted in May 1972, the month in which farm labourer Bruce Roddick confirmed his identification of the woman he had seen at the Crewe farm two days after the couple were murdered. There is no suggestion that these two events were connected as Walton's 'investigation' was clearly the result of the airing of the television item. The Roddick sighting of the woman at that time is relevant only because things were beginning to move in the free-Thomas campaign and both the political master of the police and the head of the force itself were sensitive to public questioning of what had gone on within the Crewe inquiry.

The late Brian Wilkinson, who was head of the CIB in Auckland as regional co-ordinator when the Royal Commission conducted its exhaustive hearings, recounted the following in an interview in 2001:

I was advised by Taffy Hugglestone [a senior detective] about an incident that had happened in Auckland in 1970 [the same year as the Crewe inquiry] when the police up there planted glass in the cuffs of a man's trousers to tie him to a crime. I phoned Bob Walton as national head of the CIB at that time and told him what was going on. Later Walton told me that there had been a meeting in Auckland and all the detectives were told there was to be *no more* fabrication of evidence.

Eight

The fabrication of evidence – notably the planting of a cartridge case from the rifle of Arthur Allan Thomas in the Crewe garden to secure his conviction for two murders he did not commit – angered the Royal Commission of Inquiry established to probe those acts:

> Mr Thomas spent 9 years in prison. That a man is locked up for a day without cause has always been seen by our law as a most serious assault on his rights. That a man is wrongly imprisoned for 9 years is a wrong that can never be put right. The fact that he is imprisoned on the basis of evidence which is false to the knowledge of police officers, whose duty it is to uphold the law, is an unspeakable outrage.

However police in the Crewe inquiry used another mechanism for defeating the course of justice, with even more devastating effect. That was the suppression of material evidence which, had it been revealed to the defence, would have led to the acquittal of Thomas at his trial. It must be wondered what the three Royal Commissioners would have concluded had they been able to draw from the police all the evidence which has been extracted over more recent years.

Not only did members of the New Zealand Police suppress vital evidence from the two juries called upon to decide the innocence or otherwise of Thomas, but other significant documents and evidence were not provided to the Thomas Royal Commission. Queen's Counsel Peter Williams, who represented Thomas at the hearings which occupied most of 1980, confirms that the police continued to frustrate and evade the search for truth, as they had done throughout the previous 10 years:

> The police were ordered to present everything they had in the Crewe file, and my colleague Kevin Ryan was very intent on delving as deeply into that file as he could, having been denied access to much of it previously. However the police tried to frustrate our endeavours by producing a whole room of documents and making it physically

impossible for us to get to the important ones. They also adopted stupid tactics, such as giving us photocopies that were so faint we couldn't read them, or giving us pages that were upside down or out of order. This was the first occasion in New Zealand history that the Crown, in a criminal matter, had been compelled to grant discovery to the defence. This was not happily received by John Henry, the counsel for the police. He did not like it, but Justice Taylor said that if they had nothing to hide, what was wrong with the evidence being disclosed? He said that had been the norm in Australia for years. We ended up with a load of junk, to be frank. I believe we only got the tip of the iceberg in respect of what the Commission really wanted to see. It was a nightmare to try to analyse it all.

Moreover, some of the documents the Royal Commission wanted to view had been destroyed, among them – according to the police – the file on Len Demler and the records of a number of crucial conferences, especially those that centred on whether to go ahead with an arrest of the murdered woman's father. [Miraculously, the 'missing' Demler documents were provided to me in December 1999, after waging an Official Information Act war with police headquarters over the preceding six and a half years].

Just how much of the information available to the police in relation to the Crewe murders was not seen by the Royal Commission can now be more accurately assessed. That inquisitorial body reported to Parliament that it had viewed the 5000 pages of documents in that homicide file – supposedly 'full discovery'. Recently, a police spokesman involved with the current review of the Crewe file was quoted as saying that this actually contains around 50,000 pages.

In 1970, the rules of the disclosure game were clearly defined, as they are four decades on. Throughout the period of the two trials of Arthur Thomas, in 1971 and 1973, the two subsequent appeals following his conviction of a double murder and two additional referrals to the Court of Appeal, Police General Instruction C134 was in force. This stated:

When police decide not to call a person as a witness for the prosecution, the defence should be advised of the name and address of the person so that, if desired, the person can be called as a witness for the defence. This Instruction, however, applies only to a person who is able to give material evidence (particularly when favourable to the accused) and not a person who, because he is unable to give any material evidence, is not being called.

In its official report, the Royal Commission sought fit to comment on a highly relevant affidavit sworn by Hutton on 25 January 1971. In it, the Crewe inquiry head attested:

That apart from any persons whose testimony is similar to that of evidence already given by witnesses at the hearing of depositions [against Thomas], such as further police officers who took part in searches, doctors who examined and supplied opinions on the condition of Rochelle Crewe, and persons who speak of movements by either of the deceased or accused, I know of *no other witnesses* who can give evidence whatsoever that has not been given.

This affidavit, prepared by then junior prosecution counsel David Baragwanath, was served on the defence prior to the first Thomas trial, which began on 15 February that year. Nine years later the Royal Commission, observed, in relation to that portion of the affidavit:

We are unable to reconcile the statements in that passage [of the affidavit] with some of our findings under this term of reference.

The term of reference in question required the Commission to inquire into and report on:

1. Whether the prosecution failed at any stage to perform any duty owed to the defence in respect of … (a) the disclosure of evidentiary material which might assist the defence?

Examples of the suppression of a number of items of very material evidence in the Thomas case fall into two broad groups. The first involves evidence which the juries called upon to decide the fate of Thomas did not hear but which was covered in the proceedings of the 1980 Royal Commission. The second is evidence which – based on an evaluation of the 3500 pages of transcripts and 210 exhibits from its hearings – neither the Royal Commission nor its counsel got to see. The first group of this suppressed material is traversed in this chapter and the second group in the next.

It is inconceivable that, as officer in charge of the Crewe inquiry, Bruce Hutton would not have been aware of the examples of material evidence which were canvassed by the Royal Commission but not heard by either of the Thomas trial juries.

It is now clear that this was suppressed by the police in their eagerness to dispose of the Crewe homicide investigation once and for all. In the light of what is now known about the inquiry conducted between 22 June and 11 November 1970, it is likewise inconceivable that the withholding of any of these pieces of evidence can be regarded as a simple act of omission or oversight, or that they were of no probative value, especially to the defence teams of Paul Temm and Brian Webb at the first trial and Kevin and Gerald Ryan at the second.

The report of a Julie Merle Priest about hearing three shots on the evening the Crewes were killed, Wednesday 17 June 1970

If Arthur Thomas was to be the killer, the timing of the murder of Jeanette and Harvey Crewe always depended on a late-night attack. An early-evening killing spree would not be supported as Thomas was still in his cowshed until after 7.30 pm and there were too many local residents out and about at ratepayers' meetings and social events for that to be a viable option – especially as his car had a distinctive differential noise which was known from one end of the district to the other.

Julie Priest lived with her poultry farmer husband and family diagonally across State Highway 22 from the Crewe house. She told her husband of hearing three rifle shots on the evening of 17 June 1970 when he retired to bed about 11pm on the night of the killings. However she did not relay this to the police until 20 August 1970. This was four days after Jeanette Crewe's body was recovered from the Waikato River – a discovery which unleashed a surge of media coverage, based on the revelation that she had been shot with a .22 firearm. However Priest's crucial evidence relating to the timing of the shots now regarded as those that killed the Crewes did not resurface until 1977, when British author David Yallop interviewed her during research into his expose of the Crewe murders, *Beyond Reasonable Doubt?*

The matter was canvassed at length by the Royal Commission, both in questioning of Priest and of Hutton, and was covered in its formal report:

> Mrs Priest told us she usually went to bed at 9.30 pm, but on this particular evening, because she was tired – the previous evening she

had been out late at a ball – she went to bed early, but probably not before half past eight. She was reluctant to be any more definite than that. When first relating the incident to the police, on 20 August 1970, she said the time of her retiring to bed would not have been before half past 8. Mrs Priest's reluctance to attempt to fix the time of returning to bed that evening at this late stage is very understandable. Accepting that her statement of 'not before half past 8' on 20 August is a reasonable starting point, it seems to us that the timing of her hearing the shots cannot be fixed more accurately than somewhere between 8.30pm and 11pm.

The critical point here is that the shots came from the direction of the Crewe house and that Priest was able to pinpoint the date of those shots as being heard by her on 17 June 1970 because of her earlier than usual retirement the evening following a ball she had attended on the evening of 16 June. It was her usual practice to retire at the same time as her husband, but on this occasion she did so much earlier. The Royal Commission noted that she had gone to the police as soon as she heard that Jeanette Crewe had been shot. The date of her doing so is confirmed by a job sheet, filed by Detective Sergeant Mike Charles on 20 August, but the Royal Commission found that the police had put little value on her account:

> The police appear to have disregarded Mrs Priest's evidence on the grounds, firstly that she did not relate it [to] them until 2 months later; secondly, that there may have been other explanations (possum shooters), thirdly, because of misgivings about the accuracy of the date and, fourthly, because as a result of a test carried out by the police, they did not believe the sounds of shots would carry from the Crewes' to the Priest's home. So far as that latter matter is concerned, Mr and Mrs Priest both related to us a test that had been carried out the evening before they gave evidence before us, in which they heard very distinctly indeed – from inside the bedroom of their house – shots fired from the Crewe house.

The Royal Commission considered that Priest's evidence may well have assisted the defence, and not only regarded it as significant, but noted it would have been up to the jury to decide if the rifle shots she heard were in fact related to the murders or not. But she was not called to give testimony on the matter at either of the two Thomas trials, the reason for which is recorded in the Royal Commission's report:

> We accept that the Crown Prosecutor and his junior did not read the police file and were not informed of this matter by the police. Mrs Priest was not called to give evidence and it was not made known to the defence that she may be able to give material evidence. In our view the defence should have been informed, and the failure to do so was a breach of the duties of the police in this respect.

Sparks seen coming from the Crewe house chimney on Friday 19 June 1970 – two nights after the murders and three days before they were reported as missing – by local lad Robert Fleming

Eight-year-old Robert Fleming, being driven home by his father Ross, saw sparks coming from the Crewe chimney around 7.30 pm on Friday 19 June. Given that the Crewes had been shot dead in the lounge of their home almost exactly 48 hours earlier, this material evidence is something both Thomas defence teams would have seized upon – had its existence not remained well beyond their reach.

Arthur Thomas and his wife Vivien were at a sister's 21st birthday at Pukekohe that evening, and they remained there until 11.30pm. Consequently, the significance to the defence of the Fleming sighting at that crucial moment in time – coming just 10 hours after farm labourer Bruce Roddick saw a woman he did not recognise at the front gate of the Crewe house enclosure and 18 hours before Rochelle Crewe was seen by a passer-by toddling around her parent's property, at 1.40pm on Saturday 20 June – cannot be underestimated.

Professor Robert Elliott's concurring opinion on the feeding of Rochelle Crewe in the five days before the disappearance of her parent was reported

At the first Thomas trial, Doctor Thomas Fox was called as a prosecution witness to provide testimony as to the condition of the Crewe's infant daughter Rochelle, 18 months old at the time her parents were murdered. Dr Fox, who specialised as a child physician and acted in that role for the Auckland Hospital Board, had seen Rochelle the day after her grandfather, Len Demler, delivered her to the Willis family following the discovery of the bloodstained house, the bedraggled child in her cot, and her parents' absence.

Dr Fox's evidence at that trial was essentially that he had examined Rochelle less than 24 hours after she was taken to the Willises and that, based on that, and what he had heard from Barbara Willis, his view was that she had been without food, or liquid, for probably 48 hours at most. This would mean Rochelle had last received sustenance on Saturday 19 June – the day she was seen running around the front paddock – or possibly 72 hours before, being about noon on the Friday. From Dr Fox:

> Assuming this child had been left without food from Wednesday evening until she was found on the Monday, I would have expected her to have been much more ill. I think the appearance of the child would have induced Mrs Willis to seek medical attention. I have seen the cot the child usually sleeps in and in my opinion the child Rochelle, I am sure, could not have got into or out of that cot without assistance.

At the first trial, it was the police case that Rochelle had been fed and cared for between the evening of her parents' murders and the day of the discovery of those crimes, meaning that if it was Thomas who had killed the Crewes, then his wife Vivien was, by inference, the woman who had fed the Crewes' infant daughter. By the time of the retrial, in 1973, however, the game plan had changed, due to the affidavit of Bruce Roddick that Vivien Thomas was categorically *not* the woman he had seen at the Crewe house two days after they were murdered. The prosecution then opted to put forward a second medical opinion, from Dr Ronald Caughey, which declared that Rochelle had *not* been fed.

What was not known at that point however was that the police actually had *four* medical opinions in their toolbox – two supporting the feeding of the child and two rejecting this. The names and addresses of the two other medical specialists – Professor Robert Elliott and Dr Samuel Ludbrook – were not supplied to the defence.

The Royal Commission looked at this issue, and the effect of Hutton's 25 January 1971 affidavit, and decided that there was no significant breach of duty by the police in failing to advise of the evidence collected from the third and fourth doctor. Surely though, had the defence been told of the evidence collected from Professor Elliott prior to the second trial, he would have been put on the stand as his evidence supported that of Dr Fox – namely that Rochelle had been fed and cared for during those five lonely and distressing days.

Dr Donald Nelson's finding that there was heavy scoring on test bullets fired from the Thomas rifle that excluded it from being used in the murders

In the course of endeavouring to locate the firearm which had been used to kill the Crewes, police collected a total of 64 rifles from the residents of the Pukekawa district and, if relevant, from others further afield. This action immediately followed the recovery of Jeanette Crewe's body, and within her head, a .22 bullet with a number 8 on the base. As a result of an examination of this bullet, the Department of Scientific and Industrial Research's forensics expert, Dr Donald Nelson, concluded that the bullet had been fired from a rifle with six lands with a right-hand twist.

It is not disputed that of the 64 rifles collected from 17 August onward, two in particular produced bullets with the six land right-hand twist characteristic which Nelson deemed could have provided a match with the fatal bullets. One of those rifles belonged to Thomas and another to the Eyre family of Pukekawa, although the latter firearm was actually owned by a close friend of that family, Jack Brewster. It was, however, in the possession of the Eyre boys at the time of the murders.

In both the Thomas trials, Nelson – called as an expert witness for the prosecution – maintained a consistent approach, giving sworn testimony that neither the Thomas rifle nor the Eyre [Brewster] rifle could be excluded from having fired the fatal shots. It was revealed much later however that there were around 800,000 .22 rifles in the Auckland district alone and the observation was made that if the police had collected all of them, the scientists may well have found hundreds, if not thousands, that could produce the same rifling characteristics.

What Nelson did not however disclose to either jury – and what the police did not make known to the defence before the two trials – was that the Thomas rifle also produced heavy scoring on bullets fired through it. This characteristic of a rifle is akin to a human fingerprint and has the effect of ruling in, or out, the use of a firearm in a particular crime. Having observed this particular characteristic of the Thomas rifle – and that this heavy scoring did not appear on either the Jeanette or Harvey Crewe bullets – Nelson recorded this very significant matter in his notes. While the police knew about this, as Dr Nelson's evidence to the Royal Commission reveals, those tasked with endeavouring to put up a credible defence of Thomas did not.

When the police returned the Thomas rifle on 8 September 1970 – following what had been a torrid interview of its owner by Detective Sergeant Phil Seaman and Detective Bruce Parkes the day before – Detective Sergeant Mike Charles told Vivien Thomas that it was not the rifle the police were looking for in connection with the Crewe murders.

Letters from former girlfriends of Thomas which would have shown that he had no consuming passion for Jeanette Crewe

On its own, the matter of the collection of letters written to Arthur Thomas by various young girls he had pursued in the years leading up to his marriage may not seem to be of great importance in the overall picture. Used to great effect by the Crown, though, was a single letter from Jeanette Crewe sent to Thomas during her overseas trip eight years earlier. The prosecution alleged that this was proof of a passion that had so inflamed Thomas that he had shot dead not only the husband of the woman he coveted so intensely, but that he had smashed Jeanette in the face with the butt of his rifle, before shooting her at near point-blank range.

Evidence provided by the other letters in a collection long forgotten by Thomas, but found by the police during one of the searches of his house, could have been used by the defence to help establish that the proclaimed passion did not exist. But like so much other material evidence collected by the police, these letters were never disclosed.

Keith Brown's observation regarding the positioning of the Crewe car on their property on Sunday 21 June 1970

While the public knew within the first week of the Crewe homicide inquiry that a woman had been seen at that property on the morning of Friday 19 June, and a young child was seen at 1.30pm the following day, dressed and running around near the road gate, the police never disclosed a significant number of statements from witnesses who had travelled State Highway 22 in the five days between 17 June and 22 June 1970. Among a number of other unusual happenings reported in and around the murder scene during that period, and in later times, shades were observed pulled down over windows on some days and up again a few days later, and the Crewe car was seen – by several witnesses – in one position for three days, but was in a different location days later. One specific example serves to illustrate the point – the statement from

Tuakau stock and station agent Keith Brown.

Brown's evidence was that at 8.30am on Sunday 21 June 1970 he had passed the Crewe farm and had seen the light at the back porch on and the couple's car at the front gate of their house enclosure. The car was in that location when Bruce Roddick saw the woman by that gate on the Friday and was in the same place the following afternoon, when Queenie McConachie passed by with her husband, seeing Rochelle in the front paddock. But when the contingent of police arrived in the late afternoon of Monday 22 June, the same car was in the garage, just to the left of the road gate. The chairman of the Royal Commission delved into the stock agent's statement:

> *Taylor:* If you had been supplied with that evidence you could have called the witness and shown where Thomas was?
> [Kevin] *Ryan:* Yes, and the suspicion would have been that there must have been someone else.

The statement of John Fisher regarding the repair of his bloody and mucus-covered watch by Pukekohe jeweller William Eggleton

In November 1971, John Fisher of Feilding read of jeweller William Eggleton's evidence and contacted the police. He said that in 1970 – he thought October or November – he had killed pigs while living in Pukekohe and took to Eggleton a watch covered in fat, slime and mucus. The police considered this of no importance, even though Eggleton had reported that it was Thomas who took a bloody watch in to him for repair, which has always been denied. The police did not report the existence of this evidence to the defence at the second Thomas trial. This was wrong in the view of the Royal Commission:

> We consider it was for the court to decide whether Mr Eggleton's evidence was affected by what Mr Fisher had to say. It was wrong for the police not to give the defence the opportunity of putting forward Mr Fisher if they wished to. Again there is no evidence suggesting that the Crown Prosecutors were aware of the existence of Mr Fisher at the time of the second trial.

According to defence lawyer Kevin Ryan, there was a distinct change of tact between the first and second Thomas trials and how the Eggleton watch evidence was handled. 'As the police found no wrist watch on the body of Harvey Crewe or at his house, only an old fob watch, it was not Thomas' watch taken to the Pukekohe jeweller but that it was one taken from Harvey Crewe. That is why I say it the evidence should have been given to the defence'. Or, in the words of the Commission's chairman:

> *Taylor:* To say the murderer would take a watch covered with the blood and mucus of his victim to a jeweller is ridiculous.

The mysterious disappearance of the coat or cover found alongside the wheelbarrow used to carry the bodies from the house.

Possibly one of the most bizarre incidents of the Crewe homicide inquiry occurred within days of police first turning out to that property. The potential evidence was variously described as an old cow cover with ragged edges, or as an old oilskin coat, as one witness remembered seeing sleeves. The exact nature of it was never established, for it disappeared off the face of the earth while the police had control of the Crewe house enclosure. Given that it was found initially next to the wheelbarrow used to remove the bodies through the front door of the murder house – rust scales from the barrow were found on the steps – it could have been potentially significant.

The old cover, or coat, found alongside the wheelbarrow used to remove the bodies of the Crewe house. This photograph was taken on the second day of the murder inquiry, but the material disappeared while police had control of the crime scene.

The evidence given by Detective Graham [Bud] Abbott, the designated officer in charge of exhibits, as to why the old cow cover, or coat, never got to be a formal exhibit, is extraordinary:

> *Abbott:* To the best of my recollection, I am the one that smokes, Mr Jeffries also smokes. I had been either walking in the back door of

the house or in the vicinity of the back door of the house when my cigarette had almost finished. Without thinking and with the door opened I threw it outside. I walked back into the lounge and the thought crossed my mind that I should not have done that as we had a receptacle for placing cigarette butts in the room. Now I am not quite sure about the exact time when all this took place but some good time later, perhaps an hour or two hours, I went outside and saw on the lawn some charred earth. I wondered what it could have been and it dawned on me that it could easily have been my cigarette butt that had burnt this canvass. I couldn't be sure that it was my cigarette butt because I didn't see it land on the canvas and presumed it was my cigarette butt.

Taylor: Do you remember at this time you had already established at the house where you using, a place where you went for lunch? [The Chitty farm cottage nearby].

Abbott: Yes.

Taylor: We have been told by Sergeant Parkes on that day he and all the men with him went there for lunch, or to some other part of the farm for lunch. Could this have happened at a time when you had gone away for your lunch and there was no-one about the place?

Abbott: Yes, I remember there was a good time lapse. Whether I was in the house or away from the house I cannot remember.

Taylor: It seems strange that a cigarette butt would have given a clean burn. According to you it was clean earth.

Abbott: Yes if I had been in the house I would have seen some significant smoke or flame. I am saying the canvas smoldered away, it didn't burn suddenly.

Taylor: You assume that?

Abbott: Yes.

The Royal Commission was informed that Abbott had told his immediate superior – officer in charge of the scene search Detective Sergeant Murray Jeffries – of this incident, but it appears the information never went higher than him and no record ever appeared on the investigation file. Defence counsel at neither the first nor second Thomas trials heard of it and thus they were denied a chance to cross-examine the five scene detectives present at that time. The Royal Commission had trouble with the police evidence on this issue, as the following from its report to Parliament makes abundantly clear:

Extraordinary as this may seem at a murder scene under control of the police team, at a time when the grounds [of the Crewe house] were being subjected to a systematic search (which, we were told, would include cigarette butts), one policeman related that having smoked a cigarette he flicked the butt away as he went into the house by the back door. Later, having found the material was burnt, this policeman concluded that his cigarette butt must have been the cause. We are told it was completely consumed, leaving only charred grass behind it. We heard a great deal about the weather at this time. Lying outside, the material must have been damp. We do not believe that an unaided cigarette butt could have caused a fire which completely consumed the material, including a long ragged tendril lying out to one side on its own. We know that at one stage the police searchers left the scene to have a refreshment break, and that it was in their absence that the material disappeared. Other evidence suggests that the murderer returned to the scene – the cleaning up inside the house, and the sightings of Roddick and the McConachies. We believe that some person with an interest in the material, rather than the police, was responsible for its destruction or removal. There is no reference whatever to these events on the police file. Mr Hutton and Mr Morris both say they were unaware of its existence. The issue for consideration is whether information concerning it should have been given to the defence. The defence was of course given the photographs which showed its existence, but we consider the police had a duty to advise the defence of its fate and witnesses who could give evidence about it.

The photograph showing this material, alongside the wheelbarrow which carried the bodies of Jeanette and Harvey Crewe away from the house in which they were murdered, raises a number of significant questions. As the Royal Commission chairman pointed out, how could such heavy material, damp from the heavy rain, fog and dew which pervaded Pukekawa in the latter part of June 1970 – the middle of a particularly wet and stormy winter that year – have combusted to the point where it disappeared altogether? Where are the photographs of the charred ground? Why did the other scene detectives not see scorched earth and ask about the disappearance of the canvas? Why was it not reported, by Abbott and Jeffries to their superior, officer-in-charge Bruce Hutton? If it was removed, who did so and why? Furthermore, how was that person able to come onto the Crewe property unseen, a compound that was supposed to be under the security of police investigating a double murder? Could this not point to the offender being someone local, able to slip over the fences of the Crewe property, acting with stealth in the knowledge that the police headed to the old Chitty farm cottage across the road for their lunch each day?

Perhaps the last word on this matter should be left to Kevin Ryan, who noted in his closing submissions to the Royal Commission:

> I know about the miracle of the burning bush, but I do not know of the miracle of the burning coat. It did not appear in any exhibit register. No report was made about its disappearance or destruction, and that is a matter of consequence.

Nine

The 1980 Thomas Royal Commission created history in New Zealand by ordering 'full disclosure' in relation to the Crewe homicide inquiry. In effect, its formal order allowed those representing Thomas to view *all* the documents within that extensive homicide file. However from examination of the transcripts of its hearings and the exhibits it received and considered, this next group of evidence appears to have never found its way in front of that inquisition, to its own counsel – Howard Keyte and Michael Crew – or to those representing Thomas, Peter Williams and Kevin Ryan.

Although several items were referred to by counsel assisting the Royal Commission and by those representing Thomas, there is nothing to suggest that the documents relating to these matters were ever provided and as a consequence no witnesses were questioned. To all intents and purposes, this evidence simply did not exist, either in 1971 or 1973 – when it really mattered as Thomas was on trial on two counts of murder – or in 1980, when the inquisition into the police investigation was being undertaken.

The finding of fresh milk in the Crewe kitchen on Monday 22 June 1970 and the subsequent experiment by Dr Thomas Fox to establish its age.

A comment by Bruce Hutton launched the same Doctor Fox who had been the first medical practitioner to examine Rochelle Crewe down a track which, had it been disclosed, could have proved crucial to the defence of Arthur Thomas. The detail of this revelation is recorded in a job sheet furnished by Detective Sergeant Mike Charles on 2 October 1970 which notes the concerns by the doctor about a bottle found, on Monday 22 June, in the kitchen of the Crewe house which contained milk that was *not* sour.

> Having looked through the house and noticing that there is a heater near the kitchen, depending of course on the temperature prevailing at the time, he [Fox] wonders whether milk in an open bottle can last

for five days without going sour. He doubts this. Naturally, if milk cannot last for five days without going sour in such circumstances, this bottle must have been opened by somebody *after* the Crewe's deaths.

The record shows that considerable effort was then put into obtaining the temperatures and weather conditions that prevailed at the time the Crewes were murdered and Fox conducted an experiment which replicated these conditions in his home workshop. He furnished a report of this experiment to Hutton on 5 October 1970, having undertaken his tests between 5.17pm on 30 September and 8.30am on 5 October. The temperature, condition and pH level of the milk was recorded after 24 hours and 48 hours [1 and 2 October respectively] then at 11am and 5.30pm on the third day, at 9am and 5.30pm on the fourth day and at 6.30am on the fifth day. In summary, the milk tasted and smelt satisfactory after 24 and 48 hours, but by the third day it smelt sour. Fox's test – conducted in an environment that simulated, as closely as possible, that of the Crewe house in mid June – showed that by the fourth day, the milk both smelt and tasted sour and by the fifth day, it was solid curd and had a 'very unpleasant smell'.

Thus working backward from about 4pm on Monday 22 June – which is when the first squad of detectives arrived at the Crewe farm on that date – for the milk to be observed as being fresh on that Monday, as Hutton reported to the medical practitioner, it would have had to be fresh on the previous Saturday, three days earlier. It was in the afternoon of that day that Queenie McConachie saw Rochelle running around in the front paddock.

The one-third full bottle of fresh milk is captured in police scene photographs, to the left of the saucepan on the bench in the kitchen. The subsequent experiment showed that it must have been fresh on the Saturday, three days after the murders.

Clearly, the fresh milk found in the bottle on the Monday the police were called could not have been part of the consignment delivered to the Crewes on the morning they died, Wednesday 17 June. Two full bottles containing sour milk were found in the kitchen on that Monday, as was the one-third full bottle of fresh milk to which Fox turned his attention on learning of it from Hutton four months later.

Doctor Fox appeared at both Thomas trials to give his opinion about Rochelle's condition and whether she had been fed during the five days she was 'alone' in the house – one given, as we have seen, in the affirmative – but he was not asked about this other crucial matter by either of the defence teams, who remained ignorant of the existence of the fresh milk, or the experiments done in relation to it. The prosecution did not raise these matters at the Thomas trials either.

Dale McConachie's sighting of an infant girl in the front paddock of the Crewe farm around 4.30pm on Saturday 20 June 1970

A local farmer's wife, Queenie McConachie, had seen a small girl, dressed like Rochelle Crewe, in full-length overall trousers, while being driven to rugby at Tuakau by her husband Dale on Saturday 20 June 1970. Her account of seeing the young Crewe toddler out and about in the early afternoon – Rochelle's parents had been shot and their bodies probably removed from their house by then – was covered in a statement taken on the afternoon of 25 June, three days after police first moved into the Pukekawa district. Queenie McConachie went on to be called as a prosecution witness at both the first and second Thomas trial.

Observed around 1.40pm, the child was then at the road gate, by the milk box adjacent to State Highway 22. Queenie McConachie told the first Thomas trial jury:

She was standing, holding on like that [to the gate]. She was wearing a pair of trousers with a bib front. She [then] turned and went back to the house.

At the second trial, this witnesses added:

As we got near the gate, she reached up to the gate. I did look back and she turned to walk … run back to the house.

Queenie McConachie's sighting of Rochelle that afternoon is

significant for a number of reasons. One is that it validated, from the very start of the Crewe homicide inquiry, Bruce Roddick's sighting of a woman at the scene of the murders the day before, at about 9am on Friday 19 June. Of equal importance is that Rochelle did not give any impression of being highly distressed or agitated – the inference being, of course, that she was being cared for by someone (or some people) whom she knew and trusted.

But the defence line of questioning may have taken on a new dimension had those charged with trying to get Thomas acquitted of double murder charges known of the evidence of her husband. The reality is that none of the defence counsel ever knew such a statement existed. Dale McConachie's statement was, in fact, made the day before his wife's, suggesting that his may have led to her's. On 24 June Queenie's husband told Detective Constable Les Higgins that he had also seen Rochelle in the paddock:

Approximately opposite Chitty's house [the near neighbour of the Crewe's] I looked up the road ahead of us. I saw what appeared to be a little girl with fair hair almost to her shoulders. The hair appeared to be wavy and somehow seemed too mature for the child. The child was standing at a steel gate by the Crewe garage. The gate was closed and the child was standing on the inside of the gate with her hands on the netting or mesh of the gate. As the vehicle came closer the child turned and ran toward the house. She definitely ran and it was though the vehicle had frightened her. When we took the veer to the right on the main road, we lost sight of the child. At this stage she would have run about 10 yards up the grass toward the house.

Rochelle Crewe, photographed in the week following the murder of her parents. The clothing she is wearing is that described by Dale McConachie as he passed the Crewe farm about 4.30pm on the Saturday. His statement was never revealed.

After describing the child and how she was dressed, including the pair of grey overalls with shoulder straps that buttoned up over the front – he saw enough as he drove by to believe that the two buttons at the front were white, although he could not be sure – McConachie then went on to provide a vital detail, revealing that his own sighting of the child at the Crewe's was 'close to *4.30pm*'. He was able to verify this because the rugby game at Tuakau ended at 4pm – he left the match 10 minutes beforehand with his wife –his chat with a barman at the nearby pub for five minutes, and then the time it took to drive the 22 kilometres or so back to Pukekawa, en route to his farm:

Normally the drive home [from Tuakau] takes 25 to 30 minutes. The Crewe house is only about five minutes from our house.

Significantly, unlike the sighting of Rochelle by his wife, Dale McConachie saw the Crewe child on his way *back* from Tuakau, not on the way there, as he attested to in that statement.

Documentary evidence now shows that the 4.30pm sighting of Rochelle was not only known by the officer-in-charge of the Crewe inquiry, Hutton, but by the national head of the CIB, Assistant Commissioner Bob Walton, and by the Crown Prosecutor, David Morris. From the 15 July 1970 conference they all attended:

Morris: Accepting this baby was fed – but when you get to court you are not going to get that proved.
Hutton: We ran up against this sighting – you won't shake the two McConachies.
Walton: One saw her *on the way to* football and one *on the way home*.
Hutton: Defence problem, the sighting of the child.

This discussion – the conference was centered on Demler, and his involvement in caring for Rochelle Crewe – is testament to not only Hutton having knowledge of Dale McConachie's 4.30pm sighting of Rochelle, but that the Crown's prosecuting officer and an Assistant Commissioner of Police were aware of this significant information also. But none of the three imparted this key evidence to the Thomas defence teams, the two trial juries nor the 1980 Royal Commissioners.

Had it been known that a witness had seen a child running around in the front paddock of the Crewe farm at 4.30pm on that Saturday, evidently being fed and cared for by a third person or persons, Arthur and Vivien Thomas would have been able to prove conclusively that they were at home, tending sick cows, feeding calves and milking a few of their cows, at that very time in June 1970.

Furthermore, the Crown Prosecutor would not have been able to assassinate the character of Vivien Thomas during his summing up at the second Supreme Court trial of her husband. That David Morris so blatantly inferred that the wife of the accused Arthur Thomas was the woman who had fed Rochelle Crewe when he knew categorically that someone else had been at their property, attending the infant and having her out of her cot and running around in the paddock from 1.40pm till at least 4.30pm – a period of about three hours – deserves condemnation. This is yet another example of a senior officer of the court not only failing to disclose a key witness statement, but then setting out to defame an innocent party, knowing that what he was putting to a jury had no foundation whatsoever.

Separate sightings by Colin Ross Eyre and Raymond Leslie Fox of an unknown woman driving the Crewe car on Thursday 18 June 1970, the morning immediately following the murders

Local woman Ruth Eyre's youngest son, Ross – then aged 16 and a student – had been waiting for the school bus outside their home on the corner of State Highway 22 and Te Ahu Road, several kilometres from the Crewe home, when around 8am on Thursday 18 October 1970 he saw the Crewe car coming toward him round the bend. Driving the Crewe car was a fair-haired woman he did not recognise. [Jeanette Crewe had dark hair]. The woman looked 'straight through' him and the car went into a pothole on the left hand side of the road – a nasty one that locals knew to avoid. Ross Eyre recognised all the cars in the Pukekawa district at that time and he knew both Jeanette and Harvey Crewe well, having been to their farm to collect for the Scouts, and having worked for Len Demler on his farm next door several times prior to the murders.

After hearing about Ross Eyre's sighting, his mother contacted police and reported the incident, with Detective Sergeant Mike Charles being sent to interview the schoolboy. That interview took place in the first week of the Crewe investigation.

Forty two years after the event, Eyre remains adamant that he saw an unfamiliar woman driving the Crewe car that day in mid-June 1970 and that what he told Charles in an interview the following week was accurate in every respect. He also remains angry that Charles adopted an attitude that he was a policeman and Eyre was 'just a boy', pointing out that if the detective had taken his information seriously, crucial evidence may have been recovered.

Eyre now says that he had wished the car being driven by a woman he did not recognise as being from their district had crashed after hitting the pothole. Had it done so, the mystery of the Crewe murders may have been resolved the morning after the killings, rather than being still unsolved 42 years on.

It is not known if the Eyre information ever made it from Charles' notebook to a formal job sheet, as was the practice when interviews were conducted. What can be said however is that the police have constantly denied that such a job sheet exists.

A statement that does, however, exist in relation to the Crewe's car and the day of Eyre's early-morning sighting of an unknown woman driving it came from Raymond Leslie Fox, a sharemilker living just to the south of the property on which two people had just been murdered. Fox was interviewed by Detective Sergeant Phil Seaman on 24 June, two days after police were called to Pukekawa. Seaman spoke with other parties who corroborated Fox's movements on that day. The Fox statement revealed that about 10.30am on the previous Thursday – the day after the murders – he had seen a Hillman car coming toward him (travelling south). In it were two women, one whom he took to be Jeanette Crewe and the other an older woman, probably in her forties. Fox knew the Crewes – he had met Harvey about half a dozen times in the two years he had been in the area, speaking with him for several hours on one occasion, and had met Jeanette once at their home – and he knew what type of car they owned and its colour.

Neither Eyre's statement nor Fox's were tendered at the lower court hearing against Thomas, at his subsequent two Supreme Court trials, nor at the 1980 hearings of the Royal Commission. Once again, the defence teams did not know they existed.

Various sightings of a combination shotgun-rifle at the Chennells' farmhouse (later to become the Crewe property) in the 1950s

Toward the end of September 1970, the Crewe inquiry squad had in its possession statements from those who had managed or worked on the Chennells Estate and the Demler farm during the 1950s and 1960s. Two of these statements are significant – but once again the Thomas defence was not advised of them. Each of these statement relates to the combination firearm owned by Len Demler's father-in-law, Newman Chennells, and subsequently by his brother-in-law, Howard Chennells, until May 1950, when the latter died in a tractor accident on the adjoining farm. Such a firearm is exactly what the term implies, a combination of one calibre and another – in this case a 410 shotgun and a .22 rifle.

The two witnesses to the existence and description of such a firearm were Ted Bennett and Steve Mackay and the effect of their evidence was that they had seen the *combination* firearm at the Chennells farm – which Jeanette Crewe and her husband took over in 1966 – and they gave detailed descriptions of its features, including that it fired [bird] *shot* from one barrel and *bullets* from the other. Both had seen the long thin shot cartridges, just a little larger than a .303 bullet as they described them, and Mackay went even further by revealing that he saw *old .22 bullets* in the case that contained the combination firearm.

Both Paul Temm, at the first Thomas trial, and Kevin Ryan two years later at the retrial, tried desperately to get information about this firearm from police witnesses and from Demler himself, with little success. Had either lawyer known of the statements from Bennett and Mackay, the cross-examination on the issue of this firearm – at the Chennells' farm until 1950, then taken by Demler to his own house after the death of his brother-in-law that year – could have played a crucial role in the defence of the man accused of the Crewe murders.

Police knowledge of the whereabouts of the missing Chennells Estate combination firearm prior to the second Thomas trial in 1973

The entry for 16 March 1973 in the work diary of Detective Len Johnston – a key player in the Crewe inquiry – is relevant to the issue of the Chennells Estate combination firearm as it reveals that Jack Handcock, a relieving manager at the Crewe farm for several months after the murders, possessed crucial evidence about it. From Johnston's notebook:

Present whereabouts [of] combination rifle known to him [Handcock]

The second Thomas trial began 10 days later but once again the defence was not told of the existence of this very material evidence, which again could have had a significant bearing on the outcome of that retrial.

Police knowledge of an axle on the Demler farm which was similar to that recovered on the riverbed beneath Harvey Crewe's body in September 1970

In his 29 September 1970 statement – the second he had made but the first time he had actually been shown this specific exhibit – Steve Mackay advised that the axle he was shown by Detective Bruce Parkes was similar to one which he had first-hand knowledge of as a regular user of a trailer on the Demler farm from 1958 to 1962 or 1963, when he worked as a labourer on that property.

Mackay could never have gone beyond saying that the axle Parkes brought to him was *similar* to the Demler trailer axle, because many of the car parts made in the 1920s were mass produced, some being used by several different vehicle manufacturers. The 'Harvey Crewe axle' was identified as being from a 1928 Nash car, with hundreds of thousands of them being made and distributed throughout the world on that make and model.

Irrespective of whether the axle Mackay was shown on 29 September 1970 – alleged to have came off the body of Harvey Crewe but in fact recovered from the riverbed in that vicinity – was the one that he had seen on the Demler farm trailer or not, the knowledge of his statement was not provided to the defence at any point. Clearly it ought to have been disclosed on the grounds that it was material evidence.

Three formal statements relating to axles shown to witnesses at variance with the axle produced at trial

The axle alleged to have been found beneath the body of Harvey Crewe – but never proved with any certainty to have been connected to it – was one of the key ingredients of the fabricated case against Thomas. Three witness statements on the matter of the axle are significant in that the defence was unaware of any of them at the time of either the first or second Thomas trials. For the purposes of practicality, the last of these statements, from Brian Jackson and Len Elliott, will be treated as one.

Peter Garratt, a Pukekawa farmer who also assisted with running the local school buses, had been shown an axle by two detectives, probably Jeffries and Parkes as both were engaged in axle enquiries at that time. When later shown police photographs of the axle presented at the two

Thomas trials, seven years after those events, Garrett – by then a Justice of the Peace – declared that these did not depict the axle he had been shown in September 1970. Both ends of the axle he saw originally were uniform, featuring a stub axle on either end or nothing on any end. The Thomas trial axle had a kingpin in one end and not the other.

James Gordon [Ben] Hawker, manager of the former Chennells Estate from 1951 to 1961, was another who provided a statement about axles, the existence of which never reached the defenders of Thomas. Shown an axle by Hutton at his Cambridge home in September 1970, he was able to confirm that had it been in the Crewe property, he would have seen it during the decade he was living there. He had not done so. While Hawker did give evidence to the Royal Commission – the result of a statement obtained by me in 1977 and the subsequent production of an affidavit on this matter – he was adamant that the 'trial axle' was not the one he had been shown by the police a decade earlier during the Crewe inquiry. Several significant differences existed between the two axles and Hawker was able to explain them in great detail to the Royal Commissioners. His testimony on that aspect of the Crewe inquiry was, however, not put before either jury at the two Thomas trials.

Likewise, Brian Jackson and Len Elliott, two Auckland vintage car enthusiasts, were shown an axle alleged to have been found with the body of Harvey Crewe, and were able to identify the make and model. Both men provided statements to the detectives who visited them, but a matter of weeks later, in October, they saw photographs in the *New Zealand Herald* and immediately realised that the axle being displayed was not the one they had been shown. When Thomas was arrested and then put on trial, the pair went back to the police and asked what had happened to their formal statements, only to be told that these documents had 'been lost'. They were not called to give evidence at either Thomas trial, nor at the Royal Commission in 1980, but they remain adamant that the 'trial axle' was not the one shown to them by detectives in September 1970.

It is now known that the police did have two similar axles in their possession while they canvassed that issue with vintage car enthusiasts and others in the weeks following the discovery of Harvey Crewe's body. One was the axle with the significant welding on it which had been found on the riverbed *beneath* Crewe's body on 16 September 1970. The second was borrowed from Auckland engineer David Keruse. Both axles were from a Nash car but the Keruse axle did not have any king pins, cotter pins or welding, being just a bare axle beam.

Members of the Crewe inquiry squad were hawking around at least two axles during their investigation and on the basis of the statements of Garratt, Hawker, Jackson and Elliott, it appears there were others and that neither jury at the Thomas trials were told about these, nor was the defence given the opportunity to call and question the witnesses who had been shown a variety of different axles by police officers during that period.

The chance encounter of a middle-aged woman and older man horses, dogs and two 'bundles of rubbish' on the Waikato riverbank around the time of the murders

Alexander Edwin Fletcher was an Australian engineer who came to New Zealand and married a young Samoan woman then living in Auckland. In June 1970 he was awaiting the start of the giant pulp mill expansion project in Kawerau and he spent some time doing casual farm work around the Waikato. While he was in that area he went looking for a place in which he could catch whitebait in the season that was approaching. On a late afternoon he left his car on a corner of a gravel road and walked for a short distance along the stopbank that stretches for kilometres along that section of the Waikato River. Among the willow trees on the water's edge, Fletcher saw two horses, some dogs, a man with a trilby hat and a middle-aged woman trussed up in wet weather gear. On the ground were two bundles. When he asked the couple what they were doing, the man replied sheepishly, saying that they were 'just dumping some rubbish.'

When he heard of the disappearance of the Crewes some days later, Fletcher phoned the police to report what he had seen.

Following the arrest of Arthur Thomas in November 1970, Fletcher went back to the police as he felt the description of the young farmer who had been arrested was a far cry from the elderly man he had seen at the riverbank on that dark and dismal June day, only to be told by the officer that the information he had provided was not relevant and to keep the matter to himself or he would 'find himself in serious trouble'. However the young engineer did not 'shut up'. In early 1972 he contacted Thomas Retrial Committee member Doug Vesey and arranged a meeting at which he matched the man in the trilby hat he had seen with the woman, the two horses and the dogs – and the 'bundles of rubbish' – with photographs of Len Demler in the *New Zealand Herald's* hurriedly-produced booklet on the Crewe murders. He also confirmed that the horse with the white blaze also shown in the *Herald* booklet was the one he had seen at the river. Descriptions of Demler's dogs – subsequently obtained by retrial committee chairman Pat Vesey from the Raglan County Council – closely those matched the information Fletcher had provided.

Tragically, at the age of just 32, Fletcher died of severe head injuries when a steel beam fell on him at work in Kawerau on 5 April 1973, the day after Thomas collapsed in the dock of the Supreme Court at his retrial. Although the information Fletcher provided was neither suppressed nor denied the Thomas defence team at that second trial – his counsel, Kevin Ryan, had been made aware of it by the Veseys – it was clearly not provided to Paul Temm and Brian Webb by the police before the first trial two years earlier. The police maintain that there is no record of Fletcher in the Crewe homicide file, no interview sheets and no job sheets, and no account of what he saw at the edge of the Waikato River that day in June 1970.

The photograph of Len Demler and his horse used by Alexander Fletcher in his identification of the man he saw at the Waikato River, with a middle-aged woman, dogs and 'two bundles of rubbish' in June 1970, the time the Crewes disappeared.

By way of a postscript to the Fletcher affair, evidence about the existence of a second horse, as a means of corroborating the version of events of the young Australian engineer, came to me recently via an old newspaper clipping, dated 23 June 1970. This revealed that Demler and neighbour Owen Priest had – on the day they reported the disappearance of the Crewes – ruled out an accident after examining the Crewe's tractor and 'their horse'. That same article quoted another neighbour as saying that he often saw Harvey Crewe riding around his farm on 'his horse'.

Furthermore, at a Crewe inquiry conference on 15 July 1970, the search controller reported:

> [Pat] *Gaines:* One of the farmers said that the horse belonging to Crewes looked like it had been 'ridden to hell' as there was still dried sweat on it.

This evidence confirms that there were two horses available to the man in the trilby hat and his woman friend at the precise time Fletcher saw them on the banks of the Waikato River 'just dumping some rubbish'. One horse on Demler's farm and the other on the Crewe property next door.

The identity of a woman seen at the Crewe house was revealed by police to relations and family friends in the week after the murders

Maud and Wyndham Knox were close friends of Marie Crewe, the mother of the young Pukekawa farmer whom, on 22 June 1970, was reported missing – with his wife of four years – from his farmhouse. Like other relatives and close friends, the Knoxs sped northward the next morning. Their convoy from Pahiatua that day was a sober affair, its occupants distressed and alarmed at grim news filtering down from the north.

Days later, the Knoxs, with Marie Crewe, her daughter Beverly and son-in-law Don Turner, and one of Harvey Crewe's uncles, were shown through the bloodstained farmhouse from which the couple had disappeared. The discussions in that house that day centred not only on what had happened to their kin, but on who the police felt had been responsible for their murder and the removal of their bodies. Those beliefs, however, never made it to the Thomas defence teams, nor did they enter into the public domain. Thirty years passed before that initial police version of who killed the Crewes – and who fed and cared for their infant daughter Rochelle – came to light.

In 2000, a television documentary on the Crewe murders produced a letter from a Manawatu woman, the step daughter of Maud Knox and daughter of Wyndham. She subsequently swore a formal declaration, in which she states:

> My father Wyndham Knox and step-mother Maud Knox went to Pukekawa to support Marie Crewe in the harrowing days after the murders. Upon their return from Pukekawa, I discussed with them

aspects of the murders and the investigation [at that time still in its infancy]. I remember my step-mother telling me that while she was at Pukekawa she had had a conversation with one of the chief policemen involved with the investigation. He was on the scene a few days after the murders. My step-mother asked this officer who he suspected and his reply was to the effect that Jeanette Crewe's father, Len Demler, was the murderer. The motive he offered was Demler's need to regain control of the family money that had been bequeathed to Jeanette by her mother. Maud also said she had been told by this policeman that Demler had a new lady friend and he suggested this was the woman who had fed the baby, Rochelle, and was therefore an accomplice. I remember this conversation clearly because in those days it was particularly shocking to me that a father could murder his own daughter for money. I am making this statement voluntarily and only because I have an interest in seeing the full truth of the murders revealed so that the years of pain and suffering for the Crewe and Thomas families can come to an end.

The presence of Marie Crewe, members of her family and her close friends in that first week of the inquiry was confirmed in evidence from the officer in charge of the scene, Detective Sergeant Murray Jeffries, at the first Thomas trial. He put the number of those shown through the Crewe's house that day in June 1970 at six.

In 2011, former Crewe scene detective Ross Meurant revealed his knowledge of this matter, recounting what the 'lower ranks' in that inquiry had been told by their superiors at that time:

We were told that Rochelle had to have been fed during the five days before her parent's disappearance was reported to the police or she would have died. Our superiors believed that Demler had been in the Crewe house well before the police were called, that he had attended to his granddaughter Rochelle and that he was probably accompanied by his new female partner. There was considerable discussion about a woman being involved in providing care to Rochelle and deductions that Demler's woman friend was implicated. This opinion came from Bruce Hutton. It was articulated many times – at evening conferences where all personnel involved with the inquiry convened and among we scene detectives when Hutton was with us reconstructing events.

On Friday 30 October 1970, police had, however, put Vivien Thomas in a line-up at the Pukekohe station. The purpose of this was to see if Bruce Roddick could identify the woman he had seen at the Crewe farm two days after the murders. What Roddick was able to reveal after the identification parade – although he was not asked that specific question until May 1972, when he committed it to paper by way of affidavit – was that Vivien Thomas was *not* the woman he had seen on 19 June 1970 by the front fence of the house enclosure at the Crewe farm. He knew this with certainty because he had worked on the Thomas farm prior to the murders, knew Vivien Thomas and was immediately able to say that her hair colour and description were not remotely that of the woman he had seen two days after the Crewes were shot.

With the knowledge that police were expressing uncompromising beliefs, in the first week of their investigation, about the culpability of the man they were adamant had murdered Harvey Crewe and his wife on 17 June 1970, and the identity of the woman who had cared for their by-then orphaned daughter until her discovery five days later, it now seems inexplicable that Len Demler's 'new girlfriend' was not put in the line-up of 30 October that year. It is equally inexplicable that Vivien Thomas was.

The knowledge the police had of this woman – more particularly Roddick's identification of her – is reinforced by the notes of one of its own squad members, Detective Len Johnston. His work diary covering the weeks immediately preceding the 1973 retrial of Thomas records that Roddick was naming names in relation to the woman he had seen at the Crewe farm two days after the murders. Johnston noted also that this confirmed the suspicion the police had about the identity of this person.

The Crewe inquiry squad, or more specifically senior members thereof, clearly suppressed material evidence in relation to this matter. In doing so, they denied the two Thomas defence teams, the two juries and the three Royal Commissioners of 1980 the opportunity to examine these matters with the level of intensity one would expect, given their significance.

Junior counsel at the Thomas retrial, Gerald Ryan observes:

It's almost beyond belief. If any of Thomas' counsel had known about what the police were telling family and friends of the Crewes in that first week of the inquiry in 1970, not only would Demler have been cross-examined on this, the woman herself would have been put on the stand. Paul Temm would have called her to account for her movements, as would my brother Kevin.

The issue of suppression of evidence was in fact raised by Kevin Ryan, in his closing submission to the 1980 Royal Commission:

I am directing my attention to those factual matters which best illustrate the duplicity and concealment with which Thomas and those associated with him had to contend. In our jurisdiction, 'discovery' in criminal cases is denied and it is only because this Royal Commission directed that police records be made available for inspection that much of the truth has been exposed or mined for the first time.

Royal Commission chairman Robert Taylor expressed amazement at the ability for the police and the Crown to withhold such crucial evidence from the defence, revealing that he had himself been overruled by the High Court in Australia when he decided that this should not be a requirement.

During submissions from Peter Williams, senior counsel for Thomas, at the end of those hearings, the Royal Commission chairman asked:

Taylor: Isn't there a procedure in this country [New Zealand] where at the start of a Magistrate's [depositions] hearing you can call all the evidence in the possession of the Crown Prosecutor?
Peter Williams: No.
Taylor: You mean it would not be allowed or the call would not be answered?
Williams: If a blanket letter was sent across requesting [it].
Taylor: [In Australia] A call is made in court on the first day of court, the counsel for the defence calls for the production of the *whole police file.*

Williams: I can say on behalf of all the lawyers here that if that request was made, it would be declined.

Taylor: In the Australian High Court authority it can be done. I as a judge in the first instance decided it could not and the High Court ruled you can.

Williams: The position in New Zealand is the police would conceal the file beneath the skirt of privilege.

Taylor. You cannot? I thought there was privilege.

Williams: That is the position in this country.

From this it can be seen that two neighbouring countries – both operating under the auspices of the British justice system – follow entirely different paths in terms of the discovery permitted in criminal cases. Production of the full police file in relation to the Crewe homicide inquiry would categorically have ensured that Arthur Thomas was not even arrested, let alone convicted twice of murders clearly committed by another.

It is clear that any one of these very material pieces of evidence, as outlined in these two chapters, could have served to introduce enough doubt to the mind of the jury members at both trials to have ensured Thomas was acquitted and that justice was served.

Ten

In June 1970 the New Zealand Police had at its disposal 20 detectives with the rank of Inspector or above - inspectors, chief inspectors, superintendents and chief superintendents.

But on the 22nd of that month, Auckland regional CIB co-ordinator Detective Superintendent Mal Ross opted to tap one Bruce Thomas Newton Hutton on the shoulder as he emerged from a lift at Auckland Central police station just before knock-off time. His instruction to his detective inspector to 'pop down to Pukekawa' probably stemmed from his knowledge that Hutton had been a farmer – so who better to send to investigate the disappearance of a farming couple in such an isolated rural settlement?

Raised of farming stock from the Dargaville area, Hutton had first joined the police in June 1948, becoming a beat cop in Auckland at the beginning of August of that year. His formal training was limited, eight weeks being considered more than enough to get a constable onto the street in that era. However he resigned just 11 months into the job in order to marry a farmer's daughter, Dorothy, the first of the three wives he was to collect over the next half century. He returned to the force seven years later.

A mere two years after rejoining the police, Hutton became a detective constable in the Criminal Investigation Branch, the elite brigade which was at that time tasked with investigating – and almost always solving – burglaries, indecent assaults, the theft of motor vehicles, frauds and arsons. In this role he experienced his first murder inquiry, one of 30 he was involved with or which he controlled during the next 18 years. Three years later he was promoted to detective sergeant, but was returned to the uniform branch, initially in the prosecution unit, 14 months later.

It is clear that Hutton made a rapid rise up the ranks in the Auckland police – he was a senior sergeant by 1965, a relieving inspector in 1966, was authorised for 'higher duties' in 1967 and earned his inspector's rank in March 1968. From constable on beat duties to inspector in 12 years, it had been an impressive climb up the ladder to commissioned rank by any measure. In December of that year, Hutton was transferred back to his beloved CIB, a detective inspector's ranking to his name and the murder of a young couple in the remote rural settlement of Pukekawa still 18 months into the future. [On 5 October 1970, the day two out-of-town detectives arrived in Auckland to begin an overview of the inquiry that had ground on, relentlessly, from 22 June, Hutton became detective in charge of the CIB's southern division, based at Otahuhu].

The homicide file shows that Hutton arrived at the Crewe property at 5.10pm on that Monday, 22 June 1970, and that he had travelled via the Otahuhu police station where he collected Detective Senior Sergeant Les Schultz, fingerprint specialist Detective Mervyn Dedman and a police photographer, Constable Barry Stevens. On arrival at their State Highway 22 property, the first thing Hutton did was clear away the large number of locals who had congregated upon what he quickly identified as being a major crime scene. In terms of the front paddock – the little enclosure between the highway gate and the fenceline around the house – the damage had already been done. Barring a small piece of copper wire found to the right of the front gate in an August search, not a single clue was ever found in that area.

There is ample evidence now that, almost five months later, at the 'business end' of the Crewe homicide inquiry – probably following the big conference on 2 October 1970 – a switch was made from Len Demler to Arthur Thomas. The conference on that day was called to discuss whether enough had been gathered to proceed with charges against Demler. A decade later, the Demler file, understandably, became a matter of great interest to the Royal Commission, with that panel eager to see exactly what had been assembled against the father of the murdered Jeanette Crewe. But the Royal Commission was advised that the Demler file no longer existed, this erroneous evidence being provided on the basis of a telex dated 12 June 1972 in which Hutton told his boss, CIB chief Bob Walton:

> The Demler briefs of evidence appear to have been discarded at the time the file was prepared against Thomas.

But what Hutton's 1972 communique to Walton does disclose is that in the weeks leading up to that game-breaking 2 October conference – attended by Walton and Assistant Commissioner Austing, Chief Superintendent Byrne, Detectives Hutton, Cook and Tootill and Crown Prosecutor David Morris – Detective Sergeant Mike Charles had spent much of his time putting together the evidence against Demler, on 19, 21, 23, 25, 28, 29 and 30 September. [That conference ultimately concluded there was insufficient evidence to say that Demler was the offender.] In his telex, Hutton then went on to say that the Crewe file did not contain any notes from that conference and that those in attendance with whom he had discussed the matter were of the opinion that no record of the proceedings was taken. This is itself is peculiar as Walton was at that conference and the thrust of his request for the notes appears to have been based on his knowledge that a record of the discussion that day had been taken.

In evidence to the Royal Commission seven years later however, Hutton – in response to a question on a different issue – testified that records were only taken for conferences attended by the 'top brass'. The 2 October conference clearly fell into that category and indeed at the next conference, on 19 October, extensive records of the discussion – 11 pages in all – were kept. It may be significant that Hutton's telex denying the existence of any formal record of proceedings from that 2 October gathering was sent just 10 days after a petition had been lodged with the Governor-General for a retrial for Thomas.

In his June 1972 telex also, Hutton revealed something else that he later went on to deny – that Thomas was 'first considered as a possible suspect' at the 19 October conference. The record clearly shows that the movement from Demler to Thomas was, in fact, well under way by early October. The 19 October conference – called to examine the evidence for and against Demler and for and against Thomas – did not involve the top brass, as had the gathering 17 days earlier, but essentially involved the remnants of the original Crewe inquiry squad and the two officers from down south who had spent a fortnight reviewing the file, or more correctly, those parts of it with which they had been supplied. In attendance were Detective Inspector Bruce Hutton, Detective Inspector Wally Baker (Wellington), Detective Senior Sergeant Pat O'Donovan (Christchurch), Detective Senior Sergeant Les Schultz, Detective Sergeant Jim Tootill, Detective Len Johnston, Detective Bruce Parkes and Detective Stan Keith. Hutton opened the proceedings:

We have cause to have another look at the Crewe murders prior to the departure of Detective Inspector Baker and Detective Senior Sergeant O'Donovan, and the main reason for holding it is to try and collectively gather all information, both from within the squad and from an insight into the file that Mr Baker and Mr O'Donovan have conducted, in an effort to bring the inquiry to a satisfactory conclusion. I think that it can be said at this stage that there are two persons who can be considered as suspects, namely Lenard William Demler and Arthur Allan Thomas. There is no other evidence suggesting any other person, even remotely, as a possible suspect.

Hutton went on to report, in his examination of the pros and cons of the case against Demler, on the three aspects which he clearly viewed as being the essential elements of these still-unsolved murders:

Now so far as the evidence of Demler having committed the crime, there are three things that have caused me some concern and these are (a) the firearm, (b) the axle, (c) the wire found around the bodies. In regard to the firearm, strenuous efforts have been made to put a .22 calibre weapon in the possession of Demler. We all know that these enquiries covered what is described as a *combination* weapon, but even today it could not be said that we can prove that Lenard Demler had a .22 firearm with which he could have committed the murders. In regard to the axle, here again we have no evidence that an axle of a similar description as that found with the body of Harvey Crewe was ever on the Demler farm, or in his possession.

Now let's freeze the frame here. Ignoring the matter of the wire – bundles of copper and galvanized wire had been found on both the Demler and Crewe farms by police following the recovery of Jeanette's body during searches for exactly those items – the information provided by Hutton to the over-view officers is clearly at variance with the contents of statements in the possession of members of his inquiry team at that time.

The documentary record shows that on 21 September 1970, Steve Mackay provided a statement to Detective Bruce Parkes in which the matter of both a firearm and an axle were discussed. The firearm in question was later referred to as the Chennells Estate weapon. After Howard Chennells' death in 1950, Demler took this firearm to his home. According to Mackay's statement that firearm had two barrels with hammer actions, and that it was used to *shoot rabbits*. Mackay worked on the Demler farm from 1958 until 1962 or 1963, and his statement also refers, in some detail, to the two trailers on that property during his employment as a farmhand there, one of which had an axle which ought to have attracted the attention of the police:

> The axle [displayed by Parkes] is similar to one on an old home-made trailer that Demler had. The trailer was a very narrow one pulled behind a crawler tractor. I say that the axle is similar because it is the same shape as the one on the trailer. The trailer had a wonky wheel and looking at the kingpin on the axle I have been shown this appears to be where the wheel wasn't running true. The axle I have mentioned on the [narrow] trailer also had one or two bars running from the axle to the frame of the trailer. The axle I have been shown also has a lug welded onto the bottom of it to which a bar like the one I remembered could be fitted. When I used to use the trailer I wondered why the bar or bars were there as I could not see any use for them.

Mackay also provided more information on the Chennells Estate firearm, which he had first seen in 1931, but which he again personally viewed at Demler's farm after the death of Howard Chennells in the tractor accident in 1950:

> Referring to the gun I saw at Chennells' place. When I saw the gun I also saw some long thin cartridges just a shade bigger than a .303. These were cartridges that would fire *shot*. Also in the leather case in which the gun case was kept were some .22 shells. They appeared to be a greeny Verdigris colour. Both the cartridges and the shells were lying loose. I do not remember how many there were and I did not touch them at all. On the occasion I saw the gun I said something to Howard's father [Newman Chennells] about chasing rabbits with a ferret or greyhound and he said he used the gun to *shoot rabbits*.

On 20 September 1970, Hutton contacted one Ted Bennett 'as a result of information received'. According to his job sheet, filed the next day, Bennett was the first manager of the Chennells' farm following the death of Howard Chennells in 1950. The Hutton job sheet records:

> Bennett remembers a double barrel English gun in good condition in the Chennells' home during the time he was managing the property. He thinks the gun consisted of two barrels and is quite sure one

barrel fired *bird shot*. He remembers it being in the house in a polished wooden case. He said the gun was in good working order and was still in the house in the case when he left.

On 25 September Parkes – whose job sheet records that he travelled north with Hutton – interviewed Bennett. A statement by the former Chennells Estate manager records:

Among the stuff on the front porch [of the Chennells' house] there was a gun in a case. The inside of the case was lined with green felt and contained a cleaning rod as well as the gun. I would describe the gun as being two barreled, shorter than a normal shotgun. The barrels were side by side. I am not sure of it had hammers or not. The gun fired a *shot* cartridge out of one barrel and the other barrel fired a normal rifle shell. I am not sure of the calibre of the barrels but I would describe them as being 1) somewhere between a .22 and a .303. This would be the barrel firing the shell [bullet] and 2) a bore about the same diameter of the outside diameter of a .22 barrel. I would have taken the gun out of the case two or three times but never actually used it.

Had the two Thomas defence teams, or the Royal Commission, known of the existence of these highly-significant statements, it would have strongly examined Hutton and his detectives about their contents, and the documents themselves would have been entered as formal exhibits. However the existence of this evidence was never revealed by the police – not to the juries at the two Thomas trials, not to the Judges of the Court of Appeal, probably not to the Crown Prosecutor, not to the defence and, on the evidence now available, probably not to the two senior police officers sent to Auckland to specifically weigh up the case against the two suspects, as they were at that time.

Baker and O'Donovan would surely have challenged Hutton over the matter of the firearm and the axle had they viewed the two statements provided by Mackay, the Hutton and Parkes' job sheets and the Bennett statement. Because this very material evidence was obviously unknown to them, it is totally understandable that the 19 October conference came to the conclusions it did. Namely:

- Conference considered that apart from Thomas and Demler, from the enquiries there does not appear to be any other person remotely involved

- Conference concluded that every effort must be made immediately either to confirm Thomas as a suspect or exclude him altogether from the inquiry.

Baker and O'Donovan left Auckland the next day, believing that there was virtually nothing of substance that would warrant the arrest of Lenard William Demler. The Mackay and Bennett statements demonstrate something quite different.

The June 1966 marriage of Harvey Crewe and Jeanette Demler. The couple were joined by his mother, Marie Crewe (left) and her parents, Len and Maisey Demler. Within four years, three of the wedding party were dead – Maisey from a brain tumour in February 1970, and Harvey and Jeanette four months later, murdered in their house at Pukekawa. Detectives spent the following four months trying to produce sufficient evidence to justify the arrest and prosecution of Len Demler before turning swiftly, and savagely, on Arthur Thomas, a farmer from the other end of the district with little real connection to the Crewes.

The murder scene, as captured by police from an air force helicopter on 24 June, two days after Len Demler reported finding the Crewes' empty house, bar the presence of their infant daughter Rochelle, drawn but alive in her cot in the front room. The L-shaped house in which Jeanette and Harvey Crewe met their deaths was set back off State Highway 22, accessed through the small rectangular paddock in which detectives are seen standing. Their Hillman car was parked at the house enclosure gate from the Wednesday of their deaths till some time on Sunday, but when police arrived in the mid afternoon on Monday 22 June, it was in the garage to the right of the road gate.

Detective-on-trial Ross Meurant (left) and his immediate superior, Detective Bruce Parkes, were captured digging and raking in a garden on 24 June, the second day of the Crewe homicide inquiry. Meurant and Parkes were part of a four-man team which searched the Crewe house and the enclosure surrounding it in June, and the former was back there in August after the discovery of Jeanette Crewe's body and the revelation she had been shot with a .22 firearm. The August garden search failed to produce any evidence. But on 27 October, Detective Sergeant Mike Charles found a cartridge case, confirmed as being from the rifle of Arthur Thomas, in a garden searched twice previously.

The scene as the jury at the second Supreme Court trial of Arthur Thomas, in 1973, surveyed the Crewe house and its immediate surrounds. Detectives who had yet to give evidence were in attendance that day – Bruce Hutton (left foreground with hands on hips), Mike Charles and Jim Tootill, as was the trial judge, Clifford Perry (partly obscured). En route to the Crewe farm, the jury, two Crown Prosecutors, the judge, registrar and a group of detectives dined together at the Tuakau Hotel, with alcoholic beverages thrown in, but the defence team was not invited.

The Thomas farm and gully occupied by three rubbish tips (above), as photographed by the police on 21 October 1970. Tip number one is marked by an X at bottom right, the site where two stub axles had been 'discovered' the day before. One discarded spilt rim (right) and another recovered among an array of old junk (below) was used by Detective Len Johnston to construct a wheel assembly on a skeleton trailer, then photographed and put before the two trial juries. None of it was relevant, a fact known to Johnston when he referred to this skeleton trailer in his sworn testimony.

These official police photographs demonstrate another deception perpetrated on the public and the two Thomas trial juries. Carrying their original numbers, the full sequence of images was never provided to the defence teams. Photograph 6 was the only image released publicly, being used by the police to demonstrate the old car axle which diver Paul Spence said he had found on the riverbed below Harvey Crewe's body. Photographs 3 and 4 – now revealed for the first time publicly – shows police divers dragging the body in the cradle toward a row boat and placing it alongside this vessel.

Photograph 5 shows diver Paul Spence emerging with an axle. The body of Harvey Crewe is already in the row boat (left foreground). Photograph 6 – reproduced many times since 1970 – shows Bruce Hutton holding up an axle, and purportedly 'Crewe's body floating alongside the boat wrapped in a black polythene sheet'. This is manifestly untrue as the full frame proves. The body recovery had clearly already been completed by then and the black polythene was put in place after that action, for reasons never explained.

The atmosphere of the win-at-all-costs second trial of Arthur Thomas is aptly demonstrated through the actions of Bruce Hutton during a visit to the Crewe house. Wherever defence lawyer Kevin Ryan went, Hutton was on his tail. Police bugged the telephones of members of the Retrial Committee which had won a new hearing, shadowed civilian witnesses as they went about their business and investigated those who told the truth in a bid to discredit them. Crown Prosecutor David Morris (above right) peers through the louvre windows into the Crewe kitchen before presenting this scenario to the jury to explain the presence of a cartridge case in the garden nearby, despite it not being found in two previous searches.

The police, in an official history, labelled these upholders of law and order as their 'Crewe prosecution team'. Back row (from left) photographer Alan Arnold, exhibits officer Graham (Bud) Abbott, Detective Sergeant Mike Charles and inquiry clerk Stan Keith. Front row, the heavyweights, Detective Len Johnston, Crown Prosecutor David Morris, Detective Inspector Bruce Hutton and Assistant Prosecutor David Baragwanath. *(NZ Police)*

Police Commissioner – from 1978 till 1982 – Bob Walton (above left). At the time of the Crewe inquiry he was Assistant Commissioner and national head of the Criminal Investigation branch. On his watch as CIB chief, five murders were reported in six months, causing him great consternation. Walton was relieved when Detective Inspector Bruce Hutton (above right) 'solved' two of those murders. The certificate of merit presented to Hutton for his 'diligence and zeal' in solving the killings of Jeanette and Harvey Crewe remains in force to this day. Walton declined to rescind the granting of that certificate, despite numerous attempts by Thomas supporters to have Hutton stripped of it.

The target of four months of police investigation, Len Demler (above left) played bowls as his first wife's life ebbed away in early 1970, and he continued to do so while the search went on for his daughter and son-in-law throughout the latter part of that year. He took no part in those searches and was viewed by Hutton and his squad as 'categorically' being the murderer. When detectives failed to put a firearm of the right calibre in Demler's hands, they switched the attack to Arthur Thomas (above right). He was, and is, innocent of any involvement in the killing of the Crewes.

The Thomas Royal Commission at work. On the Waikato riverbank (above) Justice Robert Taylor and Peter Gordon. Retired Archbishop Allen Johnston (in tweed jacket) is partly obscured at left. The Australian judge Taylor (right) led the way throughout the eight months of hearings. Taylor (below) in typical stance – he constantly admonished police witnesses for their reluctance to tell the truth.

Eleven

Bruce Hutton was the most ruthless man he had ever worked with, in the view of former Crewe scene detective Ross Meurant. Former police inspector Jack Collins decreed:

> Hutton was not that ambitious as a beat cop, but this changed when he became a detective. He ended up being pretty ruthless.

The ruthlessness showed its face once the Crewe inquiry turned from Demler to Thomas and has been seen on many occasions since. From early October until 11 November, when Hutton finally got his man, one piece of significant 'evidence' after the next was discovered in relation to Arthur Thomas. A decade later, the Royal Commission noted:

> While they had been unable during the previous 4 months to uncover a single piece of hard evidence against their initial suspect, Mr Demler, they succeeded during this period [from 19 October] in building up what amounted virtually to the whole case against Mr A A Thomas.

The convincing case that Hutton and his squad built up against Thomas in a matter of weeks largely went unchallenged at the first Supreme Court trial in February 1971. His counsel, Paul Temm QC, was effectively defeated by his inability to obtain relevant statements and documents and the fact that crucial evidence was hidden from him. The December 1970 affidavit by Hutton – the one that declared that there were no other material witnesses who could provide material evidence, other than that produced at the depositions – is surely relevant to this matter. Based as it was on an injustice – with a liberal dose of fabricated evidence thrown in – the case against Thomas was, however, always likely to unravel because there were some who knew that fiction had replaced fact.

The wheels of the police juggernaut began to fall off in August 1971 when Woodville farm manager Graeme Hewson contacted Temm, declaring that the garden search story which had been given by the police at the first trial was a myth. Hewson was an old friend of Harvey Crewe's and had earlier given him work as a shepherd before his marriage. On hearing of the couple's disappearance in June, Hewson rushed north and spent the next month or so tending the stock there until a manager was appointed.

In August 1970, after the recovery of Jeanette Crewe's body from the Waikato River, Hewson returned to Pukekawa and spent two days assisting the police in their search of the Crewe house enclosure and the small paddock immediately in front, at the request of officer-in-charge Bruce Hutton. The objective of that assignment – which included digging and sieving the gardens and mowing the paddock – was to endeavour to recover a .22 cartridge, as the police knew by then that Jeanette had been shot with a firearm of that calibre. The garden search took place on 18 August and the paddock mowing the following day.

Following the arrest of Arthur Thomas in November, Hewson took little interest in the case, believing that the police had their man, until he returned from a trip hunting in the wild backcountry of the Whanganui River in mid 1971 and read a copy of the *New Zealand Herald's* booklet, *The Crewe Murders*. He then realised that the police claim that the garden in which the Thomas cartridge case had been found on 27 October 1970 had not been sieve searched in August was erroneous. Hewson knew this to be untrue as he had personally been involved with what had been an extensive and thorough search. He came forward and provided an affidavit, firstly to Temm, and then to his replacement, Kevin Ryan, and he subsequently appeared at the First Referral to the Court of Appeal in February 1973 which secured a retrial for Thomas.

However the man whom Hutton had 'planted' in the Demler home in the first week of the inquiry in order to listen for evidence – a courageous deed, as the police were at that time targeting the old Pukekawa farmer for the murder of his daughter and son-in-law – suddenly became a dog thief, a liar and an extortionist. In the blink of an eye, Hewson was transformed from a friend so trusted that he was admitted to a crime scene and was referred to as an honorary detective into being police enemy number one. As soon as his conflicting evidence became known, Hutton dispatched detectives to Woodville to interrogate family, friends, workmates and business associates. Detective Sergeant Mike Charles was one of those sent south to uncover anything at all that could discredit Hewson. This information was used at the First Referral and some of that muck, while largely untrue, undoubtedly stuck in those proceedings, in the eyes of the three judges at least. The effect of the investigation into Hewson – he was, it must be remembered a witness, not a suspect – had a devastating effect on both him and his family. His blackened character remains part of the court record to this day.

Local lad Bruce Roddick experienced similar treatment. His first 'misdemeanor' was to state that a woman he saw at the Demler farm in May 1972 – confirmed to two members of the Thomas family and then by way of affidavit – was the same woman he had seen at the Crewe farm two days after their murders, and that Vivien Thomas was categorically *not* that woman. Whereas the wife of Arthur Thomas was small and dark-haired, the woman Roddick had seen at the Crewe farm was taller, broad-shouldered and light-haired.

Having decided that Roddick was a good witness at the first Thomas trial – he was deliberately not asked about Vivien Thomas in those proceedings and thus the way was left open for the Crown to infer that she had been the woman who had fed the Crewe's infant daughter after their murders – Hutton and his team decided he was not so reliable by the time the retrial came around two years later. Contrast this with the 1979 determination of Muldoon's special investigator, Robert Adams-Smith QC, that Roddick *had* seen a woman at the Crewe farm that morning, that this woman had been there for an unlawful purpose connected with the murders, and that she had not come forward as a result of her involvement. That determination – extracts of which are reproduced as an Appendix 3 – led directly to the pardon of Arthur Thomas a year later.

Five witnesses bore the brunt of the attack in the Crewe inquiry. Apart from Hewson and Roddick, the characters and reputations of Tuakau Mayoress Ella McGuire and Pukekawa poultry farmers Julie and Owen Priest were also besmirched. A discussion between McGuire and Hutton at the end of the first Thomas trial led to her character being challenged. At that hearing, Pukekohe jeweller William Eggleton had miraculously appeared for the prosecution, a surprise last-minute witness who stunned the defence with talk of Thomas bringing in a bloody and mucus-covered watch for repair just after the Crewes were murdered. Eggleton's evidence was subsequently discredited, but at the First Referral to the Court of Appeal, and at the retrial, both in 1973, and again at the Royal Commission seven years later, Hutton denied that he had told McGuire that he was not interested in knowing that what the jeweller had told the jury was untrue. McGuire had previously ascertained this in a discussion with Eggleton and felt duty-bound to convey it to Hutton. As well as being placed under surveillance as she went about her daily chores, McGuire was ultimately labeled a 'vicious woman' solely on the basis that she was contesting the evidence put before both the Thomas trials and before the Court of Appeal hearing between them.

Owen Priest was the Pukekawa farmer who, on 22 June 1970, accompanied Demler to the Crewe house and then phoned the Tuakau police as a result of what he had found there. With his wife Julie, he ran an egg production operation located diagonally across the road from the scene of the murders. The evidence of the Priests, over the period of a decade, formed a part of the Crown case against Thomas. The suppression of Julie Priest's hearing of the rifle shots that undoubtedly killed the Crewes on the evening of 17 June 1970 has already been covered, but there are two other key pieces of evidence which conflicted with testimony provided by Hutton in subsequent years. The second, in particular, can be viewed as being very significant.

In evidence before the Thomas Royal Commission, given under oath, Hutton said he had been having lunch with the Priests on 27 October 1970 when the two detectives he had sent to sieve search the Crewe garden, Charles and Parkes, arrived at their farm. The Priests denied this. That is supported by the evidence of the two detectives, who said Hutton, and then Tootill, arrived at the Priest farm *after* the finding of the Thomas cartridge case, later designated as exhibit 350. While this is not a major deviation from the facts, the evidence presented to the Royal Commission about the roadside conversation the Priests had with Hutton and Johnston in mid October 1970 – after they had seen two men by the back door and had heard two rifle shots from that vicinity – was, however, infinitely more significant. The Royal Commission focused on this as the basis for its ultimate finding that these two police officers had planted exhibit 350 in the Crewe garden. As well as categorically denying elements of the evidence given by the Priests, Hutton attempted to denigrate the quality and reliability of their evidence, describing them as 'elderly people who were genuinely confused'. This description still angered the Priests decades later and even in their retirement they were critical of Hutton, whom they had willingly assisted during that dismal winter and spring of 1970 as he tried to unravel what had happened on their back door step.

Other examples of Hutton's propensity to treat the judicial process with cavalier disregard were brought to light during the hearings of the Thomas Royal Commission and more have emerged since as the former Crewe squad chief sought to re-write history. Some examples are recounted here:

Discrepancies over the trial foreman

Detective Sergeant John Hughes said he reported the prior association between himself and the second trial jury foreman Bob Rock – they had served in the navy together, in the same section on the same ship, for some considerable time – to Hutton at an early stage of that trial. Crown Prosecutor David Morris said that had he been made aware of this connection, the trial would have been aborted as one jury member had already gone home ill. Hutton countered that there had been a conversation between himself, Morris and Ryan, in which after learning of the relationship, the latter said he had no objection to Rock staying on as a member of the jury. The Royal Commission found:

> The foreman of the jury at the second trial had served in the navy with Detective Sergeant Hughes, one of the police witnesses. His evidence was significant. Detective Sergeant Hughes said, and we accept, that he reported the matter to Mr Hutton at an early stage in the trial as soon as he became aware of the identity of the foreman. Mr Morris, the Crown Prosecutor, said he was not aware of the matter at the time of the second trial. Mr Hutton, by contrast, said there had been a conversation between Mr Morris, himself, and Mr Kevin Ryan in which Mr Ryan had been [appraised] of the relationship and had indicated that he had no objection to Mr Rock staying on the jury. Mr Ryan strenuously disputed from the Bar that this conversation ever took place. We unreservedly accept Mr Morris' evidence in preference to that of Mr Hutton. It follows that Mr Ryan was not told of the relationship between Hughes and the foreman. In our view, Hutton as officer in charge of the case owed a duty to the defence to tell Mr Ryan either directly or by informing the Crown Prosecutor of any relationship between a material police witness and a member of the jury. It was then for Mr Ryan to decide what, if any, action he should take. It is in our view wholly irrelevant that the matter may have been reported to the judge through the registrar. We do not of course mean to imply that the foreman himself was

biased, or acted in any way improperly. The validity of the point does not depend, in our view, on proof that the trial was actually affected. It is a salutary maxim that justice must not only be done, but it must also be seen to be done. In our view that fact that the defence was not told of the relationship between Detective Sergeant Hughes and the foreman of the jury on its own justifies the description of the second Thomas trial as a miscarriage of justice.

Muldoon 'hijacks' the Royal Commission

On 24 June 2000, Hutton alleged in a newspaper interview that the findings of Judge Taylor, the chairman of the Thomas Royal Commission, were 'totally governed by interference by then Prime Minister Robert Muldoon during the hearings'. He further alleged that the reason Muldoon conferred privately with the judge 'was to ensure that the Commission's findings supported the pardon and to divert attention away from the economy', in effect interference by a Prime Minister in the tribunal process.

Hutton stated:

We were convinced that Judge Taylor believed he was dealing with Australian police, who were known to be corrupt. He likened us to them.

Jim McLay is now the head of New Zealand's permanent delegation to the United Nations in New York, but in the Muldoon Government, he was Justice Minister. His response to Hutton's claims:

I do know that Taylor met only once with Muldoon – when he and his fellow Commissioners handed over their report.

This account of a single meeting between Muldoon and Taylor has now been found to be in error. No challenge to McLay's integrity is intended, nor should it be taken, as he undoubtedly did not know of the brief chance meeting between the two in 1980. Royal Commissioner Peter Gordon was the source of this information:

Muldoon had met Taylor once, outside an Auckland church during the National Party's annual conference in July of 1980. Taylor had been a regular attendee at that church during the time he was in New

Zealand and I introduced the two, outside and in front of 20 people. The *only other occasion* where the [Royal] Commission chairman met Mr Muldoon was when the Commission's report was signed and presented to the Prime Minister.

Beattie's 'pardon' of Thomas

In another newspaper interview, published on 29 May 2010, Hutton repeated a conversation he allegedly had with former Governor-General Sir David Beattie. The former Queen's representative in New Zealand had been a lawyer who appeared regularly in the Court at Auckland when Hutton was a police prosecutor there. Hutton claims that Beattie took him aside in the president's room at the Trentham racecourse and said:

'Bruce, I want you to know that having to sign that pardon for Thomas was the hardest thing I have ever had to do in my life. I just want you to know that Muldoon insisted.'

This was another attempt to discredit Muldoon but again it is at variance with the facts. Thomas was pardoned on 17 December 1979. The Governor-General who signed that document was Keith Jacka Holyoake, who stayed on as the Queen's representative in New Zealand until 25 October 1980. Upon his retirement – almost a year after Thomas was freed – Beattie replaced him.

Saga of the starving baby

In a television interview on Friday 7 September 2001, while attempting to support an ill-conceived and erroneous finding that Rochelle Crewe had not been fed during the five days following her parents' murder, Hutton declared:

The other thing that struck myself and the investigators was, in an attempt to survive those five days, baby Rochelle had bitten most of the varnish off the top rails of that large cot. And in addition to that, and remarkably so, she had somehow got her wet napkins off, stained with urine of course, and had sucked on those to the extent that she had quite serious discolouration and sores starting to form around her lips and under her nose. Today, as I think back, the more compelling than ever is why would that evidence be present, and why would Rochelle's appearance be like that if she had been regularly fed, as alleged by other parties. No, I am convinced beyond any doubt in my mind that baby Rochelle was never fed and hence the mystery woman [who fed and cared for her] does not exist.

The facts are that the 'evidence' Hutton refers to never existed. Police records show that Hutton, along with two other detectives and a police photographer, arrived at the Crewe farm at 5.10pm that day, Monday 22 June 1970, about half an hour before it got dark. By then, Rochelle had been at the home of Barbara Willis for more than three hours. On her delivery to that family by her grandfather, the nappies Hutton was to later claim she had 'removed and sucked urine from to keep herself alive' had been taken off her by Mrs Willis. There is no record that Hutton even saw Rochelle that day. With two people missing from a house containing copious bloodstains, the last thing likely to have been on his mind was the little girl he knew had been taken to a caring family nearby. He certainly did not see her in the nappies, plastic overpants and top she was found in by her grandfather, Len Demler, and neighbour Owen Priest just after 1.30pm.

Barbara Willis' testimony at the lower court hearing:

On that day when I saw her, she had a pink wincyette pyjama top, singlet, two nappies and a pair of plastic pants. I took her straight inside and undressed her. I then put her in the bath. The nappies on the child – she had two, one a triangle nappy and a rectangular nappy down the middle, we call it a night nap – and there was one safety pin. The nappies were very wet, had a large amount of motion. I did not keep the nappies, *I burnt them*. I couldn't have cleaned them. I rang a doctor about the rash on her bottom, but apart from that I did not consider it necessary for medical attention. She seemed more emotionally in need of help than physically in need of help. Apart from the cream which was applied, there was no further treatment.

Nor did Rochelle give any impression of being starved:

Before I gave her anything to eat she showed no signs of wanting anything to eat but she was pleased when she got it.

Consider now the evidence of Priest, who was called to the Crewe house by Demler on the afternoon of Monday 22 June 1970:

When I first saw the child she was lying on her right side, could have been on one elbow, I'm not sure, and she was in the cot. The child looked alright when I saw her. She was wearing [a] pyjama top, nappies and a plastic cover over the nappies.

Under cross-examination at that same hearing:

Temm: You have described her [Rochelle's] condition as disorderly, but would it be accurate to say you had no cause for alarm in her state of health?
Priest: I would not.
Temm: Just to clarify that a little Mr Priest, you didn't immediately feel that you had to get a doctor to the child?
Priest: No.
Temm: She did not look like a child who had been without food for five days?
Priest: I did not know how long it was. She did not look hungry.
Temm: And more particularly thirsty?
Priest: Not more particularly, just thirsty.

Rochelle Crewe's cot, in which she lived for five days, apart from three hours outside on the Saturday after her parents were shot in an adjacent room. Inquiry head Bruce Hutton later claimed the starving infant had eaten the varnish off the top.

At that depositions hearing, and the two subsequent trials of Thomas that followed, Priest confirmed that photograph 27 – presented in evidence on those occasions – 'shows the condition of the cot as I entered'. What photograph 27 clearly shows is that Rochelle had not 'bitten most of the varnish off the top rails of that large cot'. In fact the cot in which the Crewe's infant lived that part of her life is not varnished at all. It is painted and is white. More tellingly, the coating on the cot is not bitten or damaged in any way, as the photographs taken on 24 June, two days later, attest.

The issue of whether Rochelle Crewe was fed and cared for is, in the mind of many to this day, central to who killed her parents. As has previously been revealed, senior officers on that inquiry told members of the Crewe family and their close friends who they considered the killer was, and who had assisted him to care for Rochelle, in the first week of that investigation.

Thus Hutton's insistence, on national television on 7 September 2007, that he had never believed Rochelle had been fed, should be measured against what he was telling his superiors and other members of his squad on that matter earlier. From the record of the conference of 15 July 1970:

Hutton: The child [Rochelle] has been examined by three specialists. The one that appeals to us most is Dr Fox who had the advantage of examining the child on the Tuesday, the day after she was found by Mr Demler. He [Fox] has given us a full and detailed report and he is not prepared to go back any further than the Saturday previous to the Monday on which the child was found as being the time the child last received nourishment. In fact, he does not feel that it was even that long the child was last fed. The other two specialists who saw the child some days later feel, not concerning this case, that a child of that age in a robust condition could survive from Wednesday to the following Monday without having received nourishment. But I would point out that they did not have the advantage of seeing the child until some time after she was discovered.

[Assistant Commissioner] *Walton:* Why do you prefer Dr Fox?

Hutton: Because he saw the child earlier. At the time Dr Fox examined this child he said that he would have expected, had the child not been fed from the Wednesday to the Monday, considerable dehydration, which he did not find at all. The child certainly vomited the first nourishment she received from Mrs Willis soon after Demler took the child from the cot to her place, but from then on the child had little trouble retaining fluids and soon started to increase weight again. As you will probably be aware, she only lost two and a half pounds [1134 grams] from a weighing-in which was eleven days before this incident.

[Pathologist] *Cairns:* The problem here is the lack of food. Everybody agrees that this is no big problem at all. A child of that age could go that long without food. I think the problem that is worrying Dr Fox was whether or not she could go that long without fluids and I think that the other people who have examined the child have said that a child could go four and a half days without fluids and survive, which is slightly different I think from the problem of whether the child could go four and a half days without fluids and be in the condition in which Dr Fox saw her. I think this is the important difference between seeing her later and seeing the child at the time.

Hutton: As far as I am concerned regarding the feeding of the baby, *I accept Dr Fox's report.* He examined the child within a reasonable time of this happening. To some extent he is supported by the local doctor who saw this child regularly. Knowing the child as he knew her, he is right behind Dr Fox all the way.

Total dereliction of duty

The formal report of the Thomas Royal Commission is littered with determinations about the activities and actions of Detective Inspector Bruce Hutton, who has declared, on any number of subsequent occasions, that he has always been satisfied that the Crewe homicide investigation 'was conducted in a thorough and proper manner'.

Transcripts of Hutton's sworn evidence at that 1980 inquisition make for illuminating reading, but it is appropriate to leave the Royal Commission to have the last word on this issue, with extracts from its formal report to Parliament:

On 26 October 1970 there occurred a discussion or conference, of which there are no notes in existence, at the Otahuhu police station. We find this discussion between Messrs Hutton and [Detective Sergeant Murray] Jeffries very curious. Mr Hutton must have been aware of which gardens had and had not been sieve searched, because he gave Mr Jeffries his instructions and received his report. If the police evidence that the garden was not sieve searched in August is correct, Mr Hutton would have been aware of that fact on the evening of 13 October. We find it incomprehensible that Mr Hutton waited nearly 2 weeks to order that search. We point out that the timing and circumstances of the conversation [of 26 October] between Mr Hutton and Mr Jeffries are so curious as to lead to a suspicion that it may have been staged for the benefit of those listening to it, namely

Messrs Charles and Parkes.

□□□□

Mr Hutton, however, fails to mention that he was contacted by radio-telephone and arranged to meet Mr Charles and Mr Parkes at the Priest house; his version is that he was having lunch when Charles and Parkes arrived and asked to see him. Mr and Mrs Priest, however, gave evidence, which we accept, that Mr Hutton arrived with Mr Charles and Mr Parkes and that he did not have lunch at their house. In our view, these inconsistencies are significant.

□□□□

Exhibit 343 [a .22 bullet with a number 8 on its base] was found by Detective Keith during a search of a garage on Mr Thomas' farm on 21 October. It was found in an apple box with rusty nails and bolts in a garage used by Mr Peter Thomas. It was dissected at the Otahuhu police station the same evening and it was discovered that the bullet had a number 8 embossed on its base. It was therefore of significance as being of the same type as the fatal bullets. Those present when exhibit 343 [was] examined were Mr Keith, Detective Sergeant Tootill, and Mr Hutton. All agreed some cartridges were fired that evening to remove the primer from them. Mr Keith says that exhibit 343 was fired in this way. Mr Hutton says it was not. We have no hesitation in accepting Mr Keith's evidence.

□□□□

The material which has been put before us demonstrates most graphically the atmosphere that pervaded the second trial and which has haunted this case ever since. It is quite apparent to us that considerations of honesty, fairness to the defence and proper practice were of no weight whatsoever to Mr Hutton in his desire to see Thomas convicted for a second time.

□□□□

We are quite certain that the police would have had no difficulty in obtaining access to exhibit 343 and also exhibit 318 [a box of Thomas cartridges] for the purpose of effecting a substitution. In our view, Mr Hutton must have known of the substitution, although it may have been carried out by some other person.

□□□□

We accept the evidence of Mr and Mrs Priest that Mr Priest asserted the two policemen had just fired two shots at the Crewe farm. Giving evidence before us Mr Hutton denied firing the shots but we do not believe him. We find that Mr Hutton and Mr Johnston fired two shots at the Crewe home that day.

□□□□

We conclude that on the occasion referred to by Mr and Mrs Priest, Mr Hutton and Mr Johnston planted the shellcase, exhibit 350, in the Crewe garden and that they did so to manufacture evidence that the Thomas rifle had been used for the killings. We consider that this explains why Mr Hutton described shellcase exhibit 350 as containing blue-black corrosion when it fact it did not. It also explains his odd behaviour at the Supreme Court upon discovering Dr Sprott examining one of the shellcases. Furthermore, it provides an understandable motive for the switching of exhibit 343 after it had been examined by Dr Sprott.

□□□□

On 6 September 1973 Mr Hutton had a telephone conversation with Assistant Commissioner Walton, and on that day dispatched to him a telex. This is a lengthy document and some of its paragraphs were put to Detective Keith in the witness box. Where he is in conflict with statements made by Hutton in the telex, we accepted his [Keith's] evidence. Patently many of the statements in the telex are false and could only have been designed to misrepresent the position to the Assistant Commissioner.

□□□□

He [Hutton] said he and Mr Keith sorted out the exhibits. Mr Keith said he carried out this task and prepared a list of 137 exhibits to be taken to the tip. Mr Hutton [also said] that in the company of Detective Sergeant Keith he took those 137 exhibits to the Whitford tip. This is quite untrue. Mr Keith says, and we accept him, that he took the exhibits to the tip in a police car in the boot and in the back seat. He [Keith] was unaccompanied.

□□□□

Mr Hutton's statement that he was present with Keith when they were taken to the dump and distributed was false. His description of the manner of their destruction was false to his knowledge. Hutton had both these exhibits [343 and 350] destroyed because he knew exhibit 350 had been planted and that exhibit 343 was a suspect exhibit for which an unfired shellcase had been substituted. We find the disposal of these exhibits and the reasons for it has added significance. It strongly supports the case against Hutton of planting exhibit 350 to procure the conviction of Thomas. The destruction of exhibits 343 and 350, and the telex report from Hutton, constitute impropriety on the part of the police. The telex sent by Hutton to Assistant Commissioner Walton was in part false and [was] intended to misrepresent the position so that a further search for exhibits 343 and 350 would not be undertaken by the police.

In its formal findings, the Thomas Royal Commission targeted Hutton specifically, making its clear it did not believe much of the testimony that he had given before it, or the credibility of the evidence he had, as officer-in-charge of the Crewe homicide investigation, put before two Supreme Court trials and two referrals to the Court Appeal. The key findings, in relation to Hutton, included:-

a) The shellcase exhibit 350 was planted in the Crewe garden by Detective Inspector Hutton and Detective Johnston

b) The shellcase exhibit 343 was switched on two occasions, the first probably accidentally but the second deliberately

c) The destruction of some of the exhibits at the Whitford tip was an improper action designed to prevent any further investigation of exhibit 350. Detective Inspector Hutton improperly misled his superiors concerning the chances of recovering the exhibits from the tip

e) Detective Inspector Hutton's behaviour in the courtroom at the time of Dr Sprott's examination of one of the shellcase exhibits was unacceptable.

Perjury was clearly committed at the two Thomas trials, at one of the two referrals to the Court of Appeal and at the Royal Commission. To this date, no-one has ever faced a court of law for those acts – and given that the Crewe inquiry squad has now almost reached the point of extinction, the chances that they will do so are diminishing.

The ultimate judgment has yet to be made on their commander-in-chief, one Bruce Thomas Newton Hutton, in respect of whose testimony the Royal Commission said:

The cornerstone of the Crown case, exhibit 350, was not put in the Crewe garden by the hand of the murderer. It was put there by the hand of one whose duty was to investigate fairly and honestly, but who in dereliction of that duty, in breach of his obligation to uphold the law, and departing from all standards of fairness, fabricated this evidence to procure a conviction of murder. He swore falsely, and beyond a peradventure, was responsible for Thomas being twice convicted, his appeals thrice dismissed, and for his spending 9 years of his life in prison; to be released as a result of sustained public refusal to accept these decisions.

In a recent interview, Hutton declared that he and Thomas would in future be going to very different places. Whether Hutton should ultimately be called upon to answer for his actions in the same court where he once appeared as a chief witness for the Crown in its erroneous, fatally-flawed and fabricated prosecution of Arthur Thomas, or before some higher tribunal, has yet to be determined.

Twelve

Three sworn Police officers colluded to convict an innocent man – the one who collected his rifle, the one who was tasked with keeping it under lock and key and the one who had it in his possession contrary to recognised procedures. A small band of others, numbering half a dozen, were called upon to cover up a fabrication of evidence, or more correctly a number of fabrications, perpetrated against that innocent man. Their transgressions were ones of giving, on oath, contradictory or untrue evidence or simply acquiring lapses of memory at convenient times.

On the findings of a Royal Commission of Inquiry, Detective Inspector Bruce Hutton was involved in the fabrication of evidence in order to secure a conviction against Arthur Thomas. As the head of the Crewe inquiry, it was his job to be fully aware of what his detectives were doing. It can be legitimately argued that this included certain knowledge of their unlawful acts. Detective Len Johnston was the lynchpin in the Crewe inquiry, the game-breaker who in the space of less than four weeks created an entire case against Thomas when there had previously been only the most tenuous of links. Detective Stan Keith, clerk of the inquiry, completed this unholy triumvirate.

The actions of Hutton have been detailed in the previous chapter, and the role of Keith will be considered in the next. It is now appropriate to examine the acts and evidence of Len Johnston, who, while not the architect of a conspiracy to arrest, prosecute and convict an innocent man, was the executioner.

Johnston, along with Hutton, was adjudged to have planted a cartridge case from the .22 rifle of Arthur Allan Thomas – 75 millimetres under the soil – by the side gate of the Crewe garden for the purposes of linking him with the unsolved double murder. A Royal Commission of Inquiry made this determination a decade after the event.

There is now demonstrable evidence that Johnston also planted two stub axles on the Thomas farm dump which were then matched to a crucial axle found beneath Harvey Crewe's body.

Johnston had not been involved in the Crewe inquiry until 19

September 1970 – three days after Harvey Crewe's decomposing body was recovered from the Waikato River – when he was appointed, by Hutton, as officer in charge of the axle inquiries.

One of the fixtures of the Otahuhu police station, Johnston was a plodder, prepared to put in long hours to ferret out 'evidence'. He could always be relied on to get the job done, no matter what, but like so many of his ilk at that time, he was destined to always to hold the rank of detective and he did so when he died in 1978.

The arrival of this old-style cop on the scene not only changed the dynamics of an investigation that was going nowhere, it dramatically influenced its eventual outcome – in a way few could have imagined. Within barely a month of Johnston's arrival, an entire case had been stitched together against Thomas. Johnston played the leading role in this turnaround and there is a school of thought that he was brought in for exactly that purpose.

To this day, a question mark hangs over the recovery of the body of Harvey Crewe, the 29-year-old farmer who had been missing for a day short of three months, and of the axle discovered with him. Whether that old car axle was ever actually connected to the body of Harvey Crewe is a matter of speculation – it certainly was not attached to that body when police diver Paul Spence found it resting on the riverbed. Be that as it may, Johnston was assigned the responsibility of trying to trace the origin of the axle which Hutton later claimed he had dreamed of in the days before Harvey Crewe's remains were found jammed up against a submerged tree trunk.

Hutton insisted later that Thomas had not become a suspect until 19 October. But it is now clear that the attack had swung firmly toward the unsuspecting young farmer from the other end of the Pukekawa district from much earlier in October. Within one month the case had been wrapped up. The arrest of Arthur Thomas was then only a formality.

The only connection established between Thomas and Jeanette Crewe as at the end of September was the infatuation he had for her as a young man, a brush-and-comb set he had given her on her return from Britain and America at Christmas 1962, and a letter she had written to him while she was overseas. Clearly, those charged with solving the murder of not only Jeanette, but her husband Harvey, had to find new evidence linking one with the other.

During the next two weeks, with Johnston directing the play, detectives scoured the countryside seeking information on the axle.

They showed two different axles – perhaps three – around in the hope that someone would be able to give them another break. Parkes, Jeffries, Tootill and Hutton himself were all engaged in these inquiries at various times, demonstrating the huge reliance the police were then putting on that exhibit, the only solid lead they had at that time.

Remnants of Nash and Overland cars – which used identical front axles – were numerous at that time, many fitted to the frames of home-made trailers, and how one axle could then be linked to a particular recipient structure was never explained. But on 13 October, the police learned that the Thomases had once owned a trailer with a Nash axle. This came via a phone call from Heather Cowley, the stepdaughter of a Te Puke man, Charles Shirtcliffe, who had once built a trailer with a 1928-29 Nash axle. That trailer was sold to Gordon Whyte and then, in 1959, to Allan Thomas [senior] of Pukekawa. However not only did Shirtcliffe tell Johnston that the axle he was carting around the district was not the one from his original trailer – it carried welding on it which he had not done – but the police had knowledge of a number of other home-made trailers with the same Nash axles. The riverbed axle could have come from any one of them, or from any other dismantled Nash or Overland car anywhere in the country. Nash alone made 140,000 series 320 and 420 cars with that exact same axle and thousands of them ended up in New Zealand.

On 13 October, Johnston uplifted a box of live .22 ammunition from the Thomas farm. This ammunition – no record was kept by him of how many rounds that box contained – was to become a key link in the deed perpetrated nine days later. That evening, just before 10pm, a contingent of police and DSIR scientists descended upon the Crewe house with the intent of exploring a new theory put forward by Johnston two days earlier. This theory – subsequently discredited, even by high-ranking police officers such as Auckland CIB chief Brian Wilkinson who rejected it completely – was that Harvey Crewe had been shot through the upper section of the Crewe kitchen louvres, which were open when photographed on 24 June. Scientists Donald Nelson and Johnston himself clambered up into position to prove that, with one foot on the brick wall by the back door and the other on the window sill, Harvey Crewe could have been shot from that position. All that was now needed was for a cartridge case from the Thomas rifle to be found in the nearby garden. Two weeks later, to the day, it was.

[At the risk of breaking this sequence of events, it should be recorded that at the first Thomas trial, defence counsel Paul Temm and Brian Webb demonstrated – after a reconstruction of their own at the Crewe house – that a louvres shooting was near impossible. Their reason for saying so was demonstrated by way of a bloodstain on the carpet in the Crewe lounge. When the blood which had seeped down Harvey Crewe's arm chair was positioned above this unlabelled stain, the police version was shown to have been impractical. Nonetheless, the Crown put before two juries photos of Bruce Hutton sitting in a chair – which was not the original Harvey Crewe arm chair – for the purposes of its shooting through the louvres theory. It did so to explain how the Thomas cartridge case had got into the Crewe's garden – a much more serious work of fantasy].

The reconstruction photo put by police to a jury 'proving' that Thomas shot Harvey Crewe through the louvre windows. This was not the actual chair Harvey Crewe was sitting in when he was murdered and nor was it positioned correctly to depict the scene as it was that night.

On 14 October, Johnston and Parkes headed north, to Matakana to interview Thomas senior and his sons, Richard, Lloyd and Des, about their family trailer. This trailer had in fact been on their leased farm north of Auckland since 1966, when the family handed the running of their Pukekawa property to Arthur and Vivien. While there, Johnston uplifted a number of documents, including books of cheque stubs. The whereabouts of some of those documents, deemed crucial to the defence of Thomas later, remains a mystery. The Thomases however believe they were withheld by Johnston so as to deny them the ability to prove that the replacement of the old running gear on their trailer – undertaken by engineer and part-time trailer maker Rod Rasmussen in July 1965 – had remained with him as a trade-in and had never come back to their Pukekawa farm.

On 15 October at 10.45am Rasmussen was again visited by Johnston.

Three days earlier, on 12 October, the Meremere engineer had stated categorically that he knew nothing about the axle the detective had brought to him, but on the second visit Rasmussen 'recalled' the axle replacement job he had done five years earlier and said he believed parts of the original running gear had been returned to the Thomases. [Those living on the Thomas farm at that time have always denied this assertion]. That afternoon Johnston went back to see Arthur Thomas at Mercer Ferry Road and the detective was taken to one of the three farm dumps on that property where, according to police job sheet, a cursory search was made for the trailer and parts left over from the 1965 repair job. Thomas left Johnston fossicking around on the farm dump while he went to do the evening milking and in a job sheet filed a few days later, Johnston recorded that there was nothing of relevance located by him at that time.

This search by Johnston on that day requires examination as the detective told Thomas on arrival that he was looking for the *family trailer*. This is an extraordinary statement – one which must be viewed with the utmost suspicion – because not only was Johnston advised that this trailer had been on the Matakana property since 1966, he had actually seen it in that locality the previous day. Johnston also advised Thomas that day that he was looking for parts returned after the axle replacement job undertaken by Rasmussen in 1965. The Royal Commission, in 1980, ruled that an explanation of this issue was required given what occurred five days later, on 20 October. None could be given because by then Johnston was dead.

The only viable explanation is that Johnston took the two stub axles to the farm then occupied by Arthur Thomas and he did so following his visit to Rasmussen that day.

Rasmussen later testified that he first remembered doing a job for the Thomases when Johnston 'came up with the stub axles'. On any analysis of the totality of the evidence now available, the original running gear from the Thomas trailer – the original axle, stub axles, wheels and tyres – did not go back to their farm in 1965 and thus these parts had no further connection, other than a concocted one, with that family after that date.

In any event, the riverbed axle was not the original Thomas trailer axle. This can be determined with certainty because the welding which was a major feature of the axle recovered beneath Harvey Crewe's body – this had been done with stainless steel rod and amounted to no more than tack welds – had not been undertaken, at any time, on the axle of the trailer bought by Thomas (senior). This was attested to by the man who built that trailer in 1956, Shirtcliffe, by its second owner Whyte, and by Thomas senior, who acquired it in 1959 and took it to Matakana in 1966. That Johnston was able to show the axle and stub axles to Rasmussen and discuss the Thomases with him on 15 October – and that he was the only police officer at the Thomas farm tip on that afternoon, by himself – clearly demonstrates that the stub axles which were proven to match the axle found in the river were yet another strand in the fabricated case against the young Pukekawa farmer.

This stainless welding, which is replicated on the other end of the axle recovered from the river bed below Harvey Crewe's body, was not on the Thomas farm trailer at any time while in the possession of its three owners. This axle is unrelated to the Thomases.

On 20 October, Johnston and Detective Bruce Parkes were instructed by Hutton to return to the Thomas farm – the former to collect samples of galvanised wire and the latter to uplift the .22 Browning rifle which had been returned on 8 September, having been ruled out of having any connection with the Crewe murders. Hutton was to say later that Johnston repossessed the rifle on his own volition that day, after finding the stub axles. The evidence of Johnston and Parkes – confirmed by both Arthur and Vivien Thomas – was that they had told the Thomases when they first arrived that they were there to collect the rifle again. This occurred *before* the stub axles were 'located' *not after*.

That day did prove to be a groundbreaker in another way, with Johnston inexplicably breaking off from his task of collecting wire samples to leap off an earth bank into a scrub-covered gully and 'right onto' the two stub axles, which had not been located when he searched that same area with Thomas on 15 October, according to his own subsequent testimony.

That miraculous find, described by Parkes to the Royal Commission ten years later, was a huge breakthrough in the hunt for the killer of the Crewes. Johnston knew what the stub axles were, Parkes said from the witness box, and when they were taken back to the Otahuhu police station late that afternoon, the welds on each fitted exactly with the axle the police had recovered from the riverbed a month earlier.

The Royal Commission made its own observations on this far-reaching development in its formal report:

> Mr Parkes very fairly agreed that it was an extraordinary piece of luck that the two stub axles, which were to become such significant exhibits, just fell into Detective Johnston's hands. We can only agree, particularly having regard to the fact that he had searched that tip only 5 days before. We find the circumstances in which the stub axles were located peculiar in the extreme.

The final word on the matter of the stub axles should be left with Hutton himself. In a May 1972 report to CIB national head Bob Walton – delivered at the time the Assistant Commissioner from headquarters in Wellington went to Auckland to investigate televised allegations that the cartridge case from the Thomas rifle had been planted in the Crewe's garden – Hutton wrote:

> I instructed Detectives Johnston and Parkes to travel to the farm of Arthur Allan Thomas at Mercer Ferry Road, Pukekawa, on the 20th of October 1970. Their instructions were that they were to make a search of any rubbish tips on the farm or in that area, in an effort to locate stub axles which would fit the welding that had been broken on the main axle previously found tied with wire to the body of David Harvey Crewe. At approximately 4.30pm that day, I was at the Otahuhu police station when the two detectives returned from Pukekawa with exhibits from the farm of Arthur Allan Thomas. In their presence I examined the two stub axles which had been found on the Thomas farm tip and as Detective Johnston pointed out, the welding on the stub axles *fitted like a jigsaw puzzle* to the welding on the main axle from the body of David Harvey Crewe. This was a startling discovery of course, and the two detectives, after fitting the stub axles to the main axle while at the Thomas farm that day, were convinced of the importance of such a find.

Not only did this report directly contradict the instructions that Parkes and Johnston both attested to in their court testimony at the subsequent proceedings against Thomas – they swore on oath that they had respectively been sent to retrieve his rifle and samples of wire from his farm – but Hutton's report could be considered, on face value, to be tantamount to being a direction to find crucial items of evidence *before* they were known to exist.

Before leaving the issue of the stub axle recovery however, the contrast between the evidence of Hutton and that of Parkes on the matching of those vital exhibits with the 'river bed' axle can be examined.

Hutton's 18 May 1972 report to Assistant Commissioner Bob Walton records:

> This was a startling discovery of course, and the two detectives, after fitting the stub axles to the main axle *while at the Thomas farm that day*, were convinced of the importance of the find.

It must be remembered that Parkes was the detective with Johnston on the day the stub axles were recovered from the Thomas farm – 20 October 1970. His sworn testimony at the Thomas Royal Commission in 1980 revealed:

> [Commission counsel Michael] *Crew:* Can you remember that day on the Thomas farm, actually trying to match up the stubs and the axle?
>
> *Parkes: Certainly not on the Thomas farm.*
>
> *Crew:* Where, if at all?
>
> *Parkes:* I can recall when we were back at the Otahuhu police station matching them up.
>
> *Crew:* That was later in the day was it?
>
> *Parkes:* Yes when we returned [to Otahuhu] that day.
>
> *Crew:* Are you saying that you might have had the axle in the boot or not?
>
> *Parkes:* Yes I have a suspicion that we did, but I can't be positive about that now.

Not surprisingly Johnston was involved in every one of the major developments in the Crewe inquiry during the four weeks it took to assemble the components for an irrefutable case. Likewise he was there at the end, travelling with Hutton to Pukekawa on 11 November 1970 to make the arrest.

Between 20 October and 11 November there had been a flurry of activity in the Crewe inquiry. The day after the miraculous stub axle finding, detectives – armed with a search warrant – poured onto the Thomas farm, and through the house, seizing another box of .22 bullets and anything that remotely resembled parts of a trailer. By the end of that day they had assembled a collection of farm junk that, when put together, amounted to an entire trailer, despite Johnston being aware that the trailer bought by Thomas senior in 1959 was in his possession at Matakana and had been in that locality since the middle of 1966. Photographs of this fabricated trailer were later used to effect 'the kill' by Crown Prosecutor David Morris in the two subsequent Supreme Court trials of Arthur Thomas, but in reality, there was no connection between this hotchpotch of old car parts and timber, and the crimes for which an innocent man was being tried.

A complete fabrication. Johnston created this trailer frame from a load of junk timber and 'tied' it to the axle and stub axles. Police then put this photograph of a trailer frame before the two Thomas trial juries to demonstrate something which, in reality, never existed.

The Royal Commission heard a great deal about the various axles during 1980. Three different axles were referred to by Peter Williams QC in his summing up to that inquiry. The Royal Commission concluded that 'the evidence as to the two stub axle and the axle beam is a morass of inconsistencies, unexplained discrepancies, and alternative possibilities' and hence it made no formal finding in relation to those three items apart from noting:

> We do find, however, that the one matter which has been clearly established is that it would be quite unsafe to draw any inference

connecting Mr A A Thomas with the axle found on [below] Harvey Crewe's body, merely because of the presence of the two stub axles on his tip.

However what is significant is that the Royal Commission heard evidence on, and compiled for its formal report, a list of *45 items* which *should* have been found at the Thomas farm by police searching there on 21 October 1970 had the old pieces of the trailer owned by Thomas senior been returned to his Pukekawa property in July 1965 as Rasmussen claimed. Not one of these was found in those farm dumps. It also determined that three of the five parts which the police located on the tip on 21 October and which they used in a reconstruction to prove their theory had no connection with the Thomas trailer either, or were irrelevant. The remaining two were old split rims, probably from the original trailer, which had been discarded due to damage, which is clearly shown in the police photographs of the 'skeleton' trailer they concocted.

The matter of protecting the one who the police had originally targeted as the killer of the Crewes – Len Demler – also fell to Johnston. He knew, months before the second Thomas trial began, of the whereabouts of the long-missing Chennells Estate *combination* firearm, which many believe was used to kill the Crewes. That is proved by his handwriting, in his own work diary from 1972-73, the original of which is now in the possession of the Thomases.

At that retrial in March and April 1973, Johnston gave evidence that he had received from Demler on 21 March 1973, a double-barrelled 360-360 calibre hammer gun. The documentary record shows that this was taken to the DSIR for testing on 2 April. Johnston had this firearm in his possession for 13 days and no explanation was ever sought nor given, at that trial, as to what he had done with it during that period.

On the basis of significant inconsistencies, and the information provided by an eminent British gunmaker, the firearm presented as an exhibit by Johnston at the second Thomas trial was *not* the Chennells Estate *combination* firearm.

The estate firearm was a combination firearm with a 410 shotgun barrel on one side and a .22 rifle barrel on the other. It was such a firearm in the 1930s, it was seen and described as such in the 1950s and 1960s – by three witnesses who, in September 1970 provided written statements about that to the police – and it was undoubtedly that on

17 June 1970, when Jeanette and Harvey Crewe were shot dead by an offender using what is likely to have been a single-shot .22. This conclusion is confirmed by the facial injuries to Jeanette caused by a blow from a rifle butt, as pathologist Dr Frank Cairns determined at her post mortem examination.

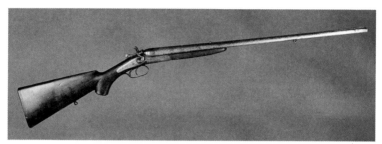

The 360-360 calibre double rifle put as an exhibit to the second Thomas trial jury by Johnston, who knew that it was not the combination firearm described by witnesses. The whereabouts of the Chennells' Estate 410/.22 shotgun-rifle was known to him before the retrial.

The Chennells Estate combination firearm was categorically not the 360-360 calibre weapon produced by Johnston at the Thomas retrial and that detective knew that the exhibit he was producing for examination by the jury was *not* a combination firearm in any shape or manner. The two are quite distinctly different firearms and the one produced as an exhibit by Johnston at the Thomas retrial at the Supreme Court in Auckland in 1973 clearly has no connection with, or relevance to, the killings of either Jeanette or Harvey Crewe. Along with the cartridge case and the two stub axles, it was merely another form of fabricated evidence.

On 14 March 1973 – twelve days before the Thomas retrial was to begin – Johnston yet again demonstrated his propensity for tampering with evidence, or more correctly endeavouring to do so. On this day he accompanied Bruce Roddick to the Chitty paddock where the farm labourer had been feeding out hay from the carry-all of a tractor when he saw a woman at the Crewes, two days after they had been murdered.

Prime Minister Rob Muldoon's special investigator, Robert Adams-Smith QC reported that this incident had generated tension between the two. Roddick subsequently revealed that the detective had kept trying to push him further up the hill, thus increasing the distance between where he actually was and where the woman at the Crewes' was standing.

After unsavoury questioning by detectives two years earlier, Roddick was by then wary of the police and he took both his mother and a neighbour with him on that day. He also stood his ground, insisting that Johnston place a stake in the ground where the tractor was actually positioned, not in the incorrect location Johnston was seeking to identify.

Roddick subsequently measured that distance at 118 of his strides – about 120 yards [109.72 metres]. But Johnston delivered, to the Thomas retrial jury, a measurement expressed in entirely different terms, being 357 feet. While this is within a meter or so of being accurate, the impression he left with that jury was that Roddick was a lot further away than 120 yards would have indicated. It could be construed that this sleight-of-hand was far from unintentional, especially as Roddick had gone from being a 'reliable' prosecution witness at the first trial, to an 'unreliable' defence witness at the subsequent retrial, simply because he was now saying, categorically, that the woman he had seen at the Crewe farm was *not* Vivien Thomas.

The view Bruce Roddick had of the Crewe house enclosure from the rear carry-all of a tractor on the Chitty farm on Friday 19 June 1970, when he saw an unknown woman standing in front of their Hillman car. He offered a good description of this woman.

Johnston died two years before the Royal Commission began hearing evidence about the part he, Hutton and other police officers had played in securing a wholly unwarranted and unjust conviction. When the Royal Commission issued its damning condemnation at the end of 1980, police officers from around New Zealand and Johnston's civilian friends rallied to the defence of the deceased Otahuhu detective. A petition was launched in a bid to restore the reputation of a 'true gentleman who would have found it impossible to have done these things'. His widow then joined action by Hutton and the two police organisations to appeal the Royal Commission's findings, an action that was lost.

However one need go no further than Johnston's work diary – written in his own hand – to confirm that he was prepared to break the law in his quest to please his superiors. That diary records, on 23

March 1973 – just three days before the second Thomas trial was to begin – that Johnston met with Demler, gave him notes on what he was to say at those proceedings and told him to bring those notes to the Supreme Court. While Demler gave no evidence at the first trial in 1971 about Thomas forcing Jeanette Crewe to flee Pukekawa and escape to Wanganui, he was very forthcoming about that issue when he took the stand in 1973 – just after Johnston delivered the notes referred to.

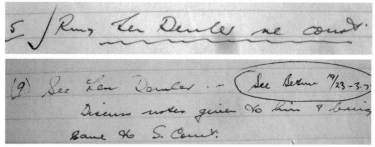

Two extracts from the notebook of Detective Len Johnston relating to the period immediately before the historic retrial of Arthur Thomas. This record reveals that Johnston was providing notes to a key witness, Len Demler, in the lead-up to the trial.

Johnston also delivered notes to the engineer Rod Rasmussen in the days preceding that second trial, according to a sworn statement from Pokeno resident Noel Ottaway, with whom the engineer had previously worked at Maramarua. From that statement:

> I was having a drink with Rasmassen in the private bar at the Mercer hotel when Johnston arrived. Johnston presented Rasmussen with a long envelope and told him 'this is what you say'.

Johnston also provided misleading information to the crucial 19 October 1970 conference, and therefore to the two out-of-town detectives who had been sent north to conduct an independent overview of the Crewe inquiry. This is confirmed by the transcript of that gathering:

> A G Thomas was subsequently seen and the ownership papers in relation to the trailer were obtained from him. When asked as to the present whereabouts of the trailer he was unable to tell us. However he thought the trailer had been left on the [Pukekawa] farm prior to him leaving in 1964 [it was 1966]. Another son, Richard Thomas, told the police that he thought the trailer had been left at Meremere when a new trailer had been made up from the parts of the original trailer.

Not only are these claims in direct conflict with the sworn testimony Johnston gave at the depositions and first Supreme Court trial of Thomas in the months that followed, they are wrong in fact. Thomas senior did not say he was unable to determine where the trailer was – it was parked outside the front door of his house when Johnston and Parkes went to Matakana on 14 October 1970, five days before the over-view conference, and shown to Johnston that very day. Neither did Thomas senior say that he thought the trailer had been left on his Pukekawa farm in 1964. A G Thomas, his wife Ivy and their two youngest sons moved north in 1966, with Arthur taking up a lease on the family property at Pukekawa in June of that year. When the senior Thomases and some of their offspring went north to Matakana, the trailer bought by them from Whyte in 1959 went with them and it was still there, being used daily, when the two Crewe inquiry detectives visited in October 1970.

Likewise, Richard Thomas did not say he thought the trailer had been left at Meremere when a new trailer had been made up from the old one. The only portion of the original trailer replaced by Rasmussen was the running gear and it was Richard Thomas who collected it from Meremere in June 1965 and took it back to Pukekawa. Richard Thomas continued to use the trailer for weekly trips to Auckland to collect bread for the pigs for a further year. Then the trailer was taken north to Matakana.

Almost 80 books of cheque stubs formed the financial records kept by A G Thomas between January 1958 and December 1972. The one book of stubs critical to proving a vital element of the defence of Thomas disappeared after Johnston's 14 October visit.

The Thomases have long believed Johnston removed a crucial book of cheque butts and an invoice, on his 14 October 1970 visit to Matakana with Parkes.

Johnston created the opportunity to take these documents by asking

Thomas senior where Richard Thomas' .22 rifle was kept, in effect creating a diversion. Allan Thomas left the room and went to another part of the farm cottage, where he believed the rifle owned by that son would be. While absent, he heard Johnston whispering to Parkes and a rustling of papers and upon rejoining them, he was told the older detective now had what he wanted. Johnston then left the farm cottage, the property and Matakana, in the company of Parkes, without advising Thomas senior of what he had seized, nor issuing any written record of the documents now in his possession. The police have always denied this theft but the Royal Commission observed:

> [On the second visit] Parkes took the precaution of submitting a complete job sheet listing all the books of cheque butts which he took. We have heard Mr Parkes give evidence before us on a number of occasions. We have been impressed by his honesty and his readiness to help the Commission. We unhesitatingly accept that Mr Parkes had no knowledge of the missing book of cheque butts.

It will be left to the reader to determine, based on such a lengthy catalogue of planting evidence and misleading superior officers in a bid to drive the investigation away from one suspect and toward another, if the description given to the late Len Johnston by his peers – that of being a 'true gentleman' – is either accurate, or appropriate.

Thirteen

While he aspired to be one of the boys, Stan Keith was, by virtue of his position, in reality just 'the boy'. As clerk of the Crewe inquiry, Keith had the least glamorous role of the 20 or so detectives involved with what remains one of New Zealand's biggest ever homicide investigations. From the moment he took possession of the first document on Tuesday 23 June 1970, the homicide file he created became, in his mind at least, his personal possession. He continued to act in that way until, in 2010, he gave up the fight in the face of continued requests for documents pursuant to the provisions of the Official Information Act.

On the face of it, Keith could be considered a bit player. His role was, however, later elevated by his being entrusted with the security of the Thomas rifle toward the end of the Crewe inquiry. This is an anomaly – there was a designated exhibits officer, Detective Graham Abbott, who should have taken exclusive control of that vital exhibit. That Keith was given that rifle was also a breach of the General Instructions and plan for running a homicide investigation, and is unlikely to have been a coincidence. The General Instructions are designed to preserve the integrity of every exhibit – although this procedure was not only bent, but broken when the need arose during the Crewe homicide inquiry.

It can now be contended, based on the closeness which existed between Keith and Hutton, that the direction to Parkes to uplift the previously-discounted Thomas rifle on 20 October 1970 came with an intention to put it in Keith's custody. Abbott may have been more diligent in relation to such a vital exhibit, but that is not what was needed when the fabrication of evidence to resolve two nasty murders was on the agenda.

The Thomas rifle, labelled exhibit 317, was given into Keith's custody on 20 October, that firearm having been uplifted by Parkes after the finding of the stub axles by Johnston at that farm in the early afternoon that day. All of Keith's subsequent evidence – to two Supreme Court trials, at the Court of Appeal, in a report produced in May 1972 and at the Royal Commission – was consistent. He was adamant that the Thomas rifle had been in his sole custody between the day he received it and 29 October 1970, when it was taken to the DSIR for testing and he swore on oath – falsely as it will be shown – that this was true.

His own testimony to the Thomas Royal Commission reveals, however, that he could not possibly have had continuous custody of the Thomas rifle because for a day and a half in that crucial nine-day period he had been out of Auckland, and away from his Government-issue locker at the Otahuhu police station, in which that firearm was said to have been secured:

Michael Crew, counsel for the Commission: Your notebook shows that you went to Wellington by plane on the morning of 22 October. You returned by train that night and were in Auckland on the morning of 23 October.
Keith: That is correct.

Subsequent testimony from Keith revealed that he had arrived back in Auckland about lunchtime on 23 October after his overnight train journey.

The truth is that Keith flew to Wellington on the morning of 22 October with a handful of wire samples from the Thomas farm. The treatment of these particular samples requires comment because in August, samples of wire from nine other farms in the Pukekawa district were dispatched by post from the DSIR in Auckland to Wellington where the Government Analyst, Harry Todd, was based. The contrast between the despatch of the August wire samples – collected when the heat was really on the main suspect at that time, Len Demler – and the second batch of wire samples, being those taken from the Thomas farm, is obvious.

Having safely delivered the Thomas farm wire to Todd, and having watched him do initial analysis work on them, Keith caught the train back through the central North Island to Auckland. He arrived at lunchtime on 23 October. This constituted a 27 or 28 hour absence from his Otahuhu base. Despite undertaking these plane and train journeys at times critical to the custody of Thomas' .22 Browning rifle, the former clerk of the Crewe inquiry did not reveal his absence to anyone outside his own squad, and then probably only to those within the inner circle. Later he provided a written report to the officer who had been charged with collecting information in response to allegations that the cartridge case exhibit 350 had been planted by members of the Crewe squad. That report, to Detective Inspector Brian James, in May 1972 states:

> The rifle was in my possession under this security up until the depositions hearing at the Otahuhu Magistrate's Court. The only occasion that it left my locker was for the re-test firing on the 29th of October [by the DSIR] as a result of the cartridge case being found at the Crewe home on the 27th of October.

If Keith's report is accepted – which it is not - then how could Bruce Hutton have showed Arthur Thomas his Browning rifle, with a packet of bullets tied to the trigger guard, in his office at the Otahuhu Police station on 25 October? The evidence of Thomas on this point at his Supreme Court trial was not challenged by the Crown Prosecutors, or Hutton himself. Clearly, despite Keith's subsequent protestations, on oath, to the contrary, the Thomas rifle had not been in his 'exclusive custody' throughout that time. The Royal Commission made this observation in 1980:

> Mr Keith gave evidence that the Thomas rifle was kept in his locker, to which he alone had the key. We do not accept that he was in a position to guarantee that no other police officer had access to the rifle. His locker was apparently of *standard* Government issue, and we have no doubt that it would not have been difficult for a determined person to gain access to it. Furthermore there is evidence given at the second trial by Mr Thomas that on 25 October 1970, Mr Hutton had the rifle in his office with a packet of ammunition attached to it. Mr Thomas gave this evidence under cross examination and was not challenged on it. That evidence indicates that officers other than Mr Keith had access to the rifle between 20 October, when it was picked up from the Thomas farm, and 27 October when exhibit 350 was found.

In a report issued in 1981 which followed his assessment of whether there were grounds for bringing prosecutions against police for crimes connected with the Crewe inquiry, Solicitor-General Paul Neazor also determined:

> Notwithstanding Mr Keith's evidence to the contrary, the Thomas rifle *could* have been in the hands of either Detective Inspector Bruce Hutton or Detective Len Johnston (or both) between 20 October

and 29 October 1970.

Keith assisted in securing convictions against Thomas in several ways over the years. He was the detective who 'found' the number 8 bullet in the Thomas garage – the only one ever found on that property to match the precise model found in the heads of the two dead Crewes. He was also the officer who had heard that often-quoted, highly-incriminating statement from Thomas to his wife on 21 October 1970: 'If they think I am guilty then I am'. That statement, said to have been uttered on the day police stormed through the Thomas farmhouse and pulled all manner of old vehicle parts out of the tip, was disputed at every subsequent court proceeding.

In 2010, in an interview for my North & South feature, Vivien Thomas once again reiterated the untruthfulness of Keith's testimony about the content of the discussion she had had with her husband that day:

> This conversation, as stated, never took place. There was certainly a conversation that day. I'd just cleaned the house and I was pretty upset. What's really strange is that Keith claims he heard me say something to Arthur that he did not hear. But he heard Arthur's reply. I find this really strange and baffling because my voice is far more penetrating that Arthur's.

Further examples of Keith's participation in the conviction of an innocent man may emerge in the fullness of time, but for now it may be sufficient to cite two ancillary matters which should provide the measure of the man.

In April 1973, Keith was one of the three Crewe detectives who dined at the Station Hotel on the eve of the Thomas retrial jury bringing down its verdict. The others were Hutton and Johnston. The Royal Commission concluded, in its formal report, that their presence in that watering hole on that evening demonstrated a clear lack of judgment on the part of the three officers concerned, while a trial was still running and while the jury was present. Hutton denied that he and Keith had been dancing with jury members at the cabaret that evening – one of the woman jurors gave sworn testimony at the Royal Commission that they had. Hutton's assertion that Thomas was clearly guilty and that the jury had a duty to find him guilty was also allegedly made during that time on the dance floor.

The second matter relates to Keith's crafty and calculated editing of documents from the Crewe homicide file after Official Information Act requests by myself. One such document formed part of the extensive file on Demler compiled by the police during the four months in which they attempted to force him to confess to killing his daughter and son-in-law. This file, of course, 'no longer existed' when the Royal Commission and counsel for Thomas wanted so much to view it in 1980, but mysteriously resurfaced after the intervention of the Chief Ombudsman just before Christmas 1999. Within the Demler file material was a transcript of a conference held a month into the Crewe inquiry. It was major event involving the 'top brass' from Auckland and Wellington and the upper echelon of the inquiry then being conducted, along with Crown Prosecutor David Morris, scientists and the like. In the original version provided to me – purporting to be *all* the evidence assembled against Demler by way of job sheets and conference records – Morris was recorded as making several comments. But that version omitted one critical finding from the Crown Prosecutor – that the police probably had enough evidence to establish a prima facie case against Demler for the murder of Harvey Crewe. The 'editor' of that document supplied under the Official Information Act to the author was one Stanley Raymond Keith.

Keith's control of the vast volumes of documents that made up the Crewe homicide file continued until 2010 when, on the eve of the fortieth anniversary of the Crewe murders, the *New Zealand Herald* interviewed the minder of the 29 boxes, which had been stored in the police archives since the Royal Commission wrapped up its hearings. In that interview, Keith had this to say:

> It has been my life. If it hadn't been for this inquiry, I would have chased promotion within the police. You get politicians, you get ghouls, you get journalists who want to write books and you get those who want to make films. You get heaps of correspondence that comes through from headquarters. I have had enough and I have told them so.

Equally, it appeared police headquarters by then may also have had enough of Keith and the complaints his actions had brought. One example is his declaration – provided to the Commissioner of Police of that day – that there was *no* schedule of exhibits destroyed by him at the Whitford tip in July 1973. That declaration, subsequently conveyed to me by police headquarters, was in direct conflict with Keith's own evidence at the Royal Commission, in which he not only discussed that schedule – which he had personally compiled – but which he produced [exhibit 110]. Other notable examples of his misrepresentation of the facts over the last three decades also exist.

Stan Keith spent 32 years as a sworn police officer but after a short stint of retirement returned to the fold. His last 14 years as a civilian employee of the New Zealand Police were as a briefing clerk, in effect a return to the role he had fulfilled on the Crewe inquiry four decades earlier. He died in June 2011, having picked up a Queen's Service Medal, ironically, for his work on the original Crewe homicide inquiry and during the Thomas Royal Commission. He finally opted out of service to the New Zealand Police just four months before he died, 'one of the boys' to the bitter end.

Fourteen

On 22 June 1970, the day Len Demler reported his daughter and son-in-law missing from the farm next door, another momentous event took place within the hierarchy of the New Zealand Police. On that day Detective Chief Superintendent Robert [Bob] Josiah Walton became an Assistant Commissioner of Police, retaining responsibility as head of the national Criminal Investigation Branch. Within two days, the police had two more Assistant Commissioners – George Austing, who took over as district commander in Auckland, and Ken Burnside, who like Walton was based at headquarters in Wellington.

Upon his arrival at police headquarters, Walton surely could not have imagined, even for one moment, just how that day would end. Not only did the new Assistant Commissioner already have three unsolved murders on his plate – a matter of gravest concern to the man who had full responsibility for the CIB – but by late that afternoon, he had five. As the national CIB chief, Walton was advised, in the early evening of 22 June 1970, of the events that were unfolding at Pukekawa.

Walton was, in both stature and reputation, a big man, one who had served in the New Zealand Army, had survived the turmoil and tragedy of the front line in Italy and North Africa during the Second World War, and was then posted to the occupation force in Japan. That link with the military continued and during his subsequent term as Commissioner of Police he remained a Colonel in the Territorial Force, a unique combination of offices. Like many military men returning to New Zealand after the Second World War, he had found his way into the police and his career advances and achievements through the 1950s and 1960s is the stuff of legends. In 1963 – he was by then a Detective Inspector – he helped establish the armed offenders squad, an elite force created to help unarmed police deal with armed criminals, and he went on to arrest John Gillies and Ronald Jorgensen for the infamous Bassett Road machine-gun murders, Al Capone-style gangland killings which fascinated a previously innocent nation.

Specialist police drug squads were formed as a result of Walton's fact-finding mission to the United States and he helped draft the

Narcotics Act 1965 which paved the way for undercover surveillance and protected officers from prosecution while they were engaged in these covert operations. By the time the Crewes were murdered, in June 1970, Walton was being viewed as a certainty to replace the aging Gus Sharp as Commissioner – and everyone in the force knew it.

Walton made his first visit to the murder scene at Pukekawa on 25 June 1970, returning on 15 July 1970, three weeks into the Crewe inquiry. That day, a major Police conference – which inquiry head Bruce Hutton subsequently labelled as one for the 'TB' [the top brass] – was held at Auckland Central police station. In attendance were Walton and the district executive – Assistant Commissioner George Austing, Auckland regional CIB co-ordinator Mal Ross, Chief Superintendent Paddy Byrne, Detective Chief Inspector Bill Cook and Chief Inspector Cliff Pentecost. Attending also were five members of the inquiry and search team – Detective Inspector Bruce Hutton, Inspector Pat Gaines, Detective Sergeant Jim Tootill, Detective Mervyn Dedman and Detective Stan Keith. Auckland Crown Prosecutor David Morris, pathologist Frank Cairns and DSIR scientists Dr Donald Nelson and Rory Shanahan completed the line-up.

Events immediately preceding that conference in Auckland that day indicate just how personally involved Walton had become in the matter of the five unsolved murders on his watch which were clearly, on the evidence now available, beginning to irritate him. On his way to Auckland for that conference, Walton visited the Rotorua police station where detectives were working to try to solve the two murders in their region – the April killing of Betty McKay and that of Olive Walker in May. Like the Crewe murders to the north, neither of these serious crimes was close to being resolved, within the ambit of the law, at least.

The second-in-command of the Olive Walker inquiry was Detective Sergeant Jack Collins. By the time Walton arrived in Rotorua that day, Collins believed that he had a solid lead on the offender. Walton had other ideas, pushing for an immediate resolution to the Olive Walker inquiry by means of an action which would have led Collins down a path he was not prepared to traverse. Ultimately, the detective sergeant's refusal to do what his boss was demanding cost him his career in the CIB, but he could not have imagined just how swift, or how prolonged, the retribution would be. In 2011 Collins related the events of that day:

Yes I remember Walton coming from Wellington and then going on to the Crewe inquiry in Auckland. I remember it like it was yesterday and I remember it very clearly. I'd been working very long hours on this inquiry and he [Walton] came up to Rotorua and started asking about this and that. We just wanted to get on with the job. He was very unhappy when he arrived, walking around the place with a glum face, but he was even more unhappy by the time he left. I told him about someone I had investigated who was close to Olive Walker's family and the opinion I had formed that this person was not the culprit. This man was a local criminal but he did not fit the evidence we had gathered. Walton kept insisting that I go back and re-investigate this known criminal. He became quite pushy and we had a heated argument. It was then that he told me I was finished in the CIB, that I would never go anywhere.

The next morning, on his arrival at work, Collins was handed a letter advising that he was being transferred back to the uniform branch. He recounted:

My immediate superior told me that morning that he thought this was most unfair, but that is what happened. Walton had seen to that. The Olive Walker inquiry was my last as a detective. Arguing with Walton was probably not a smart move on my part because we all knew he would be the next Commissioner and our fate was in his hands. He was, in effect, my boss as he was the head of the CIB at that time and I was a detective sergeant. But I had a good idea who had killed Olive Walker and Walton wanted me to focus on someone who did not fit the overall picture of what we knew. My career [as a detective] was pretty well over at that point. This is very clear in my memory and I know that when Walton left for Auckland that day he was not in a very happy frame of mind.

Collins does not believe that the Assistant Commissioner would have ever instructed the Crewe homicide inquiry squad members to fabricate evidence, but learned first hand that Walton was a champion at exerting pressure to get serious crimes resolved:

Walton was too smart to tell anyone to fabricate evidence. But he was certainly piling on the pressure. I know that because of the personal experience I had with him in Rotorua in July 1970 when he came to us on his way to Auckland. He was very unhappy that we had the Jennifer Beard murder at the end of 1969 unsolved, Betty McKay at Thornton in April and then Olive Walker in May and then the two Crewes, all unsolved.

Ironically, Jack Collins had shared a room in the barracks with Bruce Hutton during their days of detective training at the police academy some years earlier – their tutor on those courses was Bob Walton:

Hutton was always close to Walton, even at that stage. I think that what happened is that Hutton would not have wanted to let Walton and the police down and that Johnston wouldn't want to let Hutton down. That's my assessment of how that all transpired. I don't think they set out to plant evidence, but once they became desperate, something had to happen. They would have preferred to have put it on their first suspect, Demler, but it just didn't happen that way. They didn't have a firearm and without that, they had nothing.

The events of 15 July 1970 which Collins relayed were subsequently confirmed by Walton himself in evidence at the Thomas Royal Commission, although not with the same degree of detail:

I did point out that I had just come from the Walker murder in Rotorua, unsolved, and we had the Beard murder and I expected them to work toward getting evidence because I told them that evidence had to be objective.

The whole issue of what Walton had told the Crewe inquiry team – and more particularly how they interpreted his instructions – was canvassed at length by the Royal Commission. Walton was by then Commissioner of Police, having been overtaken for five years by Ken Burnside in the interim. From the Royal Commission transcript:

Walton: I was concerned that after three weeks there was no sign of the bodies, there was no positive reconstruction, and in my opinion no apparent motive, and although one [Len] Demler was regarded as the suspect, this suspicion to me appeared to be based on speculation at that stage.
Taylor: Did you give any instruction to the investigation team at that

conference?

Walton: Yes, at the end of the conference I said to the effect that there was no prima facie case against Demler and that we would need evidence to establish that.

Taylor: Did it occur to you that that instruction could have been misinterpreted by an over-ardent Policeman as a drive to create evidence instead of finding it?

Walton: No I don't think it at all possible that that misinterpretation could be placed on it because I see it as the police duty to do all possible to resolve crime.

Taylor: Let me read to you the terms as you recorded [from that conference] 'We have to drive for evidence, evidence is what we want.' I don't criticise the terms in which you gave that your instruction, that's a fairly straight instruction.

Walton: Yes, I have said it often. It is my job to motivate staff. It is our job to solve crime, but always within the law. I would add that I am quite sure that my word there would not be misconstrued by the staff there or by any other police staff. Every policeman in New Zealand would know the stand of the administration and my own personal stand against misconduct.

Taylor: You are quite sure they would not be misconstrued in the sense that people would go beyond the law?

Walton: Fabrication is not evidence and every policeman would understand that and I know of no requirement for a policeman to fabricate evidence.

Later that same day Thomas' senior counsel, Peter Williams QC, reverted to this issue:

Williams: When you used this expression at that July [1970] conference 'we have to get one' can't you see that it could have been construed by an over-zealous officer as meaning there was some mandatory obligation to get evidence to justify an arrest?

Walton: No, they would fully understand what I meant there.

Williams: Weren't you really saying that there have been these previous unsolved homicides at the present moment and it appears we have another, the reputation of our police force is at stake and I am telling you that we have to get somebody for the Crewe murders?

Walton: No they wouldn't take it that way at all. As I explained, I see it as our public duty to do our very best to solve all crimes, particularly serious crimes, but that is all within the law because we take considerable steps within the police to ensure our members [know] from the day they join the organisation, that fabrication, violence, misconduct, is not condoned. But I expect them to do their very best within the law, and having done that, the police can live with an unsolved crime and I am sure the public can. But as head of the CIB then, yes I was concerned at the number of unsolved murders.

Williams: Human nature being what it is in any large body of men, there will usually be one or two who may resort to wrongful practices if there is not a good system of checks
and sanctions?

Walton: That is a possibility. I don't like to concede that naturally because the organisation does not require that, but after all the New Zealand Police is 4932 human beings, but they are in no doubt what will happen if there should be evidence of misconduct.

Williams: So far as the history of this matter is concerned, the message from you in July 1970 was 'we have to get one' and you meant by that that they had to get proper evidence obtained by lawful means.

Walton: Yes, we had to do our utmost.

Clearly, the Crewe detectives formed a contrary interpretation to the extremely categorical exhortation – 'we have to get one' – than that which Walton says he intended in his zeal to have the five unsolved murders on his watch wrapped up.

The admission from Walton that he had *not* instructed police to 'get someone' or to 'drive for evidence' in other investigations *prior to this day* confirms that he was gravely concerned about those unsolved murders, as he relayed, in no uncertain terms, to Collins on the same day he gave that exhortation to the Crewe squad.

Walton's instructions in July 1970 may be open to misinterpretation, but that which he provided to the head of the CIB in Auckland in the months preceding the hearings of the Thomas Royal Commission are not. In the first week of the Crewe inquiry, police on the Crewe homicide inquiry were aware – and were openly telling relatives and friends of Harvey Crewe – that the woman who they considered had fed and cared for Rochelle was 'Demler's new girlfriend'.

That issue emerged again in 1979, during the inquiries by Muldoon's special investigator, Robert Adams-Smith QC. In the preparation of his second report, Adams-Smith looked at the issue of the identity of the woman who fed Rochelle, an act the police had steadfastly insisted had occurred until it no longer suited them to do so. On 8 February 1980, Walton wrote to Bernie Galvin, the head of the Prime Minister's Department, advising that he [Walton] had directed Auckland CIB regional co-ordinator, Detective Chief Superintendent Brian Wilkinson, not to make inquiries into three issues which Adams-Smith had sought information about. One of those issues was the 'possible involvement of the second Mrs Demler'. [Adams-Smith was referring to Norma Demler, whom Len Demler had married in April 1972]. On the face of it, this appeared to be tantamount to an instruction from the Commissioner of Police to the head of the CIB in Auckland not to investigate a witness.

Walton's direct intervention in this matter can be seen in both the evidence given behind closed doors by Wilkinson at the Royal Commission in the course of which he [Wilkinson] stated, unequivocally, that he had been prevented from interviewing Norma Demler by his boss, Bob Walton. Exhibit 161, tabled at the Royal Commission includes a letter which directs Wilkinson not to interview Norma Demler. That document, carrying Walton's signature, verifies this assertion.

In May 2006, in the course of an interview conducted at his home in Wellington, Walton offered me this response to Wilkinson's claim:

Walton: Well I can't give you an explanation for that. I can't see why I would stop him [Wilkinson] interviewing someone *who was very closely involved in the inquiry.* I just can't clear my mind on that at all. There must have been a damned good reason, that's all I can say.

Birt: Well I have talked with Brian Wilkinson about that and he definitely remembers being stopped, so even to this day he knows he was instructed not to. He said this to me quite recently.

Walton: Well did he say why?

Birt: No I don't know why.

Walton: I need to ask him why. He must know there is a reason. Brian has got the strength not to accept something without saying 'why the hell are you doing that.' I would know of no reason why I would do that.

Walton died two years later. His motivation for putting the brakes on an aspect of a criminal investigation which remains unresolved to this day is still a matter of speculation. However had he not done so in 1979, the facts of the Crewe murders may have been revealed then, not by way of a tortuous and expensive Royal Commission process which resulted, in the final analysis, in the reputation of the New Zealand Police – an agency committed to the observance of law and order – being so badly tarnished.

While the Thomas Royal Commission focused its primary attention on the misdemeanors of Hutton and Johnston – the front rowers who, that inquiry found had engineered the creation of evidence in order to justify the arrest of Arthur Thomas – Walton did not come out of these hearings unscathed. On 8 July 1980, the day the Royal Commission formally identified exhibit 350, the chairman determined that the Commissioner of Police had misled Prime Minister Rob Muldoon in a letter the previous year.

Walton had told Muldoon that the key to the date of the deaths of the Crewes and the timing of that tragic event was a fish meal found on the dining table in their house:

Taylor: But it wasn't the key to the date was it?

[Auckland CIB chief Brian] *Wilkinson:* No

Taylor: And it was never any part of the fixing of the time of death by the police?

Wilkinson: No.

Taylor: These two matters are completely misleading. It is a bit more than being a mistake when you give that sort of information to the Prime Minister.

The Royal Commission also scolded Walton for recommending to then Police Commissioner Ken Burnside in 1977 that material supplied by Hutton and the DSIR's Dr Nelson regarding a cartridge case not be provided to the Thomas campaigners, Jim Sprott and Pat Booth:

The then Assistant Commissioner of Police, Mr R J Walton, made a report to the Commissioner of Police giving his recommendations on the material put forward by Dr Nelson and Mr Hutton. Mr Walton is of course now Commissioner of Police. The recommendation was that the material not be disclosed to Dr Sprott and Mr Booth. It is fortunate that the Minister of Justice Dr [Martyn] Finlay, insisted that it be disclosed, otherwise that issue would not have been investigated. It does the police little credit that they were prepared to conduct behind closed doors a private investigation into this crucial matter, with themselves and the DSIR as judge and jury.

Another action which must bring into question the insistence of the then Commissioner of Police – that all members of that force must comply in every way with the law – came during the Royal Commission hearings. On the morning of 8 July 1980, one of those men most heavily involved in the search of the Crewe house and its immediate environs was approached by two of New Zealand's most senior police officers. Ross Meurant was due to give evidence before the Royal Commission that day, having been the very detective who had twice previously searched the garden where the Thomas cartridge case was found on 27 October 1970.

By 1980, Meurant was a senior sergeant in the uniform branch, working in the control room at Auckland Central police station, where he was approached in that location on that day by Police Commissioner Bob Walton and CIB regional co-ordinator Brian Wilkinson:

> Walton and Wilkinson came to see me that morning and wanted me to give evidence at the Royal Commission indicating that I had not been thorough with the search of the Crewe garden. The clear message Walton gave me on that day was that I had been careless in the garden search and that is why the cartridge from the Thomas rifle had not been found earlier. The problem was that I had given evidence twice earlier, at the First Referral to the Court of Appeal and the second Thomas trial, and had said I had been meticulous, as required by the investigation manual that Walton had himself written. The Crewe case was my first homicide investigation and as a constable-on-trial with the CIB, I scrupulously followed search procedure. I had been supervised in that and I was careful and methodical, as I was required to be. I told them that I had done the search on my hands and knees, to which Walton responded 'Come on Senior, detectives don't get down on their hands and knees and sift through dirt'. The Commissioner of Police was saying that I was not as thorough as I said I had been. I was absolutely stunned.

Meurant says that at the time exhibit 350 was found in the Crewe garden he believed that it was genuine, despite knowing that he had searched that garden in June and again in August with the degree of meticulousness that was expected of him as a police constable who wanted to forge a career as a detective, and despite reservations being expressed about its authenticity later by one of the other detectives he had worked with at the Crewe property. Rumours had also been circulating among Auckland police about 'a plant' at the Crewe farm during the years leading up to the Royal Commission:

> As soon as Walton and Wilkinson turned up and tried to persuade me to say I'd been careless, I became convinced that the cartridge had been a plant. There was no other reason for them to attempt to do what they did.

Meurant delivered his testimony to the Royal Commission on the afternoon of 8 July 1980 – it followed directly after the formal identification of exhibit 350 – and he maintained that which he had provided to two earlier Court hearings. Like Jack Collins, maintaining his stand was not good for his career:

> Looking back, I now know it was no coincidence that I was not given the rank of commissioned officer until Walton retired three years later.

At the very next change of shift following the Royal Commission's identification of what had been the most controversial cartridge case in New Zealand's history, Walton stood before 400 uniform and plain clothes officers at Auckland Central police station and declared: 'That man Hutton let us down'. But five months after making that resolute declaration behind closed doors, Walton and his headquarters executive team, acting as judge and jury, ruled out the laying of criminal charges against 'that man Hutton'

Walton went on to withstand strong demands from the Thomas family to withdrew the certificate of merit Hutton had been awarded for his 'diligence and zeal' in solving the Crewe homicides, asserting that Thomas' counsel at the second trial, Kevin Ryan, had recommended Hutton for that honour. This untruth emanated from a drinking session in Auckland at which Ryan and Walton were both present. On that occasion, the Thomas lawyer heard that Stan Keith had, on Hutton's instructions, dumped the crucial exhibits from the second Thomas trial at the Whitford tip and he jokingly quipped: 'Hutton should be awarded a bloody medal'. Kevin Ryan's twin, Gerald:

> Walton had taken a joke and made it into a reality. I personally contacted Walton and complained and he promised he would contact the newspaper and put in a retraction, but he never did.

Not long before he retired, Walton witnessed the rejection of a legal challenge by Hutton, Johnston's widow and the two police service associations against the Royal Commission's findings. Those findings still stand. Publicly, Walton died still doggedly defending the actions of the Crewe homicide squad of 1970, despite a Royal Commission's finding that his men had engaged in subterfuge and fabrication in order to bring that inquiry to the speedy end he had demanded of them.

His CIB lieutenant in Auckland, Brian Wilkinson:

> Walton says he has to defend Bruce Hutton and, 30 years on, he still feels he has to say that.

Fifteen

A small group of detectives circled the wagons when aspects of the Crewe investigation – most notably the planting of the cartridge case from the Thomas rifle in the garden of the victims – began to unravel, as happened at the First Referral to the Court of Appeal in February 1973. This group consisted of the scene detectives – Detective Sergeant Murray Jeffries, Detective Bruce Parkes, Detective Kevin Gee, Detective Len Higgins and Detective Ross Meurant.

Jeffries was the officer in charge of the scene during that inquiry, and was Hutton's appointee for both the initial close-quarters search immediately after the murders were reported in June, and again in mid August after Jeanette Crewe's body was recovered from the nearby Waikato River. Parkes was in direct control of Higgins and Meurant during the June search, but was not there in August, being assigned to other inquiries. Gee joined the scene detectives in their search of the Crewe house and enclosure on 18 and 19 August that year.

The issue of a planted cartridge case did not rear its head to any great extent at the first Thomas trial, with defence counsel Paul Temm offering it as a suggestion only, fearing that the jury would baulk at considering the possibility that the police had fabricated evidence to secure a conviction. The cartridge categorisation evidence was at that time still two years off being uncovered. It is significant that it took a decade to be confirmed as fact.

The police case against Thomas began to disintegrate in 1972, when Woodville farm manager Graeme Hewson swore an affidavit which, for the first time, challenged that squad's version of events in relation to exhibit 350, the Thomas cartridge case.

The response was predictable, with the old boys of the police club – and the new ones – being called on to 'do their duty'. That duty was, however, to their colleagues, not to the rule of law. This aspect of collegial behaviour was ultimately captured by Thomas defence counsel Kevin Ryan in his closing submissions to the Royal Commission in 1980:

Since the pardon, many people have asked who was responsible for

Thomas' convictions. The answer lies not in the specific orders of any one person, but in the spontaneous actions of many. When the Police Department closes its ranks, when authority takes up arms against one whom it mistakenly believes to be a murderer, there is no need for posting of battalion orders. Within the police team each member knows what is required of him, what he must do, and during this long investigation and trial each man did it. The proceedings against Thomas had a certain inevitability. Once put in motion, they gained a momentum of their own which it subsequently became impossible to stop. This entrenched clobbering machine continued so that any witness who may be able to assist was used to stoke the police furnace.

Without going into detail about the evidence that was produced by this small group, it can be said that the same finding the Royal Commission made about the axle – that it involved a morass of inconsistencies, unexplained discrepancies and alternative possibilities – can equally be applied to the issue of the garden searches. Not only did the key witnesses to those events differ in the evidence they each gave at the various proceedings involving Thomas, other police officers from outside that tight group contradicted them with testimony that not only put the by-then exiled Graeme Hewson at the scene at crucial times, but heavily involved in the back-breaking task of sieving wet, puggy soil in a bid to locate a cartridge case Hutton needed to create a match with the bullet that had been recovered from Jeanette Crewe's head.

The versions of events from the scene detectives involved in the August search – they varied in vital respects from each other – came into question at the First Referral to the Court of Appeal and at the retrial of Arthur Thomas in 1973 and were subsequently heavily scrutinised by defence counsel and the Royal Commissioners in 1980. That temporary farm manager Jack Handcock testified that he had seen Hewson there and that he had been loosening the soil with a fork; that Detective Bruce Parkes attested to speaking with Hewson there on that day; and that Detective Sergeant Jim Tootill recorded in a job sheet that Hewson was there 'assisting with the search' did not assist the alternative case being put by the scene detectives.

The report of the Royal Commission made the following finding, based on its hearing of testimony over many days and being able to assess the demeanor and judge the credibility of the detectives involved:

We accept the evidence of Mr Hewson and reject that of the four police officers to the effect that that garden was not sieve searched [on 18 August]. We do so with some reluctance since the four officers are men to whom a reputation for integrity is vital. Despite counsel for Mr Thomas urging that we consider a more severe approach so far as the four police officers are concerned, we find also merely that they were *mistaken*. We accordingly find that the garden where exhibit 350 was eventually found on 27 October had been thoroughly and carefully searched on 23 June, and sieve searched on 18 August. We are satisfied that had exhibit 350 been deposited in that garden on 17 June, it would have been located in either the June or August search. Since it was not so located, it follows that it did not find its way into the garden until after 18 August 1970.

In making this statement, the Royal Commission appears to have recognised that the police officers appearing before it had been pressured to deliver consistent and standardised testimony – even if that was at variance with the facts. Careers were clearly on the line and while perjury by any police officer cannot be countenanced, the Royal Commissioners were pragmatic and had clearly seen that a pattern had emerged – one recognised by their findings in relation to the 'garden searchers'.

The Royal Commission went on to make several other significant observations. One was that a job sheet produced by Jeffries recorded:

All gardens [at the Crewe house] were cleared and the earth *sifted* [sieved] and examined.

The record of the squad conference held that evening also noted that Jeffries had reported:

A search was made of the lawn and the garden was completely dug up, that is all gardens, and sieved.

The Royal Commission continued:

All four officers conceded that Mr Hewson was present on 18 August, but have said that he assisted them only by searching the roof and guttering, a task that already been completed. That task would only have taken a short time and the police say that this was the only assistance which Mr Hewson gave them. The clear implication was that Mr Hewson was an embarrassment rather than providing assistance to the police. The conference note of 18 August, to which we have referred, explicitly states however that Mr Hewson was helping the police. It does not support Mr Jeffries' evidence that he humoured Mr Hewson by allowing him to climb on the roof.

The Royal Commission's finding that the garden searches had been careful and methodical is significant for a number of reasons. Firstly it is significant because the categorisation of the Thomas cartridge case ultimately ruled out that it had been married with the fatal number 8 bullets recovered from the Crewes. Secondly because the evidence of one of that young squad, constable-on-trial Ross Meurant, confirmed that he followed the manual for homicide investigations, written by Walton himself some years before, in relation to his search the garden where the Thomas cartridge was found on 27 October. The Royal Commission recorded:

> The area of Garden A in which exhibit 350 was later found by Detective Sergeant Charles was searched by Constable Meurant. He gave evidence that his search was thorough and methodical, and that evidence was confirmed by Mr Parkes and Mr Jeffries. He said that, if exhibit 350 had been on the surface of the garden, it is most likely he would have found it, although he was not prepared to say definitely that he would have done so. We understand Mr Meurant's reluctance, as an officer still serving in the force, to state categorically that he would have found exhibit 350. In our view however, taking into account all the evidence, Mr Meurant would have almost certainly found exhibit 350 had it been on the surface of the garden. The simple fact of the matter is that the depth at which the cartridge case was found by Detective Charles points to the cartridge case having been deliberately buried in the ground.

The Royal Commission then expressed its profound displeasure at the attempt to explain the presence of the cartridge case by inferring that the searches had not been adequately undertaken:

> The evidence of Mr Hutton and Mr Jeffries, and to a much lesser extent that of [Mr] Parkes, demonstrated a tendency to denigrate the

thoroughness and care of the officers carrying out the searches. The object of this evidence was obviously to establish that it is not very surprising that exhibit 350 was not found during the June search. We find it unacceptable that the police should now say that their own investigation was casual and slip-shod, although we understand that they are anxious to avoid the conclusion that exhibit 350 was planted. The Commission is of the view that the tenor of the evidence from Mr Hutton and Mr Jeffries was quite unfair to their subordinates, Mr Parkes, Mr Higgins and Mr Meurant. The explanation of exhibit 350's presence in the garden on 27 October 1970 does not lie in any failure by these officers to carry out their instructions in a proper manner. We are of the view that they conducted the June search carefully and methodically and that they would have located exhibit 350 had it been on the garden where it was later found.

Of the original Crewe inquiry squad, Ross Meurant alone has stood up to be counted in terms of his own actions, and those he worked alongside during those miserable chilling days in the foothills of Pukekawa from June till August 1970. His emergence from the dark depths of the forest, in terms of his role in the Thomas affair at least, began with the publication of his 1989 book *The Beat to the Beehive*. In that book he resolutely declared that the finding of the Royal Commission – that the cartridge case had been planted and therefore evidence fabricated – was 'clearly an appropriate determination'. Having been the detective who searched the relevant garden, in June and again in August, he was in a position to make such a judgment.

The Crewe inquiry was the first homicide investigation Meurant had been involved with, and it is clear from his public utterances in the intervening decades that he now believes some of his former colleagues on that assignment acted in concert to ensure that two of the high-profile murders unsolved at that time were able to be crossed off the list – contrary to the law and their own oath of office. In July 2010 Meurant came out in support of the first-ever call by Rochelle Crewe to re-launch the inquiry into the murder of her parents, a bid she laced with strong criticism of the police for not actively pursuing the former officers who fabricated evidence, as determined by the Thomas Royal Commission.

Of the balance of the Crewe squad, few stand out as warranting detailed examination, but one who does is John Rex Hughes. While he was on the Crewe inquiry for just six weeks – his role largely involved interrogating Len Demler, a task for which he was more than adequately equipped – his subsequent testimony played a pivotal role in securing the conviction of Thomas.

Hughes was regarded as 'a master' of verbals, the practice of accepting, then giving sworn evidence about what a detective had been told, often in the face of strenuous denials by the accused. On the evidence now available, it appears that in the dying days of this inquiry, someone convinced Hughes that Thomas was the offender.

This belief manifested itself at the first Thomas trial when he dropped a bombshell on the defence, swearing, on oath, that Thomas had told him that he had worked at the Crewe farm, had had morning tea with the couple and that 'Harvey Crewe appeared to be a decent type of bloke'. This statement was not true and Thomas never uttered those words, indeed he told Detective Bruce Parkes that any connection he had had with the former Chennells' farm ended well before the Crewes moved there in 1966, as was indeed the case. Hughes was not, however, swayed from his fabricated account of events and Crown Prosecutor David Morris sought from Thomas at his second trial an explanation of why such a highly-regarded detective sergeant would concoct such a story. Such a question itself constitutes an impropriety, given that Morris had personally heard at the original trial two years earlier the truth – that Thomas last worked on the Chennells' estate, later to be the Crewe farm, in 1964. This was two years before the Jeanette Crewe returned to Pukekawa with her new husband.

Morris did concede, to the Royal Commission seven years later, that what he had put before the second Thomas trial jury in relation to Hughes' evidence was false. He insisted that he had sought to have that matter clarified, with two separate requests to the police to check the detail of Thomas' employment with the topdressing company concerned. Hughes blamed Hutton for not doing the necessary checks on Thomas' employment, saying it was a matter for the officer-in-charge of the inquiry to determine.

The Royal Commission criticised the police for failing to establish the truth, labelling it improper conduct, but for reasons that have never been explained, that inquisition did not make any reference to Hughes and his perjured evidence, despite him repeating the very same false 'verbal' to that inquisition in 1980.

Hughes had been the subject of a number of 'planting' allegations before the Crewe inquiry and he went on to become involved in several other high profile cases following his stint as officer in charge of suspects in 1970. The most notable was as head of the inquiry into the murders of Swedish backpackers Urban Hoghlan and Heidi Paakonen in the Coromandel 19 years later. David Wayne Tamahere was arrested, convicted and spent 20 years in prison for those murders, but that case also sparked controversy, with Hughes' sworn testimony about what the accused had told him being disputed, not only by Tamahere himself, but by the facts as they were established later. Hughes told that Supreme Court jury that Tamahere had admitted taking a wrist watch off the young Swedish man and giving it to his son, but when pig hunters found Hoglan's remains – 73 kilometres from where the police alleged the murders had taken place – that time-keeping piece was still on the victim's wrist. The finding of Hoglan's body intact, contradicting the detective's evidence that Tamahere had 'admitted' cutting the missing couple into pieces and throwing them into the ocean, added further to the suspicion many in New Zealand's community had about the bona fides of that Hughes-led investigation.

Just as this book was being completed, David Wayne Tamahere announced that he wanted a re-trial on the murders of the Swedish couple, based, in part, that he had been 'fitted up' by the police. The legacy left by the officer in charge of the inquiry that turned Tamahere into a convicted double murderer lives on.

Sixteen

The Bill of Rights Act 1990 dictates that in criminal proceedings, accused persons have 'the right to a fair and public hearing by an independent and impartial court'. That legislation was not in force in 1970, but that basic tenant had been enshrined in law for centuries. That is what the law dictated – but it is not what Arthur Allan Thomas got. The two trials he faced, and indeed even the lower court proceedings against him, were far from impartial.

From the very moment Thomas defence counsel Paul Temm and Brian Webb set foot in the Otahuhu Magistrate's Court for the taking of depositions, they were up against the system. When Temm attempted to get a copy of the inventory of items recovered from the Waikato River from search controller Inspector Pat Gaines, Magistrate Donald McLean refused to allow the witness to leave the stand. The inventory Temm required was a matter of metres away, on the desk of Crown Prosecutor David Morris. [That inventory existed then, with evidence of that given at the Royal Commission in 1980, but in 2010 the police advised me that it did no longer existed]. Later in those same proceedings, when Temm sought approval for a witness he was cross-examining to leave the stand and retrieve a job sheet which was relevant to the matter being canvassed, the request was similarly denied.

Arthur Thomas was put on trial in February 1971 in proceedings that were tame by comparison with what was to follow. Certain members of the police, of course, knew that not only was the case against him contaminated by the introduction of several key pieces of planted evidence – a cartridge case and two stub axles being the most notable – but that they had managed to deny the defence knowledge of a number of key witnesses and their statements, any of whom could have assisted with securing an acquittal.

As the case unfolded however, the prosecution need not have had any fear about the outcome. The summing up by first trial judge Trevor Henry was a masterful performance, one in which not only did he make his feelings of Thomas' guilt clear to the jury, but that Rochelle Crewe had been fed – and that Vivien Thomas had fed her.

Peter Williams QC, who came into the Thomas case for the Second Referral to the Court of Appeal in late 1974, is highly critical of that closing address by Henry at the first trial:

Henry in effect told the jury at if the cartridge case had been planted, it had to mean that someone had crept into Thomas' house, had stolen his rifle, had fired it and got the shellcase and had then gone back to his house and had put the rifle back. What he completely failed to tell the jury was that the police had demanded Thomas' rifle back for a second time and had it during the latter stages of their investigation. He also ignored the fact that the DSIR's key scientific witness, Donald Nelson, had earlier found that the Thomas rifle could *not* have fired the fatal bullets. The police had the opportunity to fire that cartridge in Thomas' rifle and obtain the shellcase and therefore had the very exhibit that could be planted. Henry knew all that because it came out in the evidence, but he did not refer to it at all in his summing up. He either deliberately, or negligently refused to deal with the possibility that the shellcase had been planted by the police.

As a further example of Henry's attempt to steer the verdict in the direction he believed was appropriate, Williams cites the judge's summation of Bruce Roddick's evidence about a woman he had seen at the Crewe house before the murders were reported. Roddick was adamant that this woman had fair hair, thus concluding that it was not Vivien Thomas, whom he knew well, because as the jury could see, she had dark hair. In the judge's summing up to the jury, this testimony became:

He [Roddick] does not tell us the colour of her locks or anything else about her clothing at all, but in his judgment, for what it is worth, a man's judgment, she gave the appearance of having light brown hair.

Williams responds:

Roddick did not say the woman gave the *appearance* of having light brown hair. He said the woman *did* have light brown hair. And what did the judge mean by 'a man's judgment'? He is implying that a man would not be as careful about his description of her appearance as a woman would be. This is complete rubbish and indicates the jaundiced view Henry took of Arthur and Vivien Thomas at that trial. The first Thomas trial makes it abundantly clear of the dangers of judges exceeding their roles and becoming emotionally involved in the facts of a case as Henry did. We know now in hindsight that not only was Henry wrong in trying to encourage the jury to believe that Thomas had fired the fatal bullets in his own rifle and that Vivien Thomas was the woman who had fed the baby, but that his inaccuracies in that regard must have been contributing factors to a grave and serious miscarriage of justice.

Martyn Finlay, who as Justice Minister became embroiled in the Thomas affair following the election of Norman Kirk's Government in 1972, later declared that Henry's summing up provided adequate grounds for the first trial to be ruled a mistrial. While not able to comment at the time he was a Minister, Finlay said later:

> The judge over-stated the case for the Crown and under-stated the case for the defence. Examples of key defence arguments were glossed over by Henry, or not mentioned at all.

The second Thomas trial was quite a different affair to that which had preceded it. Aspects of those proceedings were attacked by the Thomas Royal Commission in its report to Parliament seven years after the event. On every front, that retrial – which had never been anticipated by the police or the Crown Prosecutors – required those leading the case against Thomas to adopt tactics designed to cover up the earlier fabrication of evidence, conspiracy to defeat the course of justice, and perjury.

The first strand of this unprecedented attack on Thomas – and the 'justice' system he was relying on to secure his freedom – came via the vetting of the jury list to ensure that only those with a pro-police attitude could decide the fate of the Pukekawa farmer. In order to achieve this, police spent almost three weeks delving into the potential jury members, assigning two senior detectives to a task that had never been carried out on such a scale before – or since. By contrast, the defence was supplied with the jury list on a Thursday afternoon, just one and a half working days, or 10 business hours, before the trial was to begin.

Evidence of the extensive nature of this vetting process was given to the Royal Commission subsequently by the two detectives involved and by the Crown officer charged with running the case in the Supreme Court, David Morris. This evidence reveals, graphically, that the usual task of checking the list of potential jury panelists to ensure only that they had no criminal convictions – the practice at that time – was replaced by a much more robust, and some would say sinister, investigation into those who had been called for service. In this context, the Crown ensured that the playing field was not only uneven, but that it was manifestly tilted in favour of the prosecution, which also enjoyed the added advantage of an unlimited number of challenges, whereas the defence only had six.

On the basis of the 'intelligence' gathered, Morris graded those who had been drawn into the Thomas affair, which by then was gathering a head of steam the judiciary did not want to build up any further, and as can now be demonstrated, one it actively determined should be extinguished forever.

Determining that the jury selection process was designed to ensure that a panel would be selected that was partial to the police for what was undoubtedly one of the biggest criminal trials ever conducted in this country, the Royal Commission said:

We may observe that there was nothing in the Juries Act 1908 requiring or authorising the police to carry out any such check. In our view the thoroughness of the checking of the jury by the police was excessive, improper and calculated to prejudice the fairness of the trial. The check went well beyond the disqualifications set out [in the Act]. We do not think it correct that, because a person is ill-disposed to the police, he is therefore of 'bad fame and repute'. The right to a trial by a jury of one's peers necessitates, in our view, the possibility that the jury will include persons who are anti-police. So long as jury trials continue, that is an inconvenience which the police must accept.

While it was not the role of the Royal Commission to inquire into the conduct of the Thomas trials – it was expressly prohibited from doing so by way of its terms of reference – it did feel compelled to make recommendations on the matter of vetting of jury lists. These included its view, expressed in the strongest possible terms, that any necessary checking of jury lists should be carried out by the Justice Department not the police, and that the police should not have any access to jury lists before the defence. Its other observations were that the right of the Crown to stand aside an unlimited number of potential jurors was an anachronism which invited abuse – that the prosecution should only ever have the same number of challenges as the defence – and that where it was essential to sequester a jury, the escorts should be officers of the Justice Department, not the police.

Unsurprisingly, Bruce Hutton testified, on oath, that the checks carried out on the list of potential jury members before the second Thomas trial were restricted to those normally carried out – with the qualification that as a result of what had been occurring between the first and second trials from the Thomas side and other people, it was felt that perhaps a little bit more should be done than was normally done, to ensure a *fair trial*. On the evidence now available, much more was certainly done than was 'normal' in terms of vetting the jury list and it can be contended that it was undertaken to ensure the opposite to what Hutton claimed – namely to achieve a manifestly *unfair* trial. Indisputably, that is what Thomas received.

The placement of a police caravan on the lawn of the Auckland High Court – approved by the Law Society – was another unusual feature of this make-or-break case. While the police later insisted this was solely for the comfort of their witnesses while they were waiting to give evidence, there is ample evidence that this was much more than that. In the words of Gerald Ryan, it resembled an 'observation post', bristling with communications equipment. In this caravan, transcripts of evidence were scrutinised as quickly as they were conveyed from the courtroom, and from it, detectives were instructed to gather intelligence on what the defence was planning. An example can be found in a job sheet from Stan Keith, who in the middle of that trial reported on what five young men would be saying about an old car axle reputedly once on the Thomas farm – the police knew almost as soon as the Ryan brothers just what the thrust of that testimony would be.

Gerald Ryan also reveals the detail of a further incident which occurred during the second Thomas trial, one which, on the face of it, constitutes improper conduct:

While I was in the court with Kevin, two workmen arrived at my home to mow the lawns and during the tea break engaged my wife in conversation about my thoughts on the case and how we were going to run the defence. We found out later that they were police dog handlers from the southern area and they had been planted on our property, with the co-operation of our contractor I suppose, to ascertain information about what we would be doing in court. That's how dirty it got.

In subsequent years, questions were asked about the circumstances in which the jury foreman at the second trial, Bob Rock, was selected and why he was allowed to stay in that role despite what was clearly a close personal connection between him and one of the most senior detectives involved in the Crewe inquiry, Detective Sergeant John Hughes. As covered in an earlier chapter, the Royal Commission subsequently inquired into this matter – although it was formally prevented from investigating the conduct of the judicial proceedings involving Thomas – and in its report to Parliament it favoured the evidence from Hughes that he had told Hutton about his association with the jury foreman as soon as it was revealed.

But the Royal Commission did not know that there was a connection between Rock and another senior member of the Auckland police at that time, Detective Chief Inspector Graham Perry, had also been in the navy with the jury foreman. Gerald Ryan records this:

> Perry was sitting at the back of the court at various times and Kevin asked me what he was doing there. Perry had no active involvement with the Crewe inquiry and there seemed to be no reason for him being at that trial, other than through his previous association with Rock.

That Perry appeared in full police uniform, at the hearing of a case in which he had played no investigatory role and when, as a detective, his normal attire at that time was civilian or 'plain' clothes, serves only to confirm the Ryans' belief that he was not there as an impartial observer of events. The defence team was obviously not advised of the connection between the jury foreman and the two senior detectives – one of them a key witness for the prosecution – purely to avoid the possibility of an application being made to have the trial aborted.

The documentary evidence also demonstrated that bias was shown in that trial against the defence – not only at the hands of the prosecution and the trial judge. This was obvious from the very first day when the jury, court officials and Crown Prosecutors were taken out to the Crewe farm for a site inspection. The lunch at the Tuakau hotel included alcohol and was paid for by the Justice Department. The defence team was not invited. The folly of having a luncheon for a judge and jury, to which the Crown Prosecutors and police witnesses were invited, but not the defence – before anyone had even gone into the witness box to give testimony – is plain for anyone to see.

Moreover, in both the first and second Thomas trials, in 1971 and 1973, the juries were sequestered at the nearby Station Hotel. In each trial, the defence teams strenuously objected to this ruling, aware that where lengthy proceedings are imminent, juries can begin to resent the accused whose alleged actions have put them in that position. At the 1973 trial in particular, this questionable tactic, while lawful at that time, formed the foundation of a platform from which the Crown – in concert with its police and DSIR allies – was able to mount an attack aimed at ensuring that Thomas was convicted for a second time.

The strands of an all-out attack on Thomas, his family and supporters, and his defence team – and its ability to provide the type of overpowering case that would have won his acquittal – were many and varied, and they extended well beyond the sequestering of a jury. No controls were put in place to achieve the level of impartiality required in such serious criminal proceedings. Boozy cabaret nights, excursions to boxing matches, and fishing trips were all laid on for the second Thomas trial jury, with members of the police in attendance, and no expense spared. Evidence put before the Royal Commission shows that this imposition on the taxpayer was significant, and that the hospitality provided to the members of this jury was extended from the very first day of that trial.

One of the most questionable such acts of the second Thomas trial was the attendance of three of the most influential of the Crewe inquiry detectives at a dinner and dance just days before the jury was set to deliver its verdict. Whether the detectives or the jury members arrived first in the dining room of the Station Hotel is in conflict – at the Royal Commission the police said one thing and the jury members another. What is not disputed, however, is that this incident involved the Otahuhu CIB trio of Hutton, Keith and Johnston. Hutton and Keith were on the dance floor at the same time as members of that jury and one of those charged with deciding the fate of Thomas gave testimony that Hutton was virtually dancing with her that night. Hutton told the

Royal Commission he had not done so.

One aspect the Royal Commission did not get to consider however was the relationship between defence counsel Kevin Ryan and the judge at the second Thomas trial, Justice Clifford Perry. There had been a history of animosity between the two, caused by a series of appeals in which Ryan had three of Perry's judgments overturned. Having Perry on the Bench for what was undoubtedly the biggest case in Ryan's long criminal law career was the worst possible scenario imaginable. Instances of how this manifested itself, to the detriment of Thomas, can be readily found in the official record of that trial. Over-ruling Ryan's objection to the confinement, but not containment, of the jury was just the beginning.

Perry's actions in a number of respects during that trial can be viewed as questionable at best, if not constituting an abuse of judicial process. One example, strongly condemned by Peter Williams QC since, was the judge's action in allowing Crown Prosecutor Morris to phone a witness in Australia to check on an aspect of cartridge case manufacture and then to put that 'evidence' in front of the jury — not from the witness box, but on the basis of a telephone conversation. This episode came at the very end of the trial and was the result of the last-minute injection into the defence case of scientist Dr Jim Sprott. Clearly, Perry did not accept the proposition that the Thomas cartridge case had been planted and sought, personally, to satisfy himself that there was no mismatch between that crucial exhibit and the number eight bullet recovered from the head of Jeanette Crewe almost three years earlier.

The trial judge went much further, however, when Kevin Ryan raised the suggestion that there was a difference between the various categories of cartridge cases made at that time. Perry ordered the Ryans to his chambers and castigated Kevin Ryan for introducing such a matter, before ordering him to apologise to the jury, on threat of holding the lawyer in contempt of court. The transcript reveals that Ryan made that apology. Seven years later the Royal Commission formally ruled that the cartridge case and the bullet had *never* been a single item — the manufacturing records proved this to be a fact — after accepting that there were very distinct differences in the measurements of the lettering on the cartridges. This was precisely what Ryan had been alluding to before he had been summoned into the judge's chambers and lambasted.

Gerald Ryan remembers the all-out assault on the defence counsel by the trial judge like it was yesterday:

What Perry did, and the way he carried on was very unfair – completely unethical – absolutely grounds for a mistrial. I had, at Kevin's request, phoned through to Ian Cook, the ICI manager in Melbourne, to ask about the lettering on the cartridges. Cook told me he'd just come off the phone from the Prosecutor [Morris]. You see this cartridge evidence had come in at a very late stage and Kevin wanted to be certain about what was being said. What Dr Sprott was alluding to involved intricate detail about the size of the lettering in various cartridge cases. It was quite hard for people to grasp and Kevin thought the best way to deal with it was to seek an adjournment so we could do more work on it, but Perry refused to allow this. Perry thought we were doing something wrong and he demanded we go into chambers immediately. The judge threatened Kevin with contempt unless he went back in front of the jury and retracted his claim that there was a difference in the lettering. Kevin held his ground, I have to give him that, but he did what Perry ordered because he had to put up the best fight possible for Thomas. The public never saw what went on and nor did the jury, all of it happened in Perry's chambers. It was a terrible thing and I felt like storming out, but the defence case had concluded by then so we stayed to allow Kevin to provide his final address. The way it happened is exactly as I have recounted it, but it was very unfair and so terribly wrong.

Two and a half years later Peter Williams QC was drawn into the Thomas case when the issue of the cartridge case was put before the Court of Appeal. He is also highly critical of a number of aspects of the retrial of Arthur Thomas, many of which have left him not only appalled, but despairing that the interests of justice were so badly perverted in such a manner:

The mere fact of a judge allowing the Prosecutor to phone someone up like that during a trial and taking a statement, which was then put before a jury as fact, is appalling quite frankly. But having allowed that, to then demand that Kevin Ryan read out an agreed statement to the effect that he had misled the jury and to force him to retract what he had said seems to me to be inexplicable and I just cannot understand a judge countenancing that type of procedure. I accept what Gerald Ryan says, after all he was there at the time and is a man of impeccable integrity. Frankly I find the threat of contempt of court even worse.

Williams insists that because the theory about the size of lettering on cartridges case was only developed in the very finishing stages of the second Thomas trial, when those questions were raised, the procedure should have been to adjourn the trial until expert witnesses could have been called to give testimony:

> It was Ian Cook in Melbourne they phoned at the end of that trial, but the point I would make about Cook was that he was not a scientist, he was the manager of a very big manufacturing company. It really took a scientist to very carefully measure that lettering, the space of them, and the height and so forth. It was a very detailed job that at that stage a layman would not have appreciated.

Williams is not the only one critical of that second Thomas trial judge. Perry's performance also came under attack from a Government scientist, who claimed that the judge's insistence that the trace impurities in wire be expressed as percentages, rather than parts per million as was the scientific norm, served only to confuse the jury.

Meat Industry Research Council scientist Dr Rod Locker told the Royal Commission on the Courts in 1977:

> The former is a cumbersome, confusing way of expressing small quantities. He [Perry] was unable to appreciate the significance of difference in the small amounts. He dismissed a 20 per cent difference in a trace impurity as trivial. The analyst [Ian Devereux] presenting the evidence felt obliged to point out to the judge that this was the equivalent of claiming there was no difference between a five foot man and a six foot man.

Locker criticised several other aspects of scientific handling of the Thomas case, including the destruction of key exhibits by the police, the restriction placed on access to key exhibits by defence scientists and the tendency of the DSIR's staff to see themselves as an arm of the police and the prosecution.

Two other serious instances of judicial misconduct occurred at that trial, also at the hands of the trial judge. The first involved an attempt by defence scientist Dr Jim Sprott to relay the detail of a conversation he had with Hutton regarding the colour of the cartridge case, exhibit 350, upon its recovery from the Crewe garden. This was an important matter as Hutton's evidence was in conflict with the officer who found the cartridge, Detective Sergeant Mike Charles, and his search companion, Detective Bruce Parkes. But Justice Perry stopped Sprott in his tracks during his testimony, making a direction that this evidence was not to be given. The Royal Commission later asked: 'Was it the position that by judicial order, you were prevented from recounting a conversation between yourself and Hutton'? Sprott confirmed that this was the case, and the transcript of the second Thomas trial attests to that.

The bias against the defence was demonstrated further in relation to the examination of exhibits. Perry permitted a key prosecution scientific witness, Donald Nelson, to remove two contested cartridge cases from the court and take them to the DSIR, in effect eliminating the requirement that they be held under strict custody of the court. The court registrar, Ian Miller, who ought to have had sole custody of these exhibits, did not accompany them when they left the precincts. Their security was compromised and it is little wonder that accusations were later levelled that there had been a switch of cartridge cases, which the Royal Commission found to be a fact. The trial judge's actions in allowing a witness to take exhibits out of the court building while a trial was in progress was grossly improper. Contrast this unwarranted concession to the prosecution with a request by defence scientist, Dr Sprott. He also wanted to examine the cartridge cases in question but assistant Crown Prosecutor David Baragwanath refused to allow this, claiming that this was not permitted as the defence had by then concluded its case.

The care of those exhibits at the second trial also deserves condemnation. The crucial exhibits – the two cartridges, labelled 343 and 350 – while in the custody of the court registrar were also being examined each morning by Crewe inquiry clerk Stan Keith. No defence representative was ever invited to be part of this daily checking ritual. This type of joint custody arrangement, known to the trial judge and seemingly sanctioned by him, was open to abuse and it was significant that the Royal Commission recorded in its formal findings that exhibit 343 had been switched during that trial, beginning the hearing as a fired cartridge, then becoming unfired, only to reappear the next day as yet another unfired cartridge with entirely different lettering.

Peter Williams QC describes the second Thomas trial as being a permanent blot on the New Zealand justice system, with Crown Prosecutor David Morris being another of the key players at whom criticism can rightly be levelled. The character assassination by innuendo he presented in his closing address, when there was no opportunity for a response from those whose reputations were on the line, is also viewed with disdain by many. The inference that the carpet in front of the Crewe's fireplace was burnt to destroy semen after a sexual attack by Thomas on Jeanette Crewe – an entirely new theory that had no basis in fact as the pathology report clearly demonstrates – was callously calculated to hammer home the final nail in the coffin for the accused.

Morris went on to then paint Vivien Thomas as the woman who had fed the Crewe baby, having been fully aware that at a hearing in the Court of Appeal only two months beforehand, in his presence, Bruce Roddick had declared on oath that she was categorically not the woman he had seen at the Crewe house two days after their murders.

Vivien Thomas spent the rest of her life feeling both frustration and anger about the way Morris besmirched her name and was still calling for an apology when she died in April 2010:

> He did this in his summing up, when I had no chance to respond. Had he done so in cross-examination, I would have rejected those accusations, of course, very strongly. Naively I thought the judge would have intervened, but he didn't. That tragic summing up from Morris remains on the record. It's part of the judicial record, for all time and for anyone to see. It's part of our legal history, but when people read it now they realise just how bad it was. But this is the length to which the police and the prosecution had to go at that time. It was a nasty fight and everyone to do with the prosecution team, I believe, knew that they had to win it because of what the police had done.

Morris' questionable tactics at that second trial did not end there. He used, again to great effect, the perjured statement of Hughes about previous visits by the accused to the Crewe farm, which he knew to be untrue. The consistent testimony of Thomas himself and of Detective Bruce Parkes demonstrated that Thomas had not been on that property while the Crewes lived there and Morris allowed Hughes to go on the stand and gave false evidence, yet again at the retrial. Morris' proclamation, at that same trial, that the bullet that killed Jeanette Crewe had been contained within the cartridge case from the Thomas rifle was also an untruth. Scientific evidence had been given that contradicted this, making it yet another example of a Crown Prosecutor being neither fair nor factual.

The part Morris played in the wrongful prosecution of Thomas, not once but twice, was significant. He had been in on the action from the very start of the Crewe inquiry, attending the scene and the major conferences prior to the decision being taken to arrest Thomas. At one of those conferences, a month after the murders, the prosecutor advised his police colleagues that he believed there was enough evidence to present a prima facie case against Demler for the killing of Harvey Crewe.

David Morris' actions should be considered in the light of the following, quoted from Conduct and Etiquette at the Bar, by W W Boulton:

Crown Counsel is a representative of the State, a 'Minister of Justice'. His function is to assist the jury in arriving at the truth. He must not urge any argument that does not carry weight in his own mind, or try to shut out any legal evidence that would be important to the interests of the person accused. It is not his duty to obtain a conviction by all means; but simply to lay before the jury the whole of the facts that compose his case, and to make them perfectly intelligible and to see that the jury is instructed with regard to the law and is able to apply the law to the facts.

This general determination of such a role is further reinforced by the classic definition of the duties of a Crown Prosecutor, delivered in 1935 by Lord Hewart, the Chief Justice of England:

It cannot be too often made plain that the business of counsel for the Crown is fairly and impartially to exhibit all the facts to the jury. The Crown has no interest in securing a conviction. Its only interest is that the right person should be convicted, that the truth be known and that justice should be done.

On the basis of those established definitions, could it be said that Morris fulfilled his obligation to the public of New Zealand, to his office and especially to Arthur Thomas, in particular at the second trial?

Kevin Ryan in closing submissions to the 1980 Royal Commission – commentary that was developed following his personal exposure to the fight to the death in which he had been involved – appropriately noted:

> I recognise that frequently the partisanship of the opposing lawyers blocks the uncovering of vital evidence or leads to a presentation of vital testimony in a way that distorts it. I shall attempt to show why we have allowed the fighting spirit to become dangerously excessive. In the Thomas trials, the Prosecutors, inflected badly by this fighting spirit, produced only the evidence that they thought would obtain convictions.

In 1978, after the Privy Council turned down a bid to have the Thomas convictions reviewed in London – it did not have the jurisdiction following the lodging of an opinion, by the Court of Appeal at the Second Referral, to the Governor-General – Morris expressed his satisfaction at having won the good fight. He declared:

> The [Thomas] matter is at an end. The campaigners can try again I suppose, and they can petition the Governor-General every day of the week, but the Thomas case is now closed.

That was Morris' sentiment, but someone had forgotten to tell the Thomas clan, and its legion of supporters throughout New Zealand – or, for that matter a Prime Minister called Muldoon. Two years later the Crown Prosecutor who made his name in the Thomas trials found himself in the witness box, undergoing torrid examination by his former opposing counsel, Peter Williams QC and Kevin Ryan. The tables had finally been turned.

Morris survived the Thomas Royal Commission, and like most of the senior counsel who appeared for parties to that inquisition, he went on to become a Supreme Court judge. Not surprisingly, his first two murder trial judgments were overturned on appeal. In the first case, the President of the Court of Appeal, Sir Robin Cooke, admonished the newly-appointed judge for thinking he was still in his old role:

> When the whole summing up is analysed in terms of substance rather than somewhat formal concessions to the defence, the overwhelming impression is that it was aimed predominantly at persuading the jury

to find murder.

Morris also received official censure from the Chief Justice, Thomas Eichelbaum – the same officer of the court who had defended the Thomas Royal Commissioners in 1982 – after making a series of inflammatory comments during trials, including using the phrase 'nigger in a wood pile', and the now infamous statement that 'if every man throughout history had stopped the first time a woman said no, the world would be a lot less exciting place'.

Upon his death on 2007, Chief Justice Sian Elias labelled Morris 'a man of high courage, the utmost integrity, considerable modesty and great personal kindness'. Understandably, the Thomases have other descriptions for him.

Fifteen judges and one stipendary magistrate were involved in the various phases of the Thomas case, with Chief Justice Sir Richard Wild a significant force. Wild's part in the Thomas affair cannot be under-estimated either. The only dissenting voice of the three-judge panel which determined, in 1973, that the Pukekawa farmer should receive a re-trial, he then went on to preside over a Full Bench 'opinion' in the Court of Appeal which denied Thomas a third trial or a pardon. This Second Referral, conducted somewhat unusually over a holiday break at the end of 1974 and the beginning of 1975, has been widely criticised for requiring that Thomas prove a negative, namely that he could not exclude the possibility that his cartridge case, exhibit 350, was ever fitted with a number eight bullet. This 'opinion' – it was not a formal judgment of that court – was completely contradictory to the basic premise in criminal law that a man is deemed to be innocent until proven guilty. Peter Williams QC records that this was the first case in the history of British law where a court not only placed the onus of proof on the appellant, but made him prove his case beyond all reasonable doubt.

Wild's attitude – hardly one of an impartial umpire – is reflected in the comment he made to a friend, while fishing on Lake Taupo in the months following the arrest of Thomas: '*We had to get someone for the Crewe murders*'. That same attitude manifested itself at the start of the appeal that followed Thomas' second double murder convictions in 1973, when he admonished Kevin Ryan for withdrawing one of the grounds for appeal, thus wasting 15 copies, each containing 500 pages at 15 cents a page. The loss to the public was around $500 – the cost of justice did not appear to come into the equation.

Wild's participation in the grave injustice perpetrated on Thomas can be no more graphically illustrated than by way of the following declaration at the Second Referral, with Christmas approaching, when the issue of the cartridge case and its relevance to the murder bullets was being truly tested for the first time:

> It goes without saying that the court will always ensure a fair hearing and it is essential that counsel has full opportunity to prepare his cross-examination and final submissions. Having regard to the foregoing, it is also necessary in the interests of justice that this protracted case be brought to an end one way or the other.

Wild should not have even been on that Bench in view of the public statements he had made criticising Thomas and his supporters, insists Peter Williams, claiming that the Chief Justice's participation went against the fundamental principle of English law that judges must be impartial and independent:

> I was completely shattered at the Second Referral by the attitude Wild displayed particularly because I had appeared before him on many occasions in previous cases and personally had found him to be very fair, and a person who would listen to both sides. On a personal level I always got on very well with him and I had great respect for him, and I am talking about over a period of quite a number of years. But somehow this Thomas case seemed to have contaminated him. I really found it so inexplicable that his attitude was so dogmatic and so anti-Thomas that he just didn't seem to be the same man. At that time the general anecdotal view was that the rule of law was more important than Thomas and that it was therefore more important, from a judicial point of view, that Thomas would fail.

Former Justice Minister Martyn Finlay also clearly took a dim view of the decision of the Court of Appeal at the Second Referral, the very last segment of a judicial process that had been running for half a decade by 1976. Following his retirement from that portfolio, he was to say that he was astonished when the Court of Appeal found that Thomas' challenge over the cartridge case had been sustained, but then to rule that his case had not been proved beyond reasonable doubt:

> As Attorney General [at that time] I could not publicly disagree with

the unanimous decision of five Supreme Court judges, but I can now say that I believe it was wrong in requiring a criminal, rather than a civil standard of proof to be met and wrong in holding that this higher standard had not, on the evidence submitted to the court, been met.

On any assessment all the factors that combined to make a case against Arthur Thomas – the interference from the trial judges, particularly Perry at the second Supreme Court hearing; the over-zealousness of the Crown Prosecutors by then in win-at-all-costs mode; the suppression of relevant and critical evidence; the refusal to allow eye-witness testimony; and the effects of a police operation geared at destroying any defence arguments as soon as they had been put – also denied him the inalienable right to a fair trial. But far from recognising this, the 'system' designed to deliver justice to the good citizens of New Zealand instead reinforced the fabrication and malpractice which had been perpetrated.

In April 1975, Sir Alfred North, a former president of the Court of Appeal and the same judge who had, in May 1972, heard Thomas' first application to have his convictions overturned, declared that it was 'quite improper for anyone to continue suggesting that Thomas had been unfairly convicted.' There was ample evidence, North proclaimed, for the convictions to be upheld. 'In this case, Thomas has received justice'.

Rejecting the suggestion that the British system for conducting criminal trails was strongly weighted against the defendant, and that investigations modelled on Europe's inquisitorial system were preferable, North declared:

> This is absolute nonsense. Our system of administering justice is *far too favourable* to accused persons and should be amended. As far as the Crewe murder case is concerned, there is no justification for anyone to suggest that the dice was loaded against the accused. Thomas has, on the contrary, received great indulgence from the authorities.

He then went on to vehemently decry the granting of a retrial for Thomas, which he insisted had been provided by the authorities on the basis of very flimsy evidence:

It will be a very sorry day for New Zealand if this sort of thing happens again. Incalculable harm has been done to our criminal justice system by these events. The system would break down if it could be subjected to these continued allegations of unfairness.

No mention was made then, or afterward, of the 'unfairness' of the acts of police officers who fabricated evidence in order to gain wrongful convictions on the most serious of all possible charges, or those of officers of the court who take an oath predicated on delivery of truth as a vital part of the system they had sworn to serve. In the words of Peter Williams QC:

Again and again we find that someone who has been convicted, and whom we believe is guilty, is actually innocent. You have to realise that our system is fallible. It relies on evidence and that people do not lie. Circumstantial evidence can be the basis of wrong inferences, and miscarriages of justice do occur. As Sir Thomas Thorp said in his report [on miscarriages of justice] several years ago, there are far more miscarriages of justice than we realise. The Thomas case was one of the most notable, but it wasn't the first and, given the fallibility of our justice system, it won't be the last.

In the end, it took the courageous decisions of the Government of the day and a Royal Commission fronted by a former Australian judge, a one-time Parliamentarian and a gentleman of the cloth to deliver justice to Arthur Thomas after the New Zealand judicial system failed him at every turn.

Seventeen

The extent of the fabrication of evidence used to successfully secure the conviction of Arthur Thomas for a double murder, not once but twice, did not rest with members of the New Zealand Police alone. The Department of Scientific and Industrial Research – now the Institute of Environmental Science and Research – played an equally devastating part in his wrongful convictions. The blame can be laid at the door of one of its most experienced scientists in particular.

The DSIR was, in the 1970s, the New Zealand Police's primary scientific agency, just as the ESR is today. But as the Thomas Royal Commission noted in 1980, the officers of this agency saw themselves as a natural extension of the police and the Crown prosecution service, rather than impartial scientific advisors prepared to provide independent testimony, irrespective of whether it proved or disproved a case. Once Dr Jim Sprott entered the Thomas case for the defence in the last days of the second trial in 1973, any semblance of balance Dr Donald Nelson – the DSIR's key officer on the Crewe homicide inquiry – may have retained went out of the door.

As revealed in chapter eight, Nelson failed to disclose to either of the trial juries that Thomas' .22 Browning pump-action rifle produced heavy scoring on bullets that was not found on the remnants of the lead taken at post mortem from either of the Crewes. He told Hutton about this on 16 October 1970, but neither of them made the Crown Prosecutor aware of this critical piece of information. At the time of the examination of the Thomas rifle and test-firing in August 1970 – just days after the recovery of Jeanette Crewe's body from the river and the disclosure she had been killed by a bullet from a .22 rifle – Nelson made notes about his findings. These were produced to the Royal Commission, but had not been disclosed at the two Thomas trials earlier in the decade. These notes recorded *'no match seen'* between the Thomas test bullets and the Jeanette Crewe bullet. Those same notes also testified to the heavy scoring marks produced by the Thomas rifle during Nelson's testing, as indeed that rifle does to this day. Ten years after making these notes, Nelson conceded to the Royal Commission that he would have expected such heavy scoring to have survived and to have been seen on the bullet taken from Jeanette Crewe, but he never provided this testimony to either of the trial juries.

The Royal Commission noted:

> In our opinion [this] substantially reduced the chances that either or both of the fatal bullets could have come from the Thomas rifle, but Dr Nelson gave no evidence relating to them at either trial. His evidence was so incomplete in the light of all these matters that it presented to the juries a false picture of his examination and findings and which of itself could have resulted in a miscarriage of justice.

In October 1973, Nelson attempted to persuade George Leighton, a senior staff member of the Melbourne factory that provided engravings used in the manufacture of cartridge cases which were sent to New Zealand for loading, to sign an affidavit declaring that the lettering on two exhibits, 343 and 350, were identical and indistinguishable. The vital ingredient of this statement was that exhibit 343, which contained a number eight bullet the same as that found in the Crewes, and 350, the Thomas rifle cartridge from the Crewe garden, were the same, but they were not. Exhibit 350 never carried a number eight bullet. Leighton refused to sign that legal document, insisting that he amend the wording. The Royal Commission recorded:

> It is apparent that Dr Nelson pressed Mr Leighton to agree to the original wording. We proposed merely to comment that this incident is indicative of a tendency on the part of Dr Nelson, manifested in other areas in far more serious ways, to shape the evidence to fit his own theories rather than to shape, and if necessary to abandon his own theories in the light of the evidence.

One of those other manifestations was the false affidavit from Nelson as to the date on which he collected another .22 cartridge case, which he suggested proved that the exhibit 350/number 8 bullet combination could have existed. Nelson's declaration in that document was that he took this cartridge, labelled 1964/2, into his possession between 26 January and 6 February *1964*. The difficulty, however, was that this cartridge was wet primed and as this process had not been used in manufacturing cases of this type until 20 October *1965*, the one Nelson labelled 1964/2 could not have come into his possession until after that date. After hearing extensive testimony on this particular matter, the Royal Commission concluded:

> Dr Nelson told us he was not aware of the difference between wet priming and dry priming in 1973. It must have come as a rude shock to him when Dr Sprott established that there was such a difference, and that [exhibit] 1964/2 was wet primed, and that it could not have been produced until after 20 October 1965. At that stage Dr Nelson had the opportunity to admit his mistake. That would have probably meant admitting his theory [on exhibit 350] was wrong and that Dr Sprott's was right. He failed to take that opportunity. Dr Nelson has for many years been an expert forensic witness for the Crown in criminal cases. It is clear that the fundamental obligation of such a witness is to tell the whole truth in the interests of justice. It is irrelevant whether his evidence helps the Crown or the defence. In our considered opinion, it is grossly improper for an expert witness for the Crown in criminal trials to allow personal vanity, and a stubborn determination to be right at all costs, to colour his evidence as Dr Nelson has done in relation to 1964/2.

A request to the DSIR, in late 1980, to produce the two test bullets from the Thomas rifle and also three from the Eyre rifle in 1970, revealed that little assistance was likely to come the Royal Commission's way. The inquisitional panel was advised that the five bullets it had requested had been lost. But miraculously, the test bullets from 58 of the other rifles examined in 1970 – none of which were of any relevance whatsoever – had been retained by the DSIR and 'would be made available if that would be of assistance'.

In his book *A Passion for Justice*, Peter Williams QC compared New Zealand's DSIR with Australia's Forensic Science Laboratory, based in Melbourne. Williams visited that agency in the course of his legal representation of Thomas in 1973, and subsequently, and was impressed with the assistance provided:

> This agency was designed to assist justice, not just to promote the police side of a prosecution. I couldn't help but compare this attitude with the adversarial stance of the DSIR in New Zealand, where not only would no help be given to the defence but bias and

dishonesty – particularly in the person of Donald Nelson – would be used to assist the police case. It's worth noting that the New Zealand Police later complained to their Australian counterparts about the assistance we were given in Melbourne, especially by the officer in charge of the firearms identification section of the laboratory. The prosecution case in relation to Thomas was always flawed by the fact that their forensic team was led by Nelson. Again and again his dishonesty would pollute the whole of the Crown case against Thomas. It was this senior scientist of the New Zealand DSIR who tried to procure a false document [from Leighton in Melbourne] to support his own fabricated evidence. The false affidavit he swore in relation to the cartridge case 1964/2 was used in what became known as the Hutton-Nelson report to Justice Minister Martyn Finlay in an effort to put the kiss of death on the pro-Thomas crusade. Ultimately though, Nelson was again proved to be a liar and a perjurer. I am sure that if he had been a defence scientist he would have been criminally charged.

For his part, Nelson accepted in his testimony to the Royal Commission – albeit after almost a decade of erroneously and doggedly supporting the false police case against Thomas – that he may not have retained the impartiality expected of him. But it was a reluctant admission, one that came at the end of a frustrating period of cross examination regarding cartridge 1964/2 from counsel assisting the Royal Commission, Michael Crewe, and chairman Judge Robert Taylor:

Taylor: He [Cook] swore that 1964/2 could not have been made in his factory prior to 1965. Do you believe him or don't you?
Nelson: I don't.
Taylor: The question is if that is true and correct you are wrong when you say you picked it up on this date in 1964.
Nelson: If you accept that as correct, but I don't accept it.
Taylor: Then you don't believe Mr Cook do you?
Nelson: Not in that respect.
Taylor: Does it not come down to this. Come hell or high water you are going to stick to this theory of your's about when 1964/2 was made whatever evidence is to the contrary. You won't concede the possibility of you being wrong about that no matter what evidence is given?

Nelson: No sir.

Taylor: You don't agree you are being pig-headed.

Nelson: I have often been accused of being this.

Taylor: Or partisan?

Nelson: This matter has become so emotionally fused that I could even concede that.

The DSIR and some of its senior staff do not stand alone in being accused of wrongdoing in the Thomas case. Officers of the Justice Department, as it was then, were also accused of actions which demonstrated a pro-prosecution bias, and in some respects, a deviation from both the law and accepted practice. The Thomas Royal Commission in 1980 found Justice Department officials at fault in a number of instances.

Peter Williams QC is scathing of the actions of officials in allowing what amounted to unbridled interaction between jurors and their police escorts, as well as the cavalier attitude they appeared to display toward the level of expenditure that was occurring:

It seems that the atmosphere in the Station Hotel during the second trial was more of a bacchanalian carnival than part of a serious judicial process. It simply defies belief that members of the jury were drinking and dancing with police officers. This is an extremely serious matter and points to major issues of integrity with the entire case.

Eighteen

In the estimation of Greg Newbold, the Thomas case was 'rotten to the core'. Now a professor of sociology at Canterbury University and one of this country's most published criminologists, his exposure to the Thomas case began in 1975, amid the stark grey walls of Paremoremo prison, to which the devastated young Pukekawa farmer had been returned two years earlier after his second round of convictions for murder. Newbold, a 24-year-old university student and part-time lecturer, was sent there after his own flimsy conviction for offering to sell heroin, for which he served five and a half years in prison. [An examination of Newbold's own case reveals that he was also convicted on the basis of perjured evidence].

One of the first people Newbold met in the maximum security yards of Paremoremo was Thomas, 'the least likely murderer you could imagine.' In the following years, the circumstances of Thomas' conviction were never far from Newbold's mind:

The Thomas case was the benchmark for bad policing in New Zealand because that is what it was. It was rotten from beginning to end. Everything was bad in that investigation, all at once. Everything was in the mix. Today you get cases that are clean, with a bit of tainting here and there. But not in the Thomas case – that was a cesspit. The police initially believed that Demler killed the Crewes and then they decided that Thomas was the one. Once they decided this they got tunnel vision and every piece of evidence they saw implicated Thomas. Then they fabricated what they didn't have to secure a conviction. You can be very sure of that. Perjury was committed in the Thomas case and not only by one detective. I think they probably lied consistently all the way through, but mostly once civilian witnesses began challenging the police version of events. The evidence demonstrates that and as head of that inquiry, Hutton was ultimately responsible. The public does not know what really went on in that case, but based on what is now emerging, people should be extremely concerned. But of course it has never been fully exposed. The average member of the public does not know.

Newbold, who was at university in Auckland when the Crewes were murdered, believes he does know. He is adamant in his belief that the crucial pieces of evidence used to secure the conviction of Thomas were both planted:

> The other parts of the axle – the stub axles – were put in his farm tip. They were put there by Johnston. He had already searched that tip and found nothing of relevance, but he then went back five days later and walked straight to those stub axles. It's just like they said later 'let's have another look at the Crewe garden'. It was a case of 'let's have another look at the farm tip', and two stub axles that match exactly the axle were found.

Newbold is adamant that perjury was committed in the Thomas trials, and at the Royal Commission, and the research he has conducted over recent decades reveals that this insidious and highly-destructive crime is practised regularly by some officers within the New Zealand Police. But it is not only the police who perjure themselves in this country's courts – defendants and witnesses do too:

> It is done in our courts all the time. Defendants do it. Some police do it. The courts have turned into a lying contest and the reason the police feel justified in committing perjury is that they believe the defendants are committing perjury.

Under existing law, the penalty upon conviction for committing perjury is a maximum of seven years in prison, although if that act is committed to achieve the conviction of someone for an offence where he or she could be jailed for three or more years, the penalty can be increased to 14 years. The strength of potential penalties for perjury is sufficient as provided for in law. The issue, Newbold says, is not the penalty, but the prosecution of those committing what should be regarded as one of the most serious assaults on law and order in this country, but isn't:

> They need to be actively prosecuting perjury. Not only punishing it but they need to prosecute it because there are times when it is clear

people have perjured themselves. The courts must start prosecuting perjury, vigorously, and sending people to prison for committing perjury. But then you would have to have the police prosecuting their own. That's difficult to achieve. I've got no doubt that police will cover for police.

The question now arises as to whether members of the New Zealand Police are today doing what they did in the Thomas case? Newbold's response:

Yes, without a doubt. The police will do whatever they can do, and they need to do, to get a conviction – perjury, planting evidence, I think they will do the whole lot, there is no question in my mind – and verballing people. Of course the police committed perjury in the Thomas case. It's been proved – they were found out, but in that most serious of cases, nothing happened to them. They were protected by their own.

Perjury is simply lying under oath, whether the evidence is given in court orally, or by way of a sworn affidavit. The lying must involve something being said by the person accused, knowing it to be false and intended by that person to mislead the court or tribunal. The Crimes Act 1961 defines perjury as 'an assertion as to a matter of fact, opinion, belief or knowledge made by a witness in a judicial hearing as part of the evidence on oath, whether the evidence is given in open court or by affidavit or otherwise, that assertion being known by the witness to be false and being intended by him to mislead the tribunal hearing the proceeding'. In this action the term 'oath' includes an affirmation, and also includes a declaration made under section 13 of the Oaths and Declarations Act 1957.

But what may surprise readers is that it took more than 160 years – Governor George Grey set up the original elements of this force in 1846 – for a police officer to be convicted of perjury in New Zealand.

In April 2002, Stephen John Tresidder, a sergeant serving at Whakatane, was convicted of that crime, in the process writing himself into New Zealand's history books. With 17 years of service under his belt, he was sentenced to nine months in prison.

At the time of the Tresidder affair, Bay of Plenty Police District Commander Gary Smith noted that this was the first conviction of a serving New Zealand police officer:

> Thankfully this is an isolated case and we are pleased that justice has been done. It's a sad day for police when an officer is convicted of a criminal offence because it erodes public confidence. It is critically important to the integrity of the organisation that officers who breach the trust associated with their oath of office are appropriately dealt with.

Tresidder, however, did not go down without a fight:

> How is it that I am the first? What about the police in the Arthur Allan Thomas case?
> Why weren't they done for perjury?

Nineteen

Arthur Thomas was incarcerated, on the basis of a case consisting largely of fabricated evidence, for nine years and five weeks. Most of that time was served in the maximum security wing of Pareremoremo prison north of Auckland. After 3322 days of imprisonment, the Pukekawa farmer was pardoned by the Governor-General of the day, Sir Keith Holyoake, on the recommendation of Justice Minister Jim McLay. He was released from Hautu prison farm near Turangi that same day, 17 December 1979. At first he thought news of his release was a hoax and he only agreed to leave the prison farm after he had received a guarantee that his pardon meant he was a man completely free of conviction. In the time he was incarcerated, two Supreme Court trials had been conducted, four hearings of the Court of Appeal concluded, and an application to the Privy Council in London lodged, the latter rejected on the ground of lack of jurisdiction.

The young Pukekawa farmer had, in effect, strolled nonchalantly into the perfect storm in late 1970. Trusting of the police, even after his arrest he believed that it was all a mistake and that the evidence would soon be found to prove his innocence. It never occurred to him that the State – in the form of the police, the Crown Prosecutors and the judiciary – could ever win. The reality is that its various arms collectively acted to ensure that they would never lose.

Over the decades since Thomas first stood in the dock at the Otahuhu Magistrate's Court on 11 November 1970 – the day he was arrested for killing two people he did not kill – many have wondered whether the New Zealand justice system could ever go so badly off the rails again.

While the clock could not be turned back for Thomas, his false imprisonment did, nevertheless, prompt significant changes to the way justice is administered in New Zealand. The recommendations which followed the delivery of the Thomas Royal Commission's report to Parliament acted as the catalyst for the legislative amendments that achieved this long-overdue overhaul. These include changes in the areas of criminal discovery, guardianship of juries, rights to jury lists, jury selection, sequestering of juries, payments and other provisions to juries and disclosure of expert evidence.

While the Official Information Act in 1982 substantially enlarged the duty of the prosecution to disclose information, perhaps the biggest advance in this area has come through the enactment of the Criminal Disclosure Act 2008. Before its introduction, prosecution obligations to disclose information to the defence was governed by a mix of legislation and common law. But that common law duty of disclosure to ensure the fairness of a trial could be quite easily circumvented, as was demonstrated in the two Thomas trials. The new law, enacted almost three decades after the Thomas Royal Commission attacked elements of the Thomas prosecution and police inquiry team for their non-disclosure of material evidence in the trials of 1971 and more particularly in 1973, does not however appear to have gone as far as the Australian law highlighted by Judge Robert Taylor, its chairman.

In the Australian High Court jurisdiction, defence lawyers were entitled, as of right, to view *everything on the police file* in relation to a specific criminal investigation, not just that which the prosecutor was intending to bring to trial. Section 16(1)(a) of New Zealand's Criminal Disclosure Act, on the other hand, decrees that a prosecutor *may withhold information* to which a defendant may otherwise be entitled if 'disclosure of the information is likely to prejudice the maintenance of the law, including the prevention, investigation, and detection of offences'.

This clause appears to have been simply cloned from that which has existed in the Official Information Act – a determination which has been used to devastating effect in very recent times by the New Zealand Police to deny me, and other legitimate researchers, documents from the Crewe homicide file.

What is of particular concern under this clause of both Acts is the ability of a Prosecutor to deny information to the defence based on an assertion by the police that it could prejudice the maintenance of the law in a case where police practice is being called into question. On the face of the legislation as it stands, full access to an investigation file by defence counsel, as of right, is still not guaranteed on this side of the Tasman. This is in sharp contrast to enlightened law which, on the word of Justice Robert Taylor, was in existence in Australia pre-1980, when he chaired the Thomas Royal Commission.

Granted, the new legislation is a vast improvement on the hotchpotch of duties on the Crown which existed when Arthur Thomas was hauled into the dock for the first time in November 1970, but if justice is derived from truth, what harm can be done on providing those defending accused persons to provide full and unfettered access to all the information the police have gathered in the course of their investigation into an alleged crime? This would have the merit of consistency with Europe's inquisitorial system whose basic premise is a search for the truth – and from truth flows justice. The Thomas case demonstrated categorically that where police adopt unlawful practices, anything less than full disclosure can bring serious miscarriages of justice. Giving the investigators the chance, through a Crown Prosecutor, to slide out from beneath full disclosure via the mechanism of clause 16(1)(a) of the Criminal Disclosure Act would appear, on the experience gained from such historical cases, to be a deficiency which warrants review, sooner rather than later.

Another practice which contributed to the wrongful conviction of Arthur Thomas was the unlimited challenges permitted to the Crown in the jury selection process. In 1970, the Crown's ability to keep standing aside potential jurors, when the defence was allowed only six challenges, meant that eventually the prosecution could achieve a stacked jury. This was what was achieved, in effect, in the second Thomas trial. This added significantly to the unfairness that occurred as a result of the significant vetting of the jury list by the police over the three weeks before that crucial retrial began.

The Juries Act 1981 and the Jury Rules 1990 now govern the preparation of jury lists and determine who is responsible for the preparation of the final panel for jury selection. The Act brought in the year after the Thomas Royal Commission concluded states that the registrar must comply with a request to make a copy of the jury list available for inspection by eligible persons at a time not earlier than seven days before the commencement of the week in which potential jurors will be summoned to attend for service. The law now gives the Crown and the defence the same number of challenges – four apiece, or in the case of two or more accused being tried together, eight apiece.

A new Juries Amendment Bill was reported back to Parliament in July 2011. This seeks to change the reference to 'constable' in the eligible person definition by ensuring that only police employees who are performing the function of the police in respect of the proceedings but who are not personally concerned with the facts of the case, or closely associated with a party, witness or prospective witness are an eligible person. The Ministry of Justice advises that it expects this Bill to be reinstated in the first session of the new Parliament and that it will continue through the Parliamentary process during 2012.

The sequestering of the juries at both the first and second Thomas trials was stridently opposed by defence counsel before those hearings began. In both cases the applications for jury members to be permitted to go home at night were rejected by the trial judges, Henry and Perry. Antics such as those of some members of the second Thomas trial jury, while confined in the Station Hotel in this manner for almost three weeks in 1973, are significantly less likely to occur now that the Juries Amendment Act 2008 has abolished routine sequestering of juries and it is now only in unusual or serious cases that this can be ordered.

Strict rules around payments to jury members, the manner in which they are accommodated, and the provision of refreshments and meals have also been strengthened via the Jury Rules 1990, removing the ability for juries to be wined and dined with no apparent restrictions, as occurred in 1973. New court instructions from 2002 now dictate that juries should not be taken outside courthouses for meals, smoking breaks, or fresh air during their retirement for deliberations without the express leave of the trial judge, and court managers now have to settle on areas where jurors can get fresh air without significant possibility of coming into contact with others. Additionally, the potential for police officers to get too close to jury members, on a personal level – thereby denying the partiality that is required to achieve a fair and unbiased trial – has also been removed. The recommendation of the Thomas Royal Commission on this matter was adopted, albeit 22 years later, and jury members are now accompanied by an escort who is a court staff member sworn in for this purpose. In cases where jury breaks must necessarily be in areas to which other people have access, consideration must now be given to swearing in a second jury escort.

Sadly, in contrast to these significant legislative changes on the 'justice' side of the Crown ledger, there appears to have been no corresponding far-reaching, substantive amendments to the laws that govern how criminal investigations are conducted in New Zealand since the Thomas Royal Commission of 1980. The ability for certain police officers to suppress material evidence, to ignore information that would prove the innocence of a suspect, to fabricate and to perjure themselves appears to remain as strong today as it was in 1970. A succession of criminal investigations since the 1970s – some high profile and others generally known only within their own local communities – in which there have been serious allegations of police malpractice demonstrates that the 'modus operandi' in some sections of that law enforcement agency remains unchanged. The personnel may be different, but the methods used to secure convictions of those whom officers believe to be guilty are still as effective now as they were in the Thomas case, more than 40 years ago.

In 1989, largely as a result of years of debate about police accountability – sparked in no small way by tactics and methods adopted by the police as they slashed and smashed their way through demonstrators during the Springbok rugby tour of 1981 – a Police Complaints Authority (PCA) was established. Prior to that development, complaints against the police were investigated internally, as graphically demonstrated by then Commissioner Bob Walton and his executive team when they determined that there was no evidence to prosecute Bruce Hutton for his role in the failed Crewe investigation and the malpractice that followed.

The PCA was replaced by the Independent Police Conduct Authority in November 2007, largely due to concerns about its resourcing and the perception that it lacked independence. Those same concerns are still being openly expressed about its successor, despite appointments to that agency being governed by Parliament and having a sitting High Court judge as its chairman.

But it is the culture of the New Zealand Police that remains of greatest concern and in no more significant way than the approach that agency has taken – more correctly, not taken – toward actively pursuing the murderers of Jeanette and Harvey Crewe, gunned down in their home at Pukekawa on 17 June 1970, and in failing to put its own 'criminal' element on trial in the aftermath of the original homicide investigation. In 2011, the consultancy firm PricewaterhouseCoopers determined in the latest of a series of reports commissioned by the Government that the New Zealand Police 'at all levels needs to grasp there is a need for fundamental change.' That report went on to observe:

> Senior management lacks the confidence and adeptness to make bold, circuit-breaking, and symbolic moves that will change the DNA of the organisation, signal to staff at all levels that poor performance and behaviour will not be tolerated, and that a new type of leader in police will be fostered and advanced. Management has tolerated a continuation and even appointment of some of the wrong people in high places. Managers have sometimes failed to act decisively on

high profile incidents when a strong gesture has been required.

On that same day in 2011, Commissioner Howard Broad, just weeks off retirement, observed that his job had been to change the culture of the New Zealand Police, but that it had been a more difficult task than he had anticipated 'given the attitudes of many officers'. He went on to suggest that part of the problem was that the bad habits of some within his force were ingrained.

Pat Vesey, the uncle of Vivien Thomas who spearheaded the Thomas Retrial Committee after it was formed following the rejection of the first appeal, is best qualified to offer the last word on two issues that have enveloped New Zealand's police force in a black cloud since the middle of 1970:

It is bad enough when a guilty person is part of a family who have to come to terms with it. But to have a completely innocent person convicted on lies and made-up evidence is absolutely soul-destroying. If capital punishment had been retained, Arthur Thomas would be dead now. The damage to a falsely convicted person is tragic. But the loss of trust in the police and in the justice system by such a large number of people is just as tragic. At the end of the Royal Commission in November 1980, we expected two things – that the police who perpetrated this disgraceful misconduct would be charged, and that the police would actively re-launch their investigation into who killed the Crewes, because Arthur Thomas did not. We always expected those police to be charged and 40 years on we still expect them to be charged. This generation of police officials insists that their organisation is vastly different to the one that existed in the 1970s. If that's the case, let's see them prove it by cleaning up the mess. We also expect that for Rochelle Crewe's sake, every attempt must be made to find the person or persons responsible for the murder of her parents. As a country we owe her that.

Postscript

It is Wednesday 17 June 1970, mid-evening. The infant girl is sleeping deeply. It has been a hectic day – an hour or so of play with a visitor's daughter just before lunch, an afternoon at the stock sale at Bombay, shopping at Tuakau and then home – to a warm fire and familiarity. Only a light snack is required for dinner, followed by a warm bath and bed. Then a noise unfamiliar to her – the sharp crack of what sounds like a fire cracker exploding close by; an agonising scream, shouting, profanities like she has never experienced before, and never wants to hear again, then a solid thud, another sharp crack and a series of low moans just the width of a corridor away. Silence returns, bar the incessant driving rain on windows and winter winds howling through the trees, and the heavy breathing of a man pausing momentarily to consider the enormity of what he has just done, and contemplation of what he must do next.

Of course it is not known just what Rochelle Crewe heard that fateful June 1970 night. It was unlikely that she recognised the shots from a rifle – her father's shotgun was only ever used for duck-shooting hundreds of kilometres to the south, in the Wairapapa district where he had been raised.

It is also unlikely that at her tender age she was able to decipher the sounds that followed what had obviously been a sudden, violent and traumatic series of incidents; the dragging of something heavy across the lounge to the front door; the metallic clash of steel on brick as not one but two lifeless forms were transported by barrow from the scene of vicious crimes to a place where eyes could not pry; and the removal of bedspreads from adjoining rooms to serve as coverings on a potentially incriminating ride to the river.

Rochelle Crewe's story is, however, known to the person, or persons, who tended her during the five subsequent days – until the mid afternoon of Monday 22 June when she was taken by her grandfather to the home of a family friend to be cared for. From that time onward, the orphaned daughter of Jeanette and Harvey Crewe became public property, although it is a role she undoubtedly never courted, nor welcomed. Forty two years on, the question of who killed her parents is still regularly asked, but for many New Zealanders, the enigma of who fed the baby remains equally intriguing.

During the four decades or so since Rochelle Crewe's mother and father had their lives so cruelly ended, a good deal more has emerged about what many view as New Zealand's greatest cold case. As disclosed subsequently – and reinforced in this book – members of the New Zealand Police set about manufacturing an entire prosecution case against Arthur Thomas, a man whose only connection with Rochelle's mother had been time together at primary school and a teenage infatuation.

What can be stated, with the utmost certainty, is that justice has never been delivered – either to Rochelle Crewe or to the families of those who came forward freely to assist the police in their investigation into the murders of her parents, only to be labelled dog thieves, liars and nasty, vicious individuals.

In recent times Rochelle has, quite properly, come out strongly to condemn the New Zealand Police for failing to actively re-launch the investigation into the murder of her mother and father following the damning findings of malpractice delivered by the Thomas Royal Commission in November 1980.

Demanding that the State agency responsible for law and order in this country now fulfill that responsibility, Rochelle has sought an inquiry into why the police have so doggedly resisted this task for what has been almost the entirety of her life. She is angry about that and justifiably so. The survivor of those terrible events at Pukekawa in June 1970 insists that had the police reopened their inquiry into the killing of her parents following the pardon provided to Thomas in 1979, the unnecessary injustice to her family may have ended. It has not.

Rochelle Crewe has accused the police of seeking to avoid the truth in order to protect their image. She has questioned why the findings of the Royal Commission of Inquiry were sufficient to grant Thomas some $1 million in compensation for wrongful arrest and imprisonment but not sufficient to result in the police officers involved being charged with criminal acts. Her statements mirror those of the families who came under unjustified attack from members of the original Crewe inquiry squad. The Thomases, the Hewsons, the Roddicks, the Veseys and the McGuires have never received an apology for the unfounded and malicious allegations made against their kin by the New Zealand Police.

Other cold cases of that era – the unsolved killings of Olive Walker and Mona Blades for example – are now being re-investigated. The question has to be asked – why is the New Zealand Police so loath to actively pursue the Crewe murders?

Police Association president Greg O'Connor has publicly backed a call for an independent inquiry into the Crewe murders and the Thomas case, saying generations of law enforcers, including himself, have been tainted by that inquiry and its aftermath. O'Connor is right to object that current and future members of the New Zealand Police ought not to be tainted by the actions of a small group of the 'good guys' who in the 1970s became the 'bad guys'. Both O'Connor and the Police Commissioner appointed in 2011, Peter Marshall, insist that the culture of their agency and those who serve is now much different from that of the 1960s and 1970s. They have a rare opportunity – possibly the last ever as far as the Crewe investigation is concerned – to demonstrate that this is actually the case.

Crimes were committed at Pukekawa, during 1970 and in the years that followed. The killing of Jeanette and Harvey Crewe was chilling in its callousness. The disposal of their bodies in the flood-swollen Waikato River nearby was an act intended to obliterate those crimes – an act of obstructing the course of justice. To abandon an infant, to all intents and purposes alone, in a cold house in the middle of winter for five days is a bizarre feature of a crime that in so many respects was unlike anything police in this country have ever had to deal with. Yet, a series of equally repugnant crimes followed those acts, this time perpetrated by members of the New Zealand Police. Justice has eluded Jeanette and Harvey Crewe. Justice has never been delivered for their orphaned child, Rochelle, nor has it been done, or seen to be done, for the families mowed down by a law enforcement machine that ran so badly off the rails.

If the New Zealand Police wish to give real and genuine credence to their claim to be indeed a vastly different agency from that which existed in a less enlightened, less sincere and less honest era of policing in this country, they should utilise their twenty-first-century methods and technology, to vigorously re-investigate the execution of a loving and dedicated young couple who had everything to live for.

The Crewe murder inquiry of 1970 has been revealed for what it was, an abject failure. The Thomas case that followed those crimes has, equally, been shown to be the worst example of police malpractice New Zealand has ever seen. Only the New Zealand Police of today can remedy those historic ills – and only when that occurs will true justice be provided to all those who have spent more than 40 years seeking it.

Appendix 1

Report of the Thomas Royal Commission:
Identification of exhibit 350 [08 July 1980]

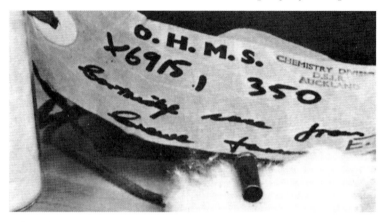

Before the Commission continues hearing evidence relating to Term of Reference 1(a), it is desirable to identify and define the cartridge case (exhibit 350).

1. Exhibit 350 was a dry primed brass long rifle cartridge case, manufactured by IMI Australia Ltd.

2. Such dry primed cartridge cases as exhibit 350 were made by IMI with a steel tool known as a bumper, which stamped the lettering ICI on the base of the cartridge case as it formed its rim. The bumper was in turn manufactured from a steel tool known as a hob, which had the letters ICI engraved on its surface.

3. The engravers of hobs used by IMI were C G Roeszler and Sons Pty Ltd, and Mr Leighton of that company gave evidence that from a practical point of view, two hobs engraved on different occasions would have lettering of distinguishable shape and appearance overall. His opinion was supported on a theoretical basis by Professor Mowbray's eloquent exposition.

4. Mr Cook's evidence, confirmed by that of Dr Sprott from his examination of the IMI records, was that:-

a. Two hobs engraved by Roeszlers arrived at IMI on 1 October 1963

b. Retained samples of cartridge cases consistent with those hobs, and with exhibit 350, first appeared in the retained samples of IMI in March 1964.
    We are satisfied that the hobs which arrived on 1 October 1963 were the source of Dr Sprott's category 4 [cartridges], and of exhibit 350.

5. Some of the .22 long rifle cartridges manufactured by IMI were then shipped to Auckland, New Zealand, where the Colonial Ammunition Co Ltd (CAC) then loaded them with projectiles and distributed them to the New Zealand market as full cartridges. Until 10 October 1963, .22 brass cartridges were loaded by CAC with their pattern 8 projectiles [lead bullets], bearing three cannelures. After that date, pattern 18 or 19 projectiles bearing two cannelures were used. It follows that exhibit 350 was loaded with a pattern 18 or pattern 19 projectile.

6. At the conclusion of his evidence, Mr MacDonald, the senior DSIR witness, accepted that it was less than probable that exhibit 350 contained a pattern 8 bullet.

7. Therefore, the Commission identifies exhibit 350 as a dry primed, .22 long rifle cartridge case, manufactured by IMI in Australia after March 1964, bearing the headstamp ICI, and loaded by CAC in Auckland with a two cannelure pattern 18 or pattern 19 projectile. It was fired in the Thomas rifle, exhibit 317, but when and where we are unable to say at this stage.

8. This identification of exhibit 350 will enable those who are concerned with the first paragraph of the Terms of Reference to be aware of the subject matter and area of inquiry into whether there was any impropriety on any person's part in the course of the investigation or subsequently, in respect of the cartridge case, exhibit 350.

Appendix 2

Police conference held at the Otahuhu CIB
[19 October 1970 - 1.30pm]

Present:
Detective Inspector Bruce Hutton
Detective Inspector Wally Baker
Detective Senior Sergeant Pat O'Donovan
Detective Senior Sergeant Les Schultz
Detective Sergeant Jim Tootill
Detective Len Johnston
Detective Bruce Parkes
Detective Stan Keith

Hutton: We have cause to have another look at the Crewe murders prior to the departure of Detective Inspector Baker and Detective Senior Sergeant O'Donovan and the main reason for holding it is to try and collectively gather all information, both from within the squad and also from an insight into the file that Mr Baker and Mr O'Donovan have conducted in an effort to bring the enquiry to a satisfactory conclusion.

I think that it can be said at this stage that there are two persons who can be considered as suspects in the enquiry, namely:-

(a) Lenard William Demler
(b) Arthur Allan Thomas

There is no other evidence suggesting any other person, even remotely, as a possible suspect.

Baker: Bearing in mind the evidence pointing toward Demler, namely the blood in his car, a motive of kinds and, of course, opportunity, I think the weakness at this stage is that we have got to put a firearm towards Demler more than we have at this stage and here again I think that you cannot put a firearm towards him. It can be said that one of two, either (1) that he has acquired one and we don't know anything about it and could be thrown in the river after use or disposed of after use, or (2) is the possibility of him acquiring a firearm like that one of

Eyre's where you have got a firearm on the back verandah of the place, and if a guy was this way inclined he could get it.

Another thing as far as Demler is concerned, because of the inhospitable nature of the two deceased, we are up against just what goes on in the house and we are dependent on Demler and because of this you just cannot contradict him. As far as the disposal of the bodies and the attempt at cleaning the place up and the burning, I would not like to theorise on that at all. As the result of our discussion with Demler the other day he could easily do it and wouldn't turn a hair, this would be my picking of him. He showed no remorse whatever about anything you spoke about and whether, of course, this is his nature or that but he just never batted an eye-lid. I think we gave him plenty of opportunity if he was ever going to show any weakness. As far as sentiment or anything like that went, there was nothing there.

O'Donovan: I felt about him a marked reluctance to talk about or volunteer any information about either of the Crewes and anything you wanted had to be extracted from direct questions whereas in fact on quite a number of occasions he turned to Mr Tootill and made conversation on other matters relating to the farm which I thought was particularly odd, as though he was not interested in the death of his daughter.

Hutton: I might mention at this stage that Mrs Crewe [senior] forwarded me a letter on date which she had previously received from Lenard William Demler and it read as follows:-

RD1 Tuakau
15th October 1970

Dear Marie
I have been wondering when Harvey's funeral would be. Did you know that we provided for Harvey to be buried with Jeanette. Could you let me know the date of the funeral and what arrangements you would like. I have been thinking about Rochelle. How is she? Hope she is settling down quite happily. Would like to get some news soon.
Yours sincerely
Len

Baker: This is in-keeping with the whole make-up of this fellow.
Hutton: As far as Demler is concerned, taking the motive, I agree

with you Wal that the motive is really weak. There is the suggestion of $12,000 worth of shares with perhaps in addition to the transfer of the motor car being a possible motive – the cause of an argument between Demler on one side and Jeanette and Harvey on the other, and the fact that Jeanette of course has entered into the running of the Demler estate in the form of a trustee as a result of Maisey Demler's will. So much for the motive.

Now so far as the evidence of Demler having committed the crime, there are three things that have caused me some concern and these are:-

  (a) the firearm
  (b) the axle
  (c) the wire found around the bodies

In regard to the firearm, strenuous efforts have been made to put a .22 calibre weapon in the possession of Demler. We all know that these enquiries covered what is described as a combination weapon but even today *it would not be said that we can prove that Lenard Demler has a .22 firearm* with which he could have committed these murders. In regard to the axle, *here again we have no evidence that an axle of a similar description as that found with the body of Harvey Crewe was ever on the Demler farm or in his possession.*

Finally, in regard to the copper wire and galvanized wire found around the bodies, tests conducted on similar gauge wire taken from the Demler farm have revealed that none of the exhibit wire came off the Demler property. Perhaps I might mention that the only similar wire found was a piece of copper wire discovered in the small paddock immediately in front of the small house gate of the Crewe household after the commission of these offences. One must surely presume from the finding of this similar wire that at the time the offender placed the bodies in a motor car he was at least in possession of the copper wire and used it to truss the bodies with and even perhaps suggests he may have had the axle also.

O'Donovan: I feel that it would be very doubtful that the axle came from the dump on that particular night. You will recall the blood under Harvey's chair – it indicates to me that at the time the blood stopped falling Harvey was still in the chair and had not been moved. You will also recall that the chair was moved back. To me it does not appear that Harvey's body was removed on the following day. If this had been so I don't think the blood drag marks would have been left on the floor, so they must have left there that night. So that if we assume that Harvey's body was removed on the night of the murders, would it not be stretching the imagination to think that the murderer went from Harvey's house to the tip, stumbled around in the dark on a windy wild night and located an axle which could weight down one body and something else unknown to weigh down the other body. I feel that we have got to consider that he went to the house prepared to dump those bodies in the river.

Schultz: I agree this is quite probable. You have got fragments of wire and that if a man had gone to all the trouble of doing this he would go prepared with wire or what you would like to tie the body up with at some stage, probably in the house or near the front gate. I think that the blood on the side of the house was from the head – it was a very faint mark and in the early part of it it faded quite a lot. I think myself that you have not got jointed bits of wire – stacks of stuff to tie bodies with.

Tootill: It is not consistent with short ends tied together – just one more piece he had not utilised.

Hutton: I am satisfied that the offender was short of wire at the time he actually trussed the bodies up. Now this is a different thing to saying he was short of wire from the source he acquired this wire from.

Parkes: I think perhaps he only intended taking one body away. I cannot help feeling that whoever did it was aiming for murder-suicide. Because there was that much blood he had to change his mind and take both of them away and that is why he ran out – went to truss up one body and had two bodies to get rid of.

O'Donovan: Taking this a step further, would that explain the attempt to clear up Jeanette's blood by the fireplace?

Baker: Furthermore, while on this aspect of it, if there had been any sexual interference here is another reason why he would want to get rid of Jeanette but not Harvey to make it look like Jeanette had knocked Harvey off. Here again we have got two bodies with two different lots of blood and I mean these are the sorts of thing Pat and I have talked a lot of this between ourselves. *We have not overlooked the possibility of two people being there.*

Hutton: So far as Harvey's body is concerned, there was copper wire wound around the shoulders, under one armpit and over the other shoulder, purely to hold clothing on the body. From the bedspread we found with wire around it we know that the wire had been wound around Harvey's neck to keep that on to stop blood getting on perhaps the offender's car. Insofar as the weight is concerned, wire passed twice around Harvey's body in the region of the abdomen had been tied and later the axle weight had been fastened to this wire with a piece of copper wire 8 inches or 9 inches long.

Further to this, Jeanette's body had just one single strand of copper wire wound tightly around the two legs just above the knees and there were clear indications that another piece of wire had been passed through for the purpose of holding a weight and had since broken off due to the constant friction of the two wires.

O'Donovan: If he went to the house with the intention of disposing of the bodies he would have plenty of wire to weigh them down but for the unforeseen circumstance of so much blood which necessitated the use of more wire to bind the bedclothes on. I think in consideration of the murders I do not think you can ignore the burglaries and the previous fires. If it is to be considered that they are relevant to the murder inquiry this would more or less indicate that Demler had nothing to do here because on one of those occasions at least Crewe was with Demler at the time of the incident – the burglary.

Baker: I also think that if we are going to consider that any of these previous incidents are connected with the murder, it tends to eliminate anyone from outside the area. This is one of the things we looked at very initially Pat, because I say you have this apparently happily married couple with a young baby visiting the old stamping grounds three weeks before the murder. This I think could tend to inflame someone that we have never attached much importance to but the thing possibly against this is that that person would have to be up here on at least one of those previous occasions if we are going to link these incidents and I don't think you can disregard them because they are three incidents dealing with only one farm in the neighbourhood and one couple in the neighbourhood.

O'Donovan: I think that in addition to the burglary you have to consider the odd stuff that was taken at the time of the burglary – a brush and comb set, engagement ring and I think a necklace, all the property of Jeanette, when there was money in the house.

Schultz: I myself don't think they are connected. They are too remote in time. It is over 18 months since the last one before the murder – that was when Jeanette was in the home with the baby.

Baker: The relevant dates are:

Burglary - 20 July 1967

Fire in house - 7 December 1968

Fire in hay barn - 28 May 1969

Hutton: Just looking at those dates, they bear no resemblance to Jeanette and Harvey's wedding anniversary, if they have any bearing to the commission of these two murders.

Schultz: I think we are clouding the issue with those things.

Baker: Here again that is why we are here. There are so many bits and pieces.

Hutton: If these fires and burglaries have any bearing into the deaths of these two people and the offender is not Demler, surely one would have expected them to have known and to have mentioned who they feared this person was as the facts must surely indicate that for a person to commit these offences and then to commit murder they must have a real grudge indeed against the Crewe couple.

Baker: I cannot agree more. Harvey was always saying 'who would do this to me?' or words to that effect. He mentioned [name deleted from conference transcript by police] that was any suspect.

Schultz: Were the words 'who would do this to me?' or 'why should this happen to me?'

O'Donovan: I don't think they really gave the intention Harvey thought he was being got at or it was something sent from above.

Tootill: I think if they had known some person had a definite grudge against them there would have been some mention of it in letters or diaries or something.

Schultz: He would be quick to seize on a point like that.

Baker: I think Demler would have been the first one in the lead.

Tootill: I think Harvey would have taken some definite action to offset any danger.

O'Donovan: I think this was committed in anger.

Hutton: So far as Len Demler is concerned, I think that it would be fair to say that against him:-

1. His actions prior to and after discovery of the blood-stained house
2. Lack of remorse
3. Non-assistance in search
4. Blood in his car of the same group as Jeanette's
5. Scratch on his back – explanation for this obviously not acceptable
6. Explanation concerning:-

    a. Blood

    b. Likely suspects [names deleted from conference record by police] and unidentified mushroom picker

    c. Movements (note found in his [Demler's] possession to assist memory)

7. Knowledge that he has sufficient strength to move two bodies

8. Proximity to the scene of offence, opportunity for, availability of ready transport and unlikelihood of detection

Hutton: Facts against Demler possibly being offender:-

a. *Lack of evidence re .22 firearm or any of this calibre of ammunition in his possession*

b. *Lack of evidence re axle being in his possession*

c. Lack of similar wire being found in his possession to that found around the bodies

d. Indications that in relation to the fires and burglaries that he is not likely to have committed one of the burglaries as there was a suggestion that he may have been home and visited by the Crewes when this crime was committed

e. Lack of other blood stains in either of Demler's vehicles, similarly lack of fibres from blankets etc

Hutton: We will now discuss the other suspect for these offences, Arthur Allan Thomas. [segment deleted from conference record by police]

Johnston: History re trailer with 1929 front axle, formerly the property of [segment deleted from conference record by police]. A Mr Shirtcliife owned a 1929 Nash car in 1956. At that stage he moved from Auckland to Pukekawa and took with him a trailer which had had made up from a 1929 Nash axle assembly with pressed steel wheels. He subsequently sold this trailer shortly after he arrived at Pukekawa to an unknown person at Meremere. This person's name is probably G A Whyte. This person in turn sold it to Allan Thomas, father of Arthur Thomas, on 14 April 1959. This was the date shown on the transfer on the ownership papers in relation to the trailer. Shirtcliffe was shown the axle recovered from the body of Harvey Crewe and he was unable to positively identify the axle. However attached to the axle was a portion of the tie rod which had been drilled in a similar manner to the way Shirtcliffe had anchored the wheels of the axle, that is the tie rod had been drilled to allow the U bolts to hold the tie rod to the axle.

A G Thomas was subsequently seen and the ownership papers in relation to the trailer were obtained from him. When asked as to the present whereabouts of the trailer *he was unable to tell us.* However *he thought that the trailer had been left on the farm prior to him leaving it in 1964.* Another son, *Richard Thomas, told the police that he thought this trailer had been left at Meremere* where a new trailer had been made up from the parts of the original trailer. Rod Rasmussen, now residing at Meremere, who made the new trailer up for A G Thomas said that he could not recall retaining the old axle from Thomas' trailer as it would have been of no use to him. As far as he could recall the axle and two wheels were taken away by Richard Thomas when the new trailer was made. Arthur Thomas has been seen and his farm searched *but the trailer could not be found there.*

Baker: Also, this trailer is registered for the 70/71 period isn't it?

Johnston: Yes. Two trailers have been registered by A G Thomas – one is in his possession now and also a second trailer which was first registered on 14 April 1959.

Hutton: This information has been obtained from an interview of [segment deleted from conference transcript by police] and has yet to be verified. Mr Parkes, concerning the previous interview of Thomas when it was considered he was a possible suspect, can you give a brief summary of your impressions of Thomas, his build and that type of thing.

[segment deleted from conference transcript by police]

Schultz: Do you think his wife would support him if he had done this murder?

Parkes: I don't think she would. I don't think she is covering up for him. I have since seen him again and have spoken with him three or four times and we have never got through to him as much as before when it was put to him that he was the offender. He is more cagey now – expecting to get his face slapped.

Johnston: Wire was taken from the old cow shed adjacent to the present one on the Thomas farm. It should be noted that a piece of copper wire was joined to galvanized type of wire, probably electric fence wire. Also a packet of .22 ammunition, hollow nose, was taken. There is plenty of electric fencing wire on the farm. There could be more copper wire. I thought the way the wire was tied on his farm was somewhat similar to the wire on the body, looped through and twisted.

Hutton: Prior to throwing it open for any other discussions, I will just briefly cover the position concerning the two suspect firearms.

As a result of further examination by Dr Nelson on Sunday the 18th, we have now reached the following stage. The two suspect firearms belong to:-

(a) Arthur Allan Thomas

(b) Eyre family

During this inquiry some 70 odd .22 firearms have been test fired and all but the Eyre and Thomas firearms have been excluded. These two firearms are both pump action

Remingtons and have lands with a right hand twist in the barrels. The lands in both weapons are identical in width. The Eyre firearm has no individual groove marks whatsoever which would help identify it as the firearm that had fired any particular bullet. The Thomas firearm has five lands with no individual markings but the 6th land in test firing has revealed two slight marks which would very likely be sufficient to identify it as the rifle that fired a particular bullet. The bullet recovered from the head of Jeanette Crewe has six lands with right handed twist suggesting that it was possibly fired from a weapon of the same make. The five lands which are clearly identifiable on the exhibit bullet have no individual groove marks and unfortunately the six land is badly scored, very likely as a result of coming in contact with bone structure.

The remains of the bullet, which I might mention were badly fragmented, recovered from the body of Harvey Crewe would indicate that in one of the three lands visible two small marks which may or may not be similar to the marks revealed on the sixth land of a test fired bullet from the rifle of Thomas. I might add that I have used the phrase that it may or may not bear some resemblance to the marks on the test fired bullets from Thomas' rifle due to the fact that the bullet which entered Harvey Crewe's skull was so badly fragmented that Dr Nelson feels he must say that the marks that are visible in one of the three lands may possibly have been caused by contact with bone structure either at the point of entry of where the bullet ultimately broke up on the right side of Harvey Crewe's skull. Dr Nelson points out it is possible that similar individual marks may have been on the sixth land of the bullet recovered from the skull of Jeanette, and that the bone structure may have caused the erasure of those marks.

O'Donovan: I think you have covered it fairly well against him – suspect rifle, previous association, and axle which *may* lead back to the Thomas farm.

Parkes: The association with Jeanette was in 1960 [deleted from conference transcript by police].

O'Donovan: Another thing which intrigues me about the brush and comb set given by Thomas to Jeanette and she had one stolen in the burglary – not the same one.

Parkes: He was living at [place deleted from conference transcript by police].

Baker: [segment deleted from conference transcript by police].

Johnston: Jeanette was working at Maramarua. He left the company he was working for after working there for five years and went into the forestry at Maramarua at the time Jeanette was working in the district.

Baker: [segment deleted from conference transcript by police].

Parkes: [segment deleted from conference transcript by police].

Johnston: At the Onewero Golf ball he saw Jeanette and Harvey there and never spoke to them - that was after they were engaged.

Baker: [segment deleted from conference transcript by police].

Johnston: [segment deleted from conference transcript by police].

Parkes: And also the Demler house.

Johnston: [segment deleted from conference transcript by police] about the same time as the Crewes.

Hutton: Points against Thomas:

1. Possible motive – jealousy
2. Previous relationship – infatuation
3. Firearm (suspect rifle)
4. Proximity to scene
5. Availability of transport
6. Knowledge of Crewe farm through having worked there
7. Axle (yet to verify whereabouts of similar axle on trailer formerly the property of A G Thomas)
8. Fire and burglaries. (If these are connected Thomas could be implicated as it will be noticed that one of these incidents has occurred for each year following the marriage of Jeanette and Harvey Crewe, culminating in the double murder in the fourth year).

Points in favour of Thomas not being the offender:-

1. Alibi for the evening of 17-6-70 – appears as though wife and boarder will verify that he was home on the night in question and did not go out
2. Well thought of in the district

3. Married man – well settled on homestead farm
4. Time lapse since association with Jeanette

Points to be covered re Thomas:

1. Finances
2. Examination thereof re possibility of being identical with no. 8 ammunition similar to bullet recovered from both bodies
3. Wire – further search to be made of farm for copper and galvanized wire similar to that found on bodies, and together with present exhibits of wire from Thomas farm to be taken or sent to Wellington for examination
4. Verify movements for all of 17 June 1970 re possibility of Thomas attending the clearance sale at Bombay and the ratepayers' meeting at Glen Murray
5. Further attempts to be made to identify as many persons as possible attending that meeting
6. Thomas' whereabouts during previous fires and burglaries – employment check may assist
7. M.O [medical officer] check
8. Reading material
9. Query re non-participation in search for bodies
10. Close inspection of transport
11. Pliers

Conference considered that *apart from Thomas and Demler*, from the enquiries *there does not appear to be any other person involved.*

Conference concluded that *every effort must be made to immediately either confirm Thomas as a suspect or exclude him altogether from the inquiry.*

Appendix 3

Extracts from the two reports of independent investigator Robert Adams-Smith QC, delivered to Prime Minister Rob Muldoon [January 1979 and in December 1979]

SCOPE OF ENQUIRY

The purpose of the enquiry was to ascertain the validity of the alleged identification by one Bruce Roddick of a woman seen at the Crewe property on Friday the 19th of June 1970.

FINDINGS

1. In the morning of Friday the 19th June 1970 there was a woman, as described to the police by Bruce Roddick, in the vicinity of the Crewe house.

2. The sighting of the woman by Roddick was sufficient for Roddick accurately to state that the woman he saw was not a person known to him.

3. Roddick was, and is, unable from that sighting to positively identify any person as the woman he saw.

4. Roddick has not purported positively to identify any person as being the woman he saw on Friday the 19th June 1970. He has selected photographs of two women as being similar to the woman he described to the police.

5. Roddick cannot and does not say that the woman he saw on the Friday morning is one and the same person as the woman he saw driving the Crewe car approximately a fortnight before the crime, or the woman he saw first at the taking of depositions at the Otahuhu

Magistrate's Court and secondly at one of the [Thomas] trials at the Supreme Court.

6. There was no proper basis for Mr [David] Yallop to state in his book Beyond Reasonable Doubt? at page 23 that he knew who fed the Crewe child or that he knew the identity of the woman that Bruce Roddick saw on Friday the 19th June 1970.

7. There was no proper basis for Mr [Pat] Booth to publish in the Auckland Star of 24th November 1978 that the woman who fed the Crewe child was seen driving the Crewe car in the week before the murders or that the same woman was seen on three other occasions.

8. In the early afternoon of Saturday 20th June 1970 a child was seen at the garden gate of the Crewe property. This child was at a stage of its development that it had recently commenced walking.

In view of my findings that there were sightings of a woman on Friday the 19th June 1970 and a child on Saturday 20th June 1970, it would appear that further enquiries are necessary in respect of this aspect of the case. While Bruce Roddick is unable to identify the person he saw, his evidence in my opinion does warrant enquiries being made.

SCOPE OF FURTHER [2nd] ENQUIRY

In my report of 17 January 1979 I had recommended, for the reasons given, that the Prime Minister should be satisfied that adequate evidence was available to establish with reasonable accuracy the time of the Crewe murders. I also felt, in view of what I considered was a positive sighting of an unidentified woman on the Friday morning the 19th June 1970 at the Crewe property, that further investigations should be made to ascertain whether there was a reasonable possibility that that unidentified woman was either of the two women who had been named as possibly being at the Crewe farm on that Friday morning. The Prime Minister requested that I carry out further investigations accordingly.

SUMMARY OF INVESTIGATIONS CARRIED OUT

It is, I concede, unlikely that a crime of this nature would be committed other than during the hours of darkness. One would need a cold-blooded arrogance to carry out such a crime other than under the cover of darkness but there are certain indications from evidence that someone reasonably openly returned to the property after the crimes; that the murderer was such a person. In my first report I advised that I was satisfied that an unidentified woman was on the Crewe property on the Friday morning the 19th June. I cannot think that there is any innocent explanation as to her presence on the property that morning; if there were I am sure she would have come forward and identified herself. That somebody did go back after the murders seems clear, for not only have we the evidence that this woman was on the property on the Friday morning but also I am satisfied that someone had the little girl Rochelle up out of her cot so that she was able to be running round in front of the property on the Saturday. That somebody did go back to the property I believe is established also from the evidence of the mailman Mr Shirley. He was quite adamant that while he was able to see into the living room on the Friday morning (the first morning he realised that the deliveries had not been collected) he was unable to see into the same room on the following Monday because some covering, which he was unable to identify, had been drawn across the windows.

I believe the totality of all this evidence, namely the sighting of an unidentified woman on the Friday morning, the independent sighting of the child on the following Saturday and the drawing of the curtains across the living room windows apparently on the Friday morning established that someone, obviously having knowledge of the murders, was on the property possibly twenty four to thirty six hours after the murders were committed. If this is so it could explain how the child Rochelle was able to survive approximately four and a half days without any serious ill-effects.

COMMENTARY

There is no evidence that the Crewes were still alive by the weekend, so that if anybody was at the scene on the Friday and/or Saturday, as I believe there was, it is properly to be inferred that this person had knowledge of the crimes. The presence of such a person, in other words, cannot be explained away by the possibility that the Crewes were still alive and perhaps temporarily away from their home.

Accepting, as I do on the evidence, that someone with a knowledge of the crimes having been committed was around the property on the Friday and possibly the Saturday, the murderer must have felt very certain that he could move about reasonably freely at the property and over a period of quite a few days. While this possible explanation of the matter may seem quite bizarre, that description might aptly be applied to the whole of the case, especially when one bears in mind the real possibility that a killer, having committed these atrocious murders, calmly followed them up by feeding or arranging the feeding of the child of his victims.

Appendix 4

Address by Peter Williams, Barrister-at-law to 2000 plus people at the Auckland Town Hall [28 August 1973]

Probably never before in the history of New Zealand has public interest been so aroused by a criminal trial than by the trials of Arthur Thomas.

Justice is a quality revered by all good citizens and the thought that an innocent man might be sentenced to life imprisonment for a crime he did not commit is surely a spine-chilling concept. It is not, however, my object in this address to defend Arthur Thomas nor my intention to vilify his accusers. Fair comment in relation to a criminal trial is always acceptable provided it is not malicious and is an expression of views honestly held. However, before a lawyer can publicly give his views in relation to a trial, a painstaking and comprehensive review of the evidence would be a necessary preliminary step.

I wish to concentrate on certain matters of general importance relating to the preparation and presentation of evidence generally in criminal trials such matters having been highlighted by the Thomas trials.

In an editorial in the *Auckland Star*, the editor stated, and I quote: 'If, as seems possible, our investigatory and adversary systems have weaknesses, an inquiry should study these. The legal profession could reflect on what assistance it could give to an inquiry'. I respectfully agree with the editor and I intend, during this address, to make certain suggestions as to how, in my opinion, the present system of criminal trials could be improved.

Within the bounds of relevance, the jury should be informed of all the factual information pertaining to the charges. The investigation is usually commenced by the police and by the time the charge is brought, the police are in possession of a voluminous file containing information both culpatory and exculpatory. Under our existing law there is no safeguard to ensure that exculpatory evidence known to the police will be adduced at the trial. It is this hiatus that should be filled.

I am reliably informed by Mr Temm QC that when he first was preparing the Thomas defence for the first trial, he experienced great difficulty in gathering information which he had reasonable grounds for believing the police held to the effect that the crimes were committed by a person other than Thomas. Mr Temm even went to the extent of asking that the police file be placed in the hands of a Supreme Court judge who could direct that any such evidence be made available to the defence. The application was, however, unsuccessful.

It did appear at that stage that the police and prosecution had some weeks earlier – ie before the charges were brought against Thomas – virtually made up their minds to charge some other person with these same crimes and it is hard to believe that this stage would have been reached without the police having collected a fair volume of evidence against that other person.

Mr Temm was unable to obtain this information nor was he able to satisfy himself that this information was not there to obtain, even though he exercised every legal and legitimate method to get these facts.

During the preparation for the second trial, similar frustration was encountered by Mr Ryan, the second trial lawyer. He has informed me that he experienced great difficulty in obtaining soil samples from the Crewe farm. These were, of course, important to test the corrosive effects upon the shellcase of the bullet.

Again Mr Ryan has informed me that in other respects he experienced great difficulty in obtaining information from the police and only on specific requests for specific items were his requests granted. The most important Crown exhibit was, of course, the shellcase allegedly found at the Crewe property. Not only was difficulty experienced in getting access to this exhibit for the defence scientists, but this important exhibit had not been kept in laboratory conditions. It has apparently been carried around by various police officers and in fact the inspector in charge of the case later told the second trial jury that he had himself cleaned the cartridge case to send it for mounting in the police museum.

The defence scientists were thus deprived of the opportunity of seeing this exhibit in the condition it was when found and also because of the date that they were supplied with this exhibit, were forced to work under great time pressure to conclude their pre-trial experimentation.

The short point is, that especially in an important criminal trial where the repercussions for the defendant are so potentially severe, not only should all exculpatory evidence be at the command of his counsel but his counsel should be able to be satisfied that the prosecution has in fact released all such information within their control and knowledge.

Our trial procedure to a large extent is emulatory of the position in England.

However, in England there is a tradition that the prosecuting counsel does not go all out for a conviction but is willing to share with the defence any information in his possession which may help the accused. This convention applies theoretically in the United States also where indeed it is a rule of law to the extent that the prosecutor's suppression at trial of evidence favourable to the accused constitutes a denial in due process of law.

The English are generally accustomed to follow informal canons of conduct and as a result a number of rules have emerged concerning disclosure to counsel for an accused of material in the hands of the prosecution. Some of these rules have been reinforced by opinions of the Court of Criminal Appeal but they depend mainly for their effectiveness on the tightly-knit character of the English Bar.

The most important of these rules are as follows:-

1. If a person who may help the accused and who has not been called at the preliminary examination has been interviewed by the police, or the prosecution, his name, but not a copy of his statement, must be supplied to the defence. If he is to be called to testify, the substance of his evidence must also be supplied to the defence.

2. If a prosecution witness has made a statement to the police which contains material favourable to the accused, a copy of that statement is ordinarily supplied to the defence.

3. If at a trial a prosecution witness gives testimony that conflicts with a statement he has previously given to the police, either the statement or the inconsistent portion of it is ordinarily supplied to the defence.

4. If a prosecution witness has a previous criminal conviction which affects his credibility, that fact must be communicated to the defence.

5. If the accused has a previous criminal conviction that fact must be supplied to the defence.

6. If the accused has made a written statement to the police which has not been put in at the preliminary examination, a copy of this statement must be supplied to the defence.

7. If an accused, while in custody, has been examined by a prison

doctor with regard to his mental responsibility, a copy of any report made by that doctor must be supplied to the defence.

8.   If a scientific laboratory examination has been conducted in the case, the results of that examination must be supplied to the defence on request. If the results are clearly favourable to the accused, they must be supplied without request.

9.   If there are documents in the case which the police have seized from the accused or obtained from other sources, they may be examined by the defence upon request. Whenever these documents may help the accused, the defence is notified and given facilities for inspecting them without having made a request.

The first submission that I make is that these rules should form the basis of a statute in New Zealand so that the defence should have a statutory right to access the place where the alleged crime has been committed, access to exhibits which are not actually produced at the trial and full discovery of documents in the possession of any person that may have relevance.

I willingly concede that some of these matters are already practice and also there may be some grounds for certain curtailment of what I have said but nevertheless, unless safeguards are written into our law, occasions may well arise where a miscarriage of justice will occur because the defence was not aware of certain information which should have been placed in its hands without demur and not in the exercise of a discretion but as of right.

The Thomas trials have again highlighted the unsatisfactory nature of evidence of police officers pertaining to verbal admissions. I do not propose in this address to review this aspect in detail but merely to say that there is a crying need for statutory clarification of the rights of the suspect in relation to police interrogation including ancillary matters as the suspect's right to use a telephone and his access to a solicitor.

The final matter which I wish to touch upon is the vexed question of jury selection. It is now common knowledge that in a major trial the prosecution is supplied by the police with a plethora of detail relating to potential jurors. This information is not made available to the defence nor is it a practical possibility for the defence to obtain this information. Furthermore, at the trial, the Crown has the unlimited right to stand aside jurors while the defence is limited to six challenges. Fairness involves equality and it is obvious that our present system of jury selection favours the prosecution. Again this anomaly in our law should be removed.

The trials of Arthur Thomas have dramatically placed our system of criminal judicial inquiry before the public eye. I say this opportunity should not be neglected for public opinion to demand that the faults that are clearly manifest under such scrutiny, should be remedied surely, efficiently, permanently and with strength.

Appendix 5

Letter to Editor, New Zealand Herald [26 June 2000]

John Andrews' Weekend Herald article on the 1970 Crewe murders has former Detective Inspector Bruce Hutton providing a dismal attempt at self-defence in relation to the planting of cartridge cases while he was officer in charge of that failure-ridden investigation. Significantly, Mr Hutton neglects to add for the benefit of a new generation that the bid by himself and the family of the late Detective Len Johnston to overturn the findings of the Royal Commission failed in the Court of Appeal. That Court determined that the Royal Commission indeed had the jurisdiction to make those findings.

The Royal Commission concluded "that Arthur Thomas was imprisoned on the basis of evidence which is false in the knowledge of Police officers, whose duty is to uphold the law, is an unspeakable outrage." Those Royal Commission's findings still stand and it is incredulous to many that Mr Hutton's actions have never been subjected to the same scrutiny, in a judicial arena, as those of the man he fought to keep incarcerated for a crime he clearly did not commit.

The official police view is that the Crewe homicide file is still open. The truth will come out – as the truth always does – and it is to be hoped that at that time, new Police Commissioner Rob Robinson and his current-day team have the courage to do what his predecessors of 1970 failed to do.

- Chris Birt, Researcher/Writer

Letter to Editor, North & South [18 October 2011]

The response to Ross Meurant's expose of the police and their practices (When the Good Guys are the Bad Guys, October 2011), while entirely predictable, demonstrates just how little has in fact changed since the former detective's day.

In the guise of attempting to demonstrate that the Police force of 2011 is an entirely different beast to that seen in the 1970s, Police Commissioner Peter Marshall and his agency's trusty mouthpiece, Police

Association president Greg O'Connor, seek yet again, to defend the indefensible.

To describe the police practices of 40 years ago – particularly but not by any means confined to those adopted in the Crewe homicide inquiry – as mistakes, O'Connor is confirming Meurant's judgment that the police put the reputation of the police before any public duty.

Let's get real here. The Crewe investigation involved a conspiracy to pervert the course of justice. Perjury was committed, not by one or two of the officers involved, but by most of those involved. Evidence was fabricated to ensure Arthur Thomas was convicted and anything that could have proved he was innocent was suppressed. All these actions were deliberate, and I say that definitively, having spent 36 years undertaking a forensic examination of the Crewe file.

What Meurant was endeavouring to demonstrate, I believe, was that the criminal actions of police in the Crewe inquiry were not isolated to that controversial cartridge case and nor did they involve just two officers, so named as the perpetrators by a Royal Commission of Inquiry. Meurant knows a lot more than he has let on so far so my advice to the police would be not to poke the tiger too hard at this present point in time. He was on the inside for 20 years and the New Zealand Police would not ever want the full extent of his knowledge exposed. I am sure about that.

I am not here to plead Meurant's case. He is more than capable of doing that himself. But I would suggest that rather than shooting the messenger, the cause of our modern-day police administration might be better served cleaning up the mess that has been created by those who have gone before, rather than describing those actions as 'mistakes'.

It is a fact that on the day that the Royal Commission delivered its damning findings against former Detective Inspector Bruce Hutton and former Detective Len Johnston, the Commissioner of Police of that time, Bob Walton, issued a public declaration that there was not sufficient evidence to put the survivor of them – Hutton – on trial. That very same day! In doing so, he and his headquarters executive team undeniably usurped the role of the Courts and acted as judge and jury. This very action served only to confirm what Meurant now claims to be the case, that the police defend the police no matter what.

Lest I be accused of defaming the dead, I made allegations about Walton while he was still alive. Walton did not take any action against me on that occasion – just as he also failed to do so when Meurant went public about the pressure applied to him to give false evidence to the Royal Commission – because in both instances the evidence was available and would have been used to defend those most sinister of revelations.

I do believe that police policies and practices have changed, to a degree, since the 'bash and stash' days of the 1970s and 1980s Meurant was personally involved in. I also accept that the police force has a diverse range of personnel, including some university graduates. That can only be good. But the culture, from what I can see after almost four decades of seeking information from the New Zealand Police, does not appear to have changed for the better, to any significant degree at least. If it had done so, why would recently-retired Commissioner Howard Broad have expressed regret that this was the one area of policing that he had been unable to change as much as he would have liked? This from the head of the police administration as recently as six months ago. I could go on ad infinitum about what Broad said at that time, but space prohibits this.

It is accepted that culture within any collegial system usually only changes when it is forced to change and the New Zealand Police is no different than the Defence Force, the Law Society, the Real Estate Institute and other like-minded bodies. None of these accept change willingly and to the contrary they resist it strenuously. Just as Peter Doone, Rob Robinson and Howard Broad have all done at the end of their terms, Peter Marshall will, I feel sure, be expressing regrets that he was unable to change the culture as much as he would have liked when the New Zealand Police eventually farewells him.

The jury is still out on his Administration, but nothing I have experienced in the six months it has been in charge of this crucial agency of law and order to date gives me any confidence that the obstruction, prevarication and indeed, the outright lies that have been told by members of the police hierarchy over recent years will now come to an end simply because a new Commissioner has taken the helm.

If the New Zealand Police want to prove that the culture of the 12,000 strong force of men and women our community is so reliant on today has changed to the extent Messrs Marshall and O'Connor insist it has, then not only will they publicly endorse the independent inquiry sort by Rochelle Crewe, but they will insist on it. Their actions – or inactions – will determine how they are recorded by history on this matter in future.

- Chris Birt, Researcher/Writer